Which Reminds Me ...

A MEMOIR

Which Reminds Me ...

A MEMOIR

Mitchell Sharp

UNIVERSITY OF TORONTO PRESS
Toronto Buffalo London

© University of Toronto Press Incorporated 1994
Toronto Buffalo London
Printed in Canada

Reprinted 1994

ISBN 0-8020-0545-4

Printed on acid-free paper

Canadian Cataloguing in Publication Data

Sharp, Mitchell, 1911–
  Which reminds me : a memoir

  Includes index.
  ISBN 0-8020-0545-4

  1. Sharp, Mitchell, 1911–   . 2. Canada – Politics
  and government – 1963–1984.* 3. Politicians –
  Canada – Biography. I. Title.

  FC626.S53A3 1994   971.064′3′092   C93-094384-8
  F1034.3.S53A3 1994

To Jeannette
who was there when so much of this happened

Contents

Contents

United States – Negotiating with the United States – The Third
Option – The battle of the flags – The FLQ crisis – The War
Measures Act – The Canadian International Development Agency and
the International Development Research Centre – The view from
Ottawa

Commonwealth summits – Diplomatic relations with the Vatican –
Recognition of the People's Republic of China – Biafra – Israel and
Canadian Jews – Vietnam and the International Commission for
Control and Supervision – The Conference on Security and Coopera-
tion in Europe – Foreign travels – Relations with Latin America –
External Affairs and the monarchy

After External Affairs, what? – Access to information – Parliamentary
reform – Televising the House of Commons – Redistribution of seats
in the House of Commons – Speeches from the Throne – MPs' salaries – An ordinary MP – Reflections on majority versus minority
government, political parties, and business and politics

The Northern Pipeline Agency – The Task Force on Conflict of
Interest – The Canada–United States West Coast Salmon Fishing
Treaty – The Trilateral Commission – East-West relations – Cambodia

Foreword

Shortly after the fall 1965 election, Prime Minister Lester B. Pearson called me to his office to tell me that I would no longer be his parliamentary secretary but would hold that position under the new finance minister, Mitchell Sharp. Noting my disappointment, the Prime Minister told me that he had made the transfer because he was convinced that if I worked hard, I could become the first French-Canadian minister of finance. Thus began my long association with that exceptional human being Mitchell Sharp.

Other public figures have had the privilege of learning their economics and politics at prestigious American or European universities. My instructor was this great public servant, and I could not have had a better teacher. At first, I thought Mitchell Sharp was an English patrician, but then I discovered he was the son of a working-class immigrant and had to complete his studies part time. He learned about public life as C.D. Howe's right-hand man and as an adviser to Louis St Laurent and Lester Pearson. He left the public service on a question of principle and soon became a prominent business person. Later, he was an indispensable minister under Mike Pearson and Pierre Trudeau.

This meticulous, calm, logical, erudite, and decisive man knows more than anyone else what are the limits and the potential of the state. When Mike Pearson wanted to give the Liberal party a new philosophical impetus, Mitchell Sharp organized the Kingston Conference. When he needed someone to build international and national confidence after Walter Gordon's difficulties at Finance, he moved Mitchell Sharp from Trade and Commerce to Finance. When Pierre Trudeau wanted to differentiate his international policies from those of his predecessor, he appointed Mitchell to External Affairs.

All who know me understand why, after my years with Mitchell Sharp, I have always turned to him whenever I face a great problem. He was always ready, despite the long hours he worked, to spend time explaining to me the reasons why he made this or that decision. During the three years that I served as his parliamentary secretary and minister of state in the Department of Finance, he involved me in everything that took place in his office. In that way, he prepared me for my own career as a minister.

In reading *Which Reminds Me ...*, you will discover a great public servant who possesses a profound knowledge of public administration. You will understand better how Canada became a country in which francophones were able to take their rightful place, and why Canada should conduct its commercial relations with the United States with the greatest possible flexibility.

Students in political science and economics will learn how and why governments sometimes act in surprising ways. And all readers, after they complete these well-written, clear, direct, and fascinating pages, will understand why I am so proud that Mitchell Sharp is my mentor. They will realize why I recall so fondly those many visits to his home, where, after serious discussions of matters of state, Mitchell would sit down at the piano and help me forget my political worries by playing some Chopin, Schubert, or Mozart, which I listened to attentively with his wonderfully generous and charming wife, Jeannette Dugal.

Perhaps the greatest surprise of all in this book is Mitchell's logical and prophetic reasons for declining to become governor general of Canada.

Upon finishing the book, the reader will understand that Mitchell Sharp, uniquely among politicians, possessed remarkable integrity, competence, sincerity, and modesty. Canada will need many more like Mitchell Sharp if it is to be a proud, independent, prosperous, and generous country in the twenty-first century.

And so, I salute this young, vigorous octogenarian whom I admire so much: Bravo for yet another work splendidly done.

THE HONOURABLE JEAN CHRÉTIEN
August 1993

Preface

Some people, I am told, know from the beginning what they want to do in life, particularly people with political ambitions. I am not one of them. It was fate and fortune rather than personal planning or ambition that led me to spend most of a lifetime in the Government of Canada – sixteen years as a senior civil servant, a so-called mandarin; fifteen years as an MP, thirteen of them as a minister of the Crown; and ten years as the head of a government agency.

There was an interlude of five years between the civil service and politics when I was a business executive in Toronto. Even during those years of observing government from the outside, however, I participated in political events that turned out to be of national significance.

As a non-partisan public servant I gave advice to three powerful cabinet ministers in Liberal governments on questions of public policy and watched them make and defend their decisions. I served for about a year as deputy to a minister in the Diefenbaker government before resigning and entering private business. A few years later I entered politics, was elected to Parliament, and became a minister myself, advised by non-partisan public servants with many of whom I had once worked as a colleague.

In cabinet I held four portfolios under two prime ministers, Lester Bowles Pearson and Pierre Elliott Trudeau.

During my time in government service, Canada was transformed into a major industrial power. From the end of the war until the 1970s the standard of living of Canadians rose dramatically, without serious interruption. In retrospect, these were 'the golden years.' The structure of the modern welfare state was put in place. The federal bureaucracy and federal expenditures multiplied. Aided by the federal government, the provinces became stronger and more independent, and French-speaking Canadians from Quebec gained the status and influence they deserved in the federal bureaucracy and cabinet. National unity and economic, cultural, and political independence, particularly from the United States, were centrepieces of national purpose around which politics and politicians revolved.

This book is based on my many-sided experience in government during that extraordinary period of Canadian history. It is not a day-by-day, month-by-month, or even year-by-year account of my official activities. It is far from comprehensive. Instead, these recollections are centred on major political events and developments in which I participated in one capacity or another.

Apart from whatever historical value they have, these recollections reflect my abiding interest in the art and practice of government. It has been said, and truly, that Canada is a difficult country to govern because of its geography and its history. For that very reason it was exciting to have been at the centre of the action as I was for so many years – and to have been paid for it (although, I might add, not lavishly).

Politicians – active or retired – write about their experiences for a variety of reasons: vanity; because other politicians write about theirs; to continue their advocacy of a point of view; and sometimes, I suspect, to give themselves something to do when they are no longer pursuing a political career.

I am not sure why I undertook to write this book – probably for at least one of the aforementioned reasons. What I hope is that it may contribute to understanding of the process of government in Canada, not from a theoretical or academic point of view, but as it happens in the nitty-gritty world of political reality.

The structure of this book is as follows: for each stage of my career, I provide an account of major events in which I was involved, interspersed with reflections on the significance of my experience in terms of the process of governing Canada. The first two chapters, for example, cover periods when I was a senior official in the Department of Finance and the Department of Trade and Commerce. There follows an essay on the role of the mandarins, of which I was one.

From time to time, I interrupt the narrative of some of the major events in which I participated as minister of trade and commerce, minister of finance, secretary of state for external affairs, and president of the Privy Council, to stand back, metaphorically, and reflect on the significance of my experience for the light it throws on contemporary questions.

The book concludes with a chapter I call 'Learning to Be a Canadian,' which describes how my ideas about Canada and the problems of national unity evolved over a lifetime of experience at the centre of government in Ottawa.

This book is about government as I observed it and as I participated in it. It is not a personal autobiography, except for chapter 1, where I give a brief account of my origins, early years, and how I got to Ottawa that may help to explain my point of view and my idiosyncrasies.

Which Reminds Me ...

A MEMOIR

CHAPTER ONE

From Winnipeg to Ottawa, 1911–1942

SHARP, Hon. Mitchell W., PC, OC, BA, DSC, LLD; born Winnipeg, Man., 11 May 1911; s. Thomas and Elizabeth S.; e. Univ. of Manitoba, BA 1934, LLD 1965; London Sch. of Economics 1937; Univ. of Ottawa DSC 1970; Univ. of W. Ont. LLD 1977; Officer, Order of Can. 1983; m. Daisy, d. late John Boyd, Victoria, B.C., 23 April 1938 (Dec.); one s. Noel; m. Jeannette Dugal, 14 April 1976; Policy Associate, Strategicon, 1988–; Commr, Northern Pipeline Agency 1978–1988; concurrently Co-Chrmn of Task Force on Conflict of Interest July 1983–May 1984; Appts incl. Offr, Dept. of Finance, Ottawa 1942–51; Dir. of Economic Policy Div. 1947–51; Assoc. Depy Min. of Trade and Commerce 1951–57; Depy Min. 1957–58; Min. of Trade and Commerce 1963–65; Min. of Finance 1965–68; Secy of State for External Affairs 1968–74; Pres. Privy Council and Leader of Govt., H. of C. 1974–76; (resigned from Cabinet 1976); resigned from Parlt 1 May 1978; Liberal; United Church; Home: 33 Monkland Ave., Ottawa, Ont. K1S 1Y8.

Canadian Who's Who, 1992

Parents

If she had been alive when I entered the Canadian cabinet in 1963, my mother would have been amused – not impressed. She was anti-estab-lishment, attended evangelical church services, and once, she admitted to me, voted Social Credit as a gesture of political unorthodoxy. She wanted me, as a youth in the early 1920s, to learn a trade and in due course become a trade-union leader. Her sympathies lay with the radical organizers of the 1919 Winnipeg General Strike, put down by the Mounties in a bloody encounter.

My father and mother migrated from Scotland to Canada a year before I was born. Like many other Scottish immigrants of their generation, they had an elementary education and little by way of possessions. Somehow or other they managed to buy a small house on the outskirts of Winnipeg, where I was born in 1911, and then moved to Toronto Street in the centre of the city, where my mother and I lived while my father served overseas, in an ambulance unit from 1915 to 1918. Soon after my father's return from overseas we moved to an apartment on Furby Street, where my sister, May, was born in 1921, then to St James, a western suburb of Winnipeg, where my brother, Harry, was born in 1923.

Unlike my mother, my father was conventional in his outlook, a conservative in politics, a 'continuing' Presbyterian in religion. He had a beautiful light tenor voice, which he displayed in church and at local concerts. Sometimes I accompanied him on the piano. In his younger days (until about age forty-five), he was an ardent soccer player. As a breadwinner he wasn't particularly successful, although in the late 1930s his fortunes improved and he was for a time the editor of the weekly *St. James Leader.*

First full-time job, age fourteen

I didn't take my mother's career advice, although in retrospect I find it remarkable that she thought I would develop the sort of political skills required by a trade-union leader. Like those of my generation living in St James, a working-class district, in a small frame house without indoor plumbing or running water, I was expected to contribute to the family income as soon as I reached the minimum school-leaving age, which was then fourteen. Even before that, from age twelve, I earned fifty cents a night working as a messenger in one of the local drugstores. When I was fourteen, my mother, through a friend found me a full-time job (8:00 a.m. to 5:00 p.m. and to 1:00 p.m. on Saturdays) as a delivery boy at the Grain Trade Press, then located on McDermot Avenue, kitty-corner from the Winnipeg Grain Exchange. Delivering parcels of printed material is heavy work, but I considered myself fortunate to be earning eight dollars a week. On my first pay-day, I walked home – some three miles – to save the streetcar fare and bought a piece of gingerbread, of which I was very fond, to celebrate the occasion with the family.

Not a particularly auspicious beginning, but, like many apparently trivial events in a lifetime, it set the course of my subsequent career. The Grain Trade Press printed the forms – cash tickets, storage receipts, etc. – for the private grain-elevator companies in western Canada. Its parent company, Dawson Richardson Publications, published daily and weekly trade papers. The Sanford Evans Statistical Service, which also served the grain trade, was located in the same building. For twelve years, from 1925 to 1937, I was to work in that building, moving from one job to another and simultaneously obtaining a higher education.

It was my good fortune, in due course, to become an employee of Sanford Evans, a distinguished former mayor of Winnipeg and at that time a prominent Conservative member of the Manitoba Legislature. Evans was a patrician in appearance and style. He would have adorned the Bennett cabinet in Ottawa, but that wily veteran the Hon. Robert Rogers outmanoeuvred him to win the Conservative nomination in the federal riding of Winnipeg South by packing the nominating convention, and went on to win the seat in the 1930 general election.

The struggle for higher education

When I advanced from delivery boy in the printing plant to office boy in the Sanford Evans statistical organization, and my pay went up from eight dollars to ten dollars a week, I determined to remedy my lack of a high-school matriculation diploma by enrolling in the night classes available at Daniel McIntyre Collegiate. I had one year – Grade eleven – to complete. At the end of two years of night classes, I had passed the necessary examinations and was eligible to enter university.

Meanwhile, my work in the Evans organization brought me under the supervision of George Laycock, an engaging economist and writer, who unfortunately suffered a mental breakdown early in his career. Laycock encouraged me to continue my education by enrolling as an extramural student at the University of Manitoba. Until then, the idea of a university education had never entered my mind. Boys from my background didn't aspire to those heights!

I called on W.B.H. Teakles, the assistant registrar, at the Broadway Avenue site of the university. He was not encouraging. (How could I hope to pass the examinations if I did not attend lectures?) But since I was willing to pay the necessary fees, he agreed to register me for three out of the required five courses in the first year. There were no lectures or correspondence courses for extramural students, so I had to supplement my reading of the prescribed texts by seeking private tuition. As a result, I made the acquaintance and became a close friend of G.P.R. (Pete) Tallin, a lawyer and Manitoba Rhodes Scholar, who was later to become dean of the Manitoba Law School. In return for tutorials in the evening on a wide range of subjects from mathematics to French, I gave piano lessons to his two sons, one of whom, Rae, became enough of a musician to lead a band during his university career and went on to become legislative counsel of the Manitoba Legislature.

Having passed the examinations for the three first-year courses at the university, I returned to see Teakles. This time he was less reluctant. He enrolled me for the balance of the first year and for some courses in the second year. These I also successfully completed and, in the third year of my extramural studies, completed the remaining requirements for the second year.

Then the axe fell. The University of Manitoba decided that it would no longer grant degrees to extramural students. I went to Sanford Evans with my problem. I could not afford to give up my job to attend lectures. It was 1932, in the depths of the Depression. My father had only intermittent employment as a printing salesman. I was a major source of family income.

I shall always be grateful to Sanford Evans for his encouragement and generosity. He allowed me time off to attend lectures in the mornings, which covered nearly all my courses, and he did not reduce my salary – $100 a month. I worked in the office afternoons and in the evening until 7:00 or 8:00 p.m., and studied at home, usually until midnight, sometimes later.

Those who take university education for granted will find it difficult to credit the elation I felt when for the first time I sat in a classroom and listened to a lecture from a professor who had written the textbook that I had struggled with on my own. And here, sitting beside me, were fellow students whose fathers were well-to-do, with names such as Tarr, Isbister, and Kilgour that were familiar to readers of the *Winnipeg Free Press* and the *Winnipeg Tribune*.

As an extramural student, I had managed to gain respectable marks at the examinations. Attendance at lectures – in mathematics, physics, and economics – enabled me, in my third year, to win an Isbister scholarship, awarded to those with the highest marks, good for tuition in the fourth and final year. Sanford Evans agreed to continue the earlier arrangement and I graduated in 1934 with a BA degree.

It had been a long grind and hadn't left much room for the usual pursuits of youth or participation in student activities. Somehow, I managed to fit in some music. Each summer, I spent a couple of weeks as a leader at Camp Stephens, the YMCA Boys' Camp on the Lake of the Woods near Kenora, in return for room and board. Fred Hubbard, then in charge of the camp, was an inspiration to all of us, embodying the ideal of a healthy mind in a healthy body. On weekends, I took my girl to the movies.

Religion

For want of any strong parental guidance as a child, I attended Sunday school at the St James Gospel Hall, which was then located almost next door to our home at 294 Ferry Road. As I grew older, I became a Sunday-school teacher and played the organ at the evangelical services on Sunday evening (the Sunday morning service was the Lord's Supper, a simple form of Communion, without clergy, when the singing of hymns was unaccompanied) and became well acquainted with the King James version of the Bible.

By my late teens, I had begun to rebel against the narrowness of this fundamentalist group. At the end of a youth meeting, I delivered myself of an offensive little speech, criticizing the sentimental evangelical literature that had been read at the meeting. My political instincts at the time were obviously underdeveloped, since the elder in charge of the meeting was also the father of two of my piano students. When I arrived at his home for the next lessons, he met me at the door and invited me to join him in prayer for the salvation of my soul! Thus ended the income from those lessons and my connection with religious fundamentalism.

Music

From my parents, I inherited a love of music. I can still recall the excitement I experienced when for the first time, at about age fifteen, I heard Beethoven's Fifth Symphony, played by the Minneapolis Symphony Orchestra. I had heard singers and violinists perform masterpieces on the discs of the day, but recordings of symphonies were rare. Beethoven's heroic themes echoed in my head for days after the concert.

My mother gave me my first lessons on the piano, and at the age of ten I began weekly lessons with a Winnipeg teacher, Edith Mary Pickford, who laid a firm foundation and coached me through the Toronto Conservatory of Music examinations up to the intermediate grade. Every Saturday morning when I was between ten and fourteen, I took the

7

streetcar to the Boys' Department of the YMCA for gymnastics and a swim. (The latter constituted my weekly bath. At home a bath required me to bring water from an outdoor pump a couple of hundred yards' distant, and to heat it in a washtub on the wood stove in the kitchen.) Following lunch I walked over to my music teacher's apartment for my weekly piano lesson. After I began working full time at the age of fourteen lessons were intermittent, but even when I was under the greatest of pressure – as a working student and later as an official and a minister – I managed to find time to play the piano. The most exciting event of my life? Getting elected? Becoming a cabinet minister? No. It was when I played the Andante movement of Mozart's Piano Concerto No. 21 (the 'Elvira Madigan' theme) at a novelty fund-raising Christmas concert in 1972, with the Toronto Symphony Orchestra under Victor Feldbrill. My first and final concert appearance.

Learning to work

During those years, I learned many things, most of all how to ration my working hours. The University of Manitoba at Fort Garry, to which the Arts and Science faculties had moved in 1932, was an hour's journey by streetcar from my home in St James. Sitting or standing in those rocking chariots, I read the assigned texts and even managed to solve some mathematical problems. My first wife, Daisy, a fellow student at the university, who also lived in St James and whose father, John Boyd, taught me mathematics in high school, said she agreed to accept a date with me to find out what I was really like. Her impression had been of a red-haired boy, immersed in books, ignoring everyone else on the streetcar. She found I was otherwise normal.

During those years with Sanford Evans, I also learned to organize my ideas and put them on paper for publication. From 1929 to 1937, the years of drought and disastrously low prices, I wrote prairie crop reports and business reports for the subscribers to the statistical service. For a time, Tom Pickersgill – a brother of Jack – and I edited the *Weekly Market News*, a grain-trade publication. Occasionally, I wrote articles for the *Financial Post* on western economic conditions, and formed a friendship with its brilliant journalist Kenneth R. Wilson, who always called me when he travelled west. Those *Financial Post* contacts were to play a pivotal role in my subsequent career.

In his autobiography, Benjamin Franklin described how he learned to write by imitating Addison, the English essayist. My model was John W. Dafoe, the editor of the *Winnipeg Free Press* and one of the foremost

Canadian journalists of his day. Following Franklin's method, I would read one of Dafoe's more persuasive editorials, jot down the leading ideas, and then attempt to reconstruct it. I may not have learned the secrets of Dafoe's vigorous prose, but undoubtedly I absorbed some of his political philosophy, particularly his brand of Canadian nationalism. For westerners of my generation, the object was to lift Canada from colonial status. To be a North American nation with a dollar rather than a sterling currency and with strong ties to the United States was a sign of national maturity. We did not worry much in the 1920s and 1930s about American economic and cultural imperialism.

Postgraduate studies at the University of Manitoba

Undergraduate studies had given me a taste for learning. They had also demonstrated the great gaps in my knowledge about Canada. At age twenty-three, therefore, immediately following my graduation in 1934, I decided to undertake some postgraduate work in economics and Canadian history in my spare time. It is a striking commentary on the place of Canadian history in the Manitoba educational curriculum that there were no courses in that subject in high school, while in elementary school the teachers did not venture beyond 1867 for fear of raising contentious political issues, such as the Manitoba language question.

Fortunately, R.O. MacFarlane, professor of Canadian history at the University of Manitoba, was willing to take me on and to give me an hour or so of personal guidance in history studies every week. He required me to scan every book and to read every significant article in learned journals on Canadian history – an undertaking that was possible in 1935 but would be quite impossible, of course, today.

Although A.B. Clark had been head of the Department of Political Economy at the university while I was an undergraduate, I had learned my basic economic theory from W.J. Waines, then a lecturer in the department. In 1934, Robert (Pete) MacQueen came from the University of Saskatchewan to replace Clark. MacQueen became my friend as well as my postgraduate tutor in economics. He was weak in mathematics, and I helped him with the equations that had begun to adorn or, if you prefer, disfigure contemporary economic texts and articles. During that academic year as my tutor (1935–6), he was engaged in trying to understand the new economic theories, particularly the ideas of John Maynard Keynes, that were emerging in response to the intractable problems of the Depression. I struggled with him.

Through MacQueen, I joined the Winnipeg branch of the Canadian

Institute of International Affairs and there sat and listened to John W. Dafoe, Edgar Tarr, Noel Fieldhouse, J.S. Woodsworth, J.B. Coyne, Tom Crerar, George Ferguson, John Bird, and other eminent Winnipeggers talking about national and international affairs and cross-examining the visiting lecturers. I became a vice-president of the Young Men's Section of the Winnipeg Board of Trade and secretary of the Winnipeg Philharmonic choir, although my singing voice, said Bernard Naylor, who then led the choir, reminded him of a hen scratching on gravel.

Winnipeg in the pre-war years

In those days, Winnipeg was in many respects at the centre of Canada, not only geographically but in terms of cultural and political ferment. It was the most polyglot city in Canada, divided geographically along ethnic lines and full of tensions and rivalries. The leader of the Co-operative Commonwealth Federation (CCF), J.S. Woodsworth, represented North Winnipeg in Parliament. The Winnipeg branch of the Canadian Institute of International Affairs was the most active and stimulating in the country. The Manitoba Musical Festival, sponsored by a group of businessmen known as the Men's Musical Club, was the largest in the British Empire, attracting leading musicians from abroad as adjudicators. Winnipeg-trained musicians, mainly from the ethnic groups in the north end, were to be found in leading orchestras in Britain and the United States. The Winnipeg school children's choruses set the standard for the country. The most influential Canadian newspaper in the pre-Second World War years, when editorials counted for something, was the *Winnipeg Free Press* under the direction of John W. Dafoe, whose thunders were heard and heeded in Ottawa. Winnipeg might have been a long distance from anywhere else in pre-aviation years, but it was nevertheless a world centre for the grain trade and had to be concerned and informed about international events.

Many years later, in 1965, when my alma mater conferred on me an honorary degree, I spoke to the graduates about the extraordinary contribution of Manitobans to national affairs. There were then four Manitobans in the Pearson government – Jack Pickersgill, William Benedickson, Roger Teillet, and myself – only one, of course – Teillet – representing a Manitoba constituency. The presidents of both our national railways, Ian Sinclair and Norman MacMillan, were Manitobans. So were the sometime governor and the deputy governor of the Bank of Canada, James Coyne and Robert Beattie, our sometime ambassador to the United States of America, Arnold D.P. Heeney, and several of the civil-servant heads of government departments in Ottawa. Why? Some people say it was because of the lack of opportunity in Manitoba. This may explain why people left the province. It does not explain why they came to play such a leading role in the national life of Canada. It must have had something to do with the intellectual and cultural environment of the Winnipeg community in those pre-war years.

The London School of Economics

Towards the end of 1936, the editor of the *Financial Post*, Floyd Chalmers, offered me a job as a reporter on economic matters at a salary twice as high as I was then earning with Sanford Evans. I went to my friend and tutor, Professor MacQueen, for advice. A typical westerner, MacQueen loathed the *Financial Post* as the journal of the eastern business establishment. 'Never accept a pass from the CPR' was his governing principle. (So strongly did MacQueen impress me that, when it was first presented to me as a minister of the Crown, I turned back a pass on Canadian Pacific Airlines.) He asked me not to reply to Chalmers until he had an opportunity to ascertain what alternative offers might be available in Winnipeg. On an earlier occasion, he had arranged a scholarship in economics for me at Harvard, which I could not accept because of family responsibilities.

Within a few days, James Richardson, Winnipeg's leading business-man, not only offered me a job as economist in his grain business but, on MacQueen's advice, sent me to undertake further studies at the London School of Economics, where, for the first time in my life, I had nothing to do but study.

My immediate supervisor at LSE was Lionel Robbins (later Lord Robbins), who occupied the principal economics chair – an elegant lecturer. I attended lectures by Friedrich Von Hayek and his protégé Nicholas Kaldor. Most of my academic contacts, however, were with Moritz J. Bonn, a German Jew who had been economic adviser to the Stresemann government at the end of the First World War, and who had left Germany in 1933. For years, until his death at an advanced age, I called on him whenever I visited London. The best advice he gave me when I was his student was to spend my time seeing London and the rest of Britain, rather than attending lectures, including his own. Occasionally I took his advice, notwithstanding a twinge of Scottish conscience. However, I always attended the Cambridge-London seminars at LSE on Keynesianism and related issues.

Professor Harold Laski was in his prime at LSE – the intellectual of the

11

left – inspiring students who would lead socialist parties throughout the world and particularly in colonies aspiring to independence. I attended his lectures from time to time. One I remember particularly, because Laski had just returned from the United States and was full of praise for John L. Lewis, the leader of the United Mine Workers. In the course of his remarks, Laski made some disparaging remarks about Canada based on his experience as a lecturer at McGill in the early 1920s. A Canadian student challenged him. Laski had obviously changed his opinion of Lewis, whom he had once categorized as a thug; hadn't he changed his opinion of Canada after so many years? To which Laski replied by describing Canadian political leaders as follows: 'About Mr. Bennett [who had been defeated in 1935] I need hardly say anything to Canadians. Mr. King: a consummate politician. Mr. Woodsworth: a fine old gentleman.'

To a young man who had left school to join the work force at age fourteen, to be in the British capital and at the London School of Economics twelve years later was a miracle. I wandered the streets just looking at the places I had read about. I heard Lord Rutherford give a popular lecture on the atom with Sir William Bragg as an assistant. I visited the art galleries and bought cheap seats at the theatres and at concerts. Before returning to Canada, I visited the Continent – Paris, Geneva, Rotterdam – calling on business associates of Richardson's under the guidance of the local representatives of the Superintendance Company, which insured, among other commodities, cargoes of grain. Imagine my thoughts as, for four hours, I ate lunch and drank vintage wines in Geneva on the lawn of a private hotel beside Lac Leman as a guest of the Salamanowitz brothers, who headed the Superintendance Company. In his diary, Alexander McPhail, the first president of the Saskatchewan Wheat Pool, remarked that Jules Salamanowitz spent as much on a meal as a Saskatchewan farmer in those days earned in a month.

Grain-trade economist with James Richardson and Sons

For the grain trade, resident economists were a rarity and, as I was to discover, even top managers in Richardson's were sceptical when at the age of twenty-six I first moved into my office and began preparing internal analyses and publishing a weekly letter on developments in the grain trade for Richardson clients and the press. Within the hierarchy, I reported to William Rait, a canny Scot, who was then general manager of Pioneer Grain Company, the country elevator subsidiary of the

Richardson firm. Wallace Brown, the principal trader for Richardson's on the floor of the exchange, cleared my manuscripts before publication. I was free to write about anything that seemed to be relevant to the grain business and, within a relatively short time, the Richardson weekly letter came to be quoted extensively, locally and abroad.

Shortly after the beginning of the Second World War, I did a note on the developing feed-grain situation for Rait, forecasting a very large increase in consumption and demand. He suggested I convert it into the next Richardson weekly letter. This I did just before departing on annual leave. On return to the office, my secretary told me that there had been a very large demand for the letter. I was pleased and said so to Jack Richardson, a vice-president and the president's cousin. He advised me to forget about the letter. Henry Gauer, who was manager of Richardson's terminal operations, he told me, doesn't believe in economists. 'He doesn't think we should have hired you,' Richardson continued. 'He never reads your stuff. The day following publication of your feed grain letter, the barley market rose three cents a bushel. He was caught short and he was very angry when he found your weekly letter, which he hadn't read, was the reason for the market jump, which cost him a lot of money.' Thereafter, Gauer changed his mind about the value of economists and read my reports before they were circulated.

Western politics

Those years with Richardson's for the first time brought me into contact with western leaders and Ottawa politicians. In 1938, John Bracken, the premier of Manitoba, organized a Western Conference on Agriculture. The participants included not only western politicians and farm leaders, but also representatives of both the farmer-owned and privately owned grain-elevator companies. Clive Davidson, who was later to become secretary of the Canadian Wheat Board, did the organizational work for Bracken. Leonard Brockington had been taken on by the private grain elevator association as its counsel, mainly to provide a respectable and eloquent voice for the private grain trade and, as it turned out, for western farmers, most of whom were ordinarily very critical of the private trade. I was attached to the conference as an adviser and I found myself working not only with Brockington but also with John Brownlee, who was on the road back from his political downfall as premier of Alberta (the juiciest sex scandal of my youth) and had become counsel for the United Grain Growers. Later he was to become its president. After meetings in Winnipeg, a delegation was formed to meet the federal government in Ottawa to urge support for the hard-pressed prairie grain farmers who had suffered long years of drought and low prices. I went along to help with the drafting of the submissions to the government.

The meeting with the government took place in the East Block of the Parliament Buildings. On the platform sat Prime Minister Mackenzie King, flanked, as I recall, by C.A. Dunning, minister of finance, J.L. Ilsley, minister of national revenue, J.G. Gardiner, minister of agriculture, T.A. Crerar, minister of mines and resources, and six other ministers. Brockington, as the spokesman for the conference, made the presentation of Western grievances, with that magnificent voice and presence, notwithstanding crippling arthritis, which required him to lean back and peer out from under his bushy eyebrows. Jack Wesson, president of the Saskatchewan Wheat Pool, followed with a hard-line demand for a minimum price of eighty cents per bushel of wheat, accompanied by bushels of petitions signed by thousands of farmers, which were wheeled into the room in small trucks. To emphasize his point, he had allocated the signatories to federal constituencies in Saskatchewan and presented the analysis to the Prime Minister.

The Prime Minister thanked the western delegation for its presentation and complimented Brockington, whom he was later to hire as a speech-writer. Then he turned to Wesson. He began by saying that he wished he could reveal the contents of the dispatches he had received about the dangers of war. I do not care, he went on, if the government loses every seat in Saskatchewan, we will do our duty in this time of peril.

At twenty-seven years of age I was impressed: my first lesson in hard-ball politics.

Offer from Ottawa

When the war got under way, I joined the Canadian Officers' Training Corps, as did many university graduates. My platoon commander was David Golden, who fought in Hong Kong, was imprisoned by the Japanese, and later became a senior official in Ottawa. I held the exalted rank of corporal. I don't think I was much of a soldier but, after a year of training in the evenings and a couple of tough weeks at summer camp under the Princess Pats, I was commissioned as a second lieutenant in the militia. Just as I was trying to make up my mind whether to accept appointment as adjutant of the University of Manitoba Training Unit,

I received a call from Clifford Clark, deputy minister of finance, asking me to come to Ottawa to discuss a wartime job.

I was startled. I didn't know that Clark even knew of my existence, although I learned later he had been one of the judges in the Royal Bank Scholarship competition, when I had placed third in my graduating year for an essay on international capital movements. MacQueen, who had become a director of the Bank of Canada before his untimely death on 5 February 1941, in the first Trans-Canada Airlines crash, and J.R. Beattie, then the head of economic research at the Bank of Canada, also had spoken of me to Clark, and one of my Richardson letters on inflation had been circulated among the Ottawa mandarins. Perhaps Clark's attention had also been drawn to a paper I presented in 1939 to the Canadian Political Science Association on wheat marketing during the First World War.

Clark was looking for someone with knowledge of western-Canadian affairs generally and of the grain trade in particular. During the interview with him, I challenged the government's wheat policy, admittedly not a very diplomatic thing to do. But, as I was to find, Clark liked people with strong views so long as they were well-informed. He offered me a job. Rait, my superior at Richardson's, said he was disappointed at my willingness to accept the offer but permitted leave of absence from the company for the duration. As it turned out, I was not to return. Mrs James Richardson, who in 1939 had succeeded her deceased husband as president of the company, wrote to me at the end of the war to the effect that they would be glad to have me back, but if I chose to stay in government service they would understand. It would never have occurred to either of us then that her son, James, and I would one day serve as ministers in the same federal government.

CHAPTER TWO

In the Department of Finance, 1942–1950

I arrived to take a wartime job in the Department of Finance at the beginning of 1942. Ottawa was already overcrowded with little to commend it by way of amenities except for magnificent ski hills and fishing lakes a short distance across the Ottawa River into Quebec. I asked my friend Bob Beattie at the Bank of Canada to help me find a house for my family (which consisted of my wife and two boys – our son, Noel, and Lawrence Holden, an English lad who had been left in our care for the duration of the war). Displaying his practical approach to problems of all kinds, Beattie asked three people who had found houses how they had done it. Through one of the local milkmen, who was looking for customers, two of them replied. The milkman found half a recently constructed double for me. I was one of his faithful customers at the same address for several years.

The Department of Finance in wartime

When Clifford Clark, the deputy minister of finance, asked me to join his department for the duration of the war I knew very little about the Ottawa scene and had only the vaguest notion of what was expected of me. The only public servants with whom I was personally acquainted were fellow Winnipeggers J.W. Pickersgill in the Prime Minister's Office, J.R. Beattie, and James E. Coyne of the Bank of Canada. In due course they were to become top advisers and administrators, like myself – 'mandarins,' to use an expression that seems to be peculiar to the Canadian media.

On arrival, I reported directly to W.A. Mackintosh, also a temporary civil servant, whom Clark had borrowed from Queen's University and who was later to become its principal. Mackintosh was a central figure in the formation of economic policy during the war and in relation to post-war reconstruction. He was the principal draftsman of the government's White Paper on Employment and Income, with Special Reference to the Initial Period of Reconstruction (issued on 12 April 1945) and later the director general of the Department of Reconstruction under C.D. Howe. When Clifford Clark was ill for nine months, Mackintosh became acting deputy minister of finance. Mackintosh was an elegant and economical draftsman, a talent that is often underestimated in relation to its influence upon decision making. His talk was similarly witty and persuasive. I recall one occasion, however, when Mackintosh's obvious communications talents were misplaced. He was directed by his minister to brief the leader of the government in the Senate on a government bill. Mackintosh was giving his normal lucid explanation when the senator raised his hand: 'Dr. Mackintosh that is enough, you will confuse the senators.'

Of the younger men in the department with whom I had the privilege of working the star was R.B. Bryce, whom Clark had also recruited. A graduate in engineering at the University of Toronto, Bryce had studied economics at Cambridge under John Maynard Keynes and had returned to North America to establish a beachhead of Keynesianism at Harvard. Bryce was one of the few economists of his day who understood Keynes. Yet, in advising on Canadian fiscal policy, Bryce was intensely practical, not theoretical. He drafted speeches for the minister in a simple, direct style and with a facility that was the wonder and despair of his contemporaries like me. His memoranda could be read and understood by those who had never read an economics textbook.

The taxation division was headed by Kenneth Eaton, a graduate of Acadia University. Eaton was a bulwark of common sense in taxation matters. He took the view – and it is a pity he did not live long enough to have had a greater influence on later developments – that taxation is primarily for the purpose of raising revenue fairly and efficiently and should not be used as a means of providing incentives to business investment or for other such purposes. His principal assistant in the taxation division was Harvey Perry, later to become one of Canada's leading taxation experts and head of the Canadian Tax Foundation.

Ross Tolmie, a Rhodes Scholar from British Columbia, had moved over from the Department of National Revenue to assume the position of solicitor to the Treasury, replacing David Johnson, who had joined the Armed Forces.

This was the core group in the Department of Finance on policy matters when I arrived. Clark tried for a good geographic mix – Tolmie from B.C., (later) Deutsch from Saskatchewan, Sharp from Manitoba, Bryce from Toronto, Eaton from the Maritimes, Johnson, before enlisting, from Montreal. Closely associated were Graham Towers, governor of the Bank of Canada, Donald Gordon, the deputy governor who had become chairman of the Wartime Prices and Trade Board, and Beattie, Coyne, and Louis Rasminsky, who were originally part of the research staff of the Bank of Canada and, except for Beattie, had been given other wartime assignments. Coyne was seconded to the Foreign Exchange Control Board and later the Wartime Prices and Trade Board until he joined the Royal Canadian Air Force, and Rasminsky, who before the war had been in the League of Nations Secretariat in Geneva, to the Foreign Exchange Control Board. The Bank of Canada and the Department of Finance worked together as a team, particularly on the wartime budgets, on financing and related bond-selling campaigns, and on price controls and foreign-exchange controls.

Fiscal and monetary policy

The issues of wartime finance were debated first within the bureaucracy, under the leadership of Clark, with participation not only of Finance officials but also of Graham Towers and leading Bank of Canada officials and, when budgets were in preparation, taxation officials from the Department of National Revenue. The recommendations were then taken to the minister, J.L. Ilsley, where the issues were again debated by the senior officials in his presence. On one such occasion the debate was in full swing and at a very lofty level: opinions were offered on the conduct of the war, the political situation in Canada, the unity of the country, the economic outlook. Ilsley had sat silent, rocking himself in his office chair. Suddenly, he stopped, leaned on his desk, put his head in his hands and said: 'Gentlemen, the trouble with the Department of Finance is that we have no civil servants, only statesmen.'

Ilsley presented seven budgets, the first in 1939 and six more between 1941 and 1946. They were extraordinary statements because they were so comprehensive and innovative and in so many ways prophetic of things to come when peace returned. Once the war effort got under way, expenditures rose rapidly to levels never before contemplated, from $681 million in the fiscal year ending in 1939 to $5.13 billion at the peak of war-related expenditures in 1944. In order to pay as much as possible of the cost out of current revenues, tax rates of all kinds – personal income taxes, corporation taxes, and consumption taxes – were raised to what were considered to be their practical limits. In 1942, the excess profits tax on corporations rose to 100 per cent. In order to soften the impact, part of personal income taxes was refunded – a form of compulsory savings. For the first time – in the fiscal year ending in March 1944 – personal income tax was collected at the source, by deduction from wages and salaries.

The provinces were paid to stand aside so that the federal government could impose the same rates of personal income tax and corporation tax in all provinces. Nevertheless, about half the expenditures had to be financed by borrowings, a highly organized patriotic effort at low rates of interest. No attempt was made to utilize monetary policy as an instrument of economic stabilization except for some deliberate expansion in the money supply in the first six months of the war.

These budget statements by Ilsley were also the occasion to bring together all the strands of wartime economic policy-foreign exchange control, price and wage controls, and restrictions on civilian industry to save materials and manpower.

Because of excess-profits taxes, profiteering of the kind that had scandalized Canadians in the First World War became legally impossible. Excess-profits taxes do not encourage economy and efficiency, but in wartime that didn't matter much; the emphasis was upon production of munitions and supply and those standard items needed to keep the civilian population supplied with food, clothing, and shelter.

C.D. Howe, the minister of munitions and supply, and under him the Wartime Industries Control Board, organized the production of munitions and supply. Donald Gordon and the Wartime Prices and Trade Board were responsible for the civilian side of production, including rationing, under the authority of the minister of finance.

In trying to reconstruct events I find it difficult to separate in my memory the problems of wartime from the problems of post-war reconstruction. Those who were advising on wartime economic policy were thinking in terms not only of what had to be done to promote the war effort but, simultaneously, about the transition from war to peace, assuming an Allied victory. I don't recall that the implications of defeat were ever discussed, although I learned later that a well-camouflaged committee led by Graham Towers did, in 1940, consider what might have to be done in that event.

Ilsley and Clark

The circumstances of those wartime years and immediate post-war years contributed to the dominant position of the Department of Finance in the Ottawa hierarchy. By present-day standards, there were few ministers and few public servants. Until the end of the war, the relatively small and old-fashioned East Block of the Parliament Buildings housed the Department of Finance, Treasury Board, the Department of External Affairs, the Privy Council Office, and the Prime Minister's Office. George Ignatieff in External Affairs and I occupied neighbouring offices. Sometimes we whistled the same tune in unison.

The minister of finance was the chairman of the Treasury Board and the staff of the board reported to an assistant deputy minister of finance as secretary of the board. Trade and Commerce was a minor portfolio with little to do in those wartime years that related to economic policy. C.D. Howe was a powerful minister and had an extraordinarily competent group of officials around him – mostly dollar-a-year men recruited from industry – but, until the war came to an end, his and their efforts were concentrated on production of munitions and industrial primary products. Prime Minister Mackenzie King's central interests were not in the field of economic policy. Louis St Laurent concentrated his attention on his department – Justice – and on the participation of Quebec in the war effort.

King and St Laurent did, of course, play major roles at the highest level in support of government financial policies, including in particular the provision of financial aid to the United Kingdom, which it was the responsibility of St Laurent to persuade the Quebec caucus to accept.

As the principal policy adviser of the minister of finance during those wartime and immediate post-war years, the deputy minister of finance would, in any event, have been a key figure in the formulation of economic policy. It was the combination of Ilsley as minister and Clark as deputy minister that gave the department its special character and its enormous influence upon the course of events and provided such an extraordinarily stimulating environment for those of us who were privileged to be involved.

Clark was the inspiration and the model for those around him. He believed profoundly in the principles of political neutrality and public anonymity for civil servants and practised these principles in relations with ministers and the press. He had been appointed as deputy minister of finance by the Conservative prime minister R.B. Bennett, and had remained to serve under Mackenzie King. Clark was not hesitant, however, to urge his views in private on his minister and on the Prime Minister when the opportunity arose.

As the war came to an end, Clark was concerned – and this concern was, I believe, shared by all the principal policy advisers and the leading ministers of those days – to do everything possible to avoid another economic depression, to establish a system of social security that would minimize the poverty and hardship that had been all too prevalent in the pre-war years, and to underpin and improve the ability of the poorer provinces to carry out their constitutional responsibilities. Those were the guiding principles that inspired us and that led over time – and a considerable time it turned out to be – to the emergence of a new kind of country that had little resemblance to the one that had entered the war at the end of the 1930s.

Stanley Knowles came to Ottawa as an MP from Winnipeg at about the same time as I arrived from the same city to enter the Department of Finance. I used to tease him by saying that the CCF (Co-operative Commonwealth Federation) claimed far too much credit for the improvements in social security that took place in the decade that followed the end of the war. Looked at from an insider's point of view, the CCF was pushing against an open door.

Clark's approach was pragmatic, not ideological, and he was very much aware that ministers had to be persuaded and Parliament had to approve before anything happened. Clark treated ministers with respect, particularly Ilsley, for whom he had great admiration. When Ilsley eventually moved to become minister of justice in 1946, Clark regarded it as the end of an era.

Ilsley was conscientious to a fault. He worried about decisions before he made them, as he made them, and after he had made them. His advisers suffered along with him, but none of us begrudged the pain, not only because Ilsley understood the kind of economic policies necessary in wartime and was prepared to defend them inside and outside cabinet, but also because, in his personal life, his standards were so austere. Ilsley practised what he preached.

He represented the Annapolis Valley in Parliament and consequently had to deal, as a member of Parliament, with the problems of his apple growers, whose major markets in Britain had been disrupted by the war. Most MPs in such circumstances would be concerned to ensure that the compensation to their constituents was adequate. Ilsley confided to me that he was equally concerned that his constituents might think he was being unnecessarily generous with public monies.

In 1946, I went with Ilsley to his constituency to meet the apple growers and to see the *aboiteaux* (dykes) that needed repairs. Just before returning, the Minister invited me, in a friendly gesture, to drive with him to a fishing village in his constituency. Since he would be meeting his political ward boss, he asked, would I mind if he introduced me not as a Department of Finance official but as someone in his office? I didn't mind. The ward boss was waiting when we arrived. Ilsley congratulated him on the results of the 1945 election in his ward. It was a tough election, the ward boss replied. 'The voters like you but do not like Mackenzie King. You know that family on the hill over there. There are seven votes and they all vote like the old man. I went to see him. We always vote Liberal, he assured me, but we are not going to vote at all unless we get five dollars each. So after some hesitation I turned over thirty-five dollars.'

Obviously embarrassed, Ilsley asked me whether I was shocked. Not particularly, I replied, but where did the ward boss get the thirty-five dollars? Some from party funds, some out of his own pocket, and, of course, when those docks down there are repaired he is the foreman, was Ilsley's reply. The old man on the hill was honest, he added. He couldn't be bribed to vote Conservative. The payments at election time began after Sir Frederick Borden was defeated in this constituency and vowed that would never happen again. After many years the payments became traditional. When I entered politics I was grateful that in urban constituencies like Eglinton there was no tradition of that kind.

Ilsley's approach to decision making was orderly and thorough. He didn't accept the advice offered to him by his advisers until he had heard the issues argued in front of him, pro and con. When appropriate, Clark would bring officials with him when he met with the Minister and did not object if their views differed from his, as occasionally they did.

My impression is that Ilsley did not enter politics or specifically take on the Finance portfolio with a program of action, with deep convictions, or with ambitions to rise to the top. His strength was his superior intelligence and his integrity. Although startled from time to time by Clark's proposed innovations and reforms and Donald Gordon's zeal for the price ceiling, once convinced, Ilsley did a masterful political job of promotion and explanation. Conversations with him took unpredictable twists and turns because of his wide knowledge and curiosity. His knowledge of the United States was profound. One day, in a conversation about Canada-U.S. relations, he named all the presidents of the United States, beginning in the middle of the nineteenth century, with their nicknames and how they earned them.

He was not an admirer of Mackenzie King. On one occasion, I talked to him about something the Prime Minister had said that I found baffling. 'Mr. King,' Ilsley replied, 'uses language for some purpose other than to express thought.' Although I came to understand better the relationship between ministers and the prime minister when I entered politics myself, I still find it extraordinary that when Ilsley, a senior minister, needed to get in touch with King on an urgent matter, he went about it so indirectly, asking Pickersgill to have the PM phone him.

During the conscription crisis of 1944, Ilsley called me to his office one day on some pretext or other and, after we had dealt with the pretext, revealed what was really troubling him by asking me as a friend what I thought he should do. I replied that if I were in his position I would resign from the cabinet unless a decision were made to send overseas the men who had been called up for national service, as the minister of national defence, J.L. Ralston, wanted to do. Ilsley replied that that was what he intended to do. He added that he would become a back-bencher. When I asked him why he would not try to form a government, since he was the senior minister, he replied that he had thought about that possibility but not enough Liberal members would follow him. He reviewed the position of the Liberal caucus, member by member, and concluded that in order to form a government he would have to enter a coalition with the Conservatives. He was not prepared to be responsible for splitting the Liberal Party and after the war to be regarded as the leader of the anti-Mackenzie King Liberals.

Before Ilsley had to make a decision, Ralston resigned and the Prime Minister appointed General Andrew McNaughton to succeed him as minister of national defence. If McNaughton, the former commander of the Army, believed that conscription for overseas service was not necessary, who am I, Ilsley confided to me, to argue with him? So he stayed, and in due course McNaughton changed his mind and the conscripts were ordered overseas.

I learned a good deal about the personality of Prime Minister Mackenzie King from Ilsley and Pickersgill, one of his secretaries. My personal contacts with him were, of course, limited. One I remember because it revealed a side of the Prime Minister that came as a pleasant surprise. Bryce and I attended a reception for federal and provincial first ministers and their advisers. Hugh Dalton, the British chancellor of the Exchequer happened to be in Ottawa at the time and was invited to the federal-provincial reception. As we circulated among the guests, Bryce and I found ourselves talking to the Prime Minister. Dalton saw us and deciding we were of no account, pushed himself in front of the Prime Minister. Mr King waved him aside, saying, 'I was talking to these young men.'

Discussion among the officials concerned with economic policy was continuous and uninhibited. It took place at the office, at social gatherings, at the Five Lakes Fishing Club (founded by Clark and his associates as an inexpensive weekend resort in the nearby Gatineau country for senior government advisers), in the Château Laurier cafeteria, at Madame Burger's, a popular restaurant in Hull. One day in the Château, when some of us were gathered for lunch, Pickersgill, then in the Prime Minister's Office, arrived accompanied by a man wearing a red tie. Pickersgill did not introduce him. We all assumed that he was well known to others at the table so our talk was, as usual, unguarded. After lunch, I got an urgent telephone call. Did I know who this man was? I didn't. Perhaps he was a spy (wearing a red tie) or a newspaperman. Finally, after several hours, Pickersgill was found. Who was this man? 'Oh,' he replied, 'that's Gerry Riddell from Manitoba who has just joined External Affairs. I couldn't remember all your names so I didn't bother introducing him.'

I came to know and work with Riddell when he and I went to Atlantic City in March 1946 with L.B. Pearson, then the secretary of state for external ffairs, for the first meeting of the United Nations Relief and Rehabilitation Agency. It was my task to provide some of the basic information about the post-war world food situation. This material Riddell converted with great skill into a text for a highly successful speech by Pearson that helped to establish his reputation and Canada's reputation as a constructive force in the post-war world.

The price ceiling

I joined the Department of Finance as the resident expert on the grain trade and on western Canadian matters generally, and in due course was given other assignments in widely differing fields. The overall price ceiling had come into effect in October 1941, under the authority of the War Measures Act, replacing the system of selective controls hitherto in effect. When I arrived in Ottawa, the Wartime Prices and Trade Board was in process of being expanded to cope with the resulting need for surveillance and regulation. The general rule was that there were to be no more price increases on consumer goods and no more rent increases on existing houses and apartments. Every housewife doing her shopping became an inspector with a duty to report any price increases. Donald Gordon had taken over the chairmanship of the board and was beginning to exercise the vigorous and flamboyant leadership that in time identified him in the public mind as the personal defender of the price ceiling.

Canada had been the first Allied country to move from selective price controls to an overall price ceiling, and I was told when I arrived how the government had been persuaded, principally by Clark, Mackintosh, and Towers, to accept the concept. It took them the summer of 1941 to do so. After the decision had been made, Mackintosh was instructed to prepare the announcement for Prime Minister King to make by radio, Parliament not being in session, and, since the War Measures Act was in force, parliamentary approval not being required. After reading the opening paragraphs of the draft, King turned to Mackintosh and said with great seriousness: 'Dr Mackintosh, this is important, isn't it?'

Shortly after my arrival, Clark asked me to be the liaison between the minister and the chairman of the Prices Board. In that capacity, I discussed the agenda for meetings, first with Gordon and in turn with Ilsley, so that Ilsley would be prepared for the decisions that had to be made. There were many. Sometimes those meetings lasted until close to midnight, particularly when the price of agricultural products had to be determined, a decision that inevitably involved a contest with Gardiner, the minister of agriculture. In retrospect it was worth it. The Canadian record on control of wartime inflation was probably the best among the Allied nations. From the application of the price ceiling in October 1941 to the end of the war, the cost of living index rose only 4 per cent.

The Wheat Committee of cabinet

Western economic problems, and particularly wheat, occupied the attention of the government and Parliament to a remarkable extent in those days. The Prairies were still a one-crop economy that had not yet recovered from the effects of drought and the Depression of the 1930s. Prairie MPs on the Liberal side and in the opposition parties were vocal. There were more speeches on wheat in Parliament than on any other subject, and the minister of agriculture, Jimmy Gardiner, with his stentorian voice, was the champion of prairie farmers. In the days before the amplification system was installed in the House of Commons, Gardiner, when he was in full flight, could be heard in the lobbies.

As the resident expert in Finance on the grain trade. I accompanied Ilsley to meetings of the Wheat Committee of cabinet, which, during the war years, consisted of James MacKinnon, minister of trade and commerce, as chairman, Gardiner, minister of agriculture, Crerar, minister of mines and resources, and Ilsley. All except Ilsley were ministers from the Prairies, one from each of the three provinces, in those days when there were prairie Liberal MPs to choose from. Charles F. Wilson, head of the Grain Division in the Department of Trade and Commerce, was secretary of the committee.

Wilson was a permanent civil servant; I was a temporary civil servant. His salary was frozen. On arrival in Ottawa I had agreed that mine would be fixed for the duration. When the salary freeze began to be lifted towards the end of the war, Ilsley told me that Treasury Board was considering a salary increase for Wilson. I thought that was appropriate. Wilson deserved it. But was that fair to me? Ilsley enquired. I had no complaint. Wilson was permanent. I had agreed to a fixed salary for the duration and didn't know whether I would stay in Ottawa. That night my super-conscientious minister telephoned me at home to tell me not to worry, that Wilson's salary was not being increased. Which illustrates, among other things, the frugal attitude that prevailed in government in those far-off wartime days and the attention that was paid by ministers to details of administration. Every telephone installation, for example, was approved by Treasury Board at its periodic meetings. In my East Block office I answered my own door and my own telephone. The secretary assigned to me was in the stenographic pool. There was no carpet on the floor.

At the end of the war, I decided to stay in government rather than return to work for the James Richardson Company in Winnipeg. The only difference it made was to unfreeze my salary which had been $4,800 per year and subject it to the ordinary public-service rules.

James MacKinnon was a gentleman but, although chairman, he was not the strongest member of the Wheat Committee of cabinet. That distinction belonged to James G. Gardiner, who found himself throughout the war fighting in the interests of the prairie farmer against the Canadian consumer and the Canadian taxpayer, and, on a personal basis, against Ilsley and Donald Gordon, chairman of the Prices Board. T.A. Crerar, who had been the leader of the Progressive Party before joining the Liberals, had his own ideas and supported the prairie producers but not always Gardiner.

As the grain adviser to Ilsley I found myself on many occasions in the Wheat Committee having to take issue with Gardiner. One day, Ilsley advised me to be careful, that Gardiner might attack me personally. That didn't happen, but Gardiner never forgot or forgave and much later, when in 1948 he was a candidate to succeed King as leader of the Liberal Party, he told a journalist friend – Max Freedman of the *Winnipeg Free Press* – that I was on the list of those to be fired if he became prime minister. Freedman added that the list was a very distinguished one. Gardiner had little regard for the leading public servants in the

Department of Finance, the Bank of Canada, and the Department of External Affairs. Nor did Crerar, who greeted Mackintosh and me one day with: 'How are the Braintrust?' To which Mackintosh replied: 'Sir, you don't think we have any brains and you don't trust us.'

Closing the Winnipeg wheat market

At the outset the overall price ceiling did not apply to wheat because, in October of 1941, when the ceiling came into effect, the wheat market, which had until then been adversely affected by the war, was depressed. Flour prices were subject to the price ceiling, however, as were the prices of all consumer goods, and flour millers were paid a drawback equal to the difference between the price of wheat in October 1941, when the price ceiling came into effect, and the price the millers had to pay on the open market.

When the phoney war came to an end in 1940 and was replaced by German advances west and east, wheat prices rose, increasing the cost of the drawback paid to flour millers. Meanwhile the Canadian government had entered into an arrangement to help the British government finance its purchases in Canada, including wheat. As wheat prices rose, so, too, did this particular drain on the Canadian Treasury.

The Department of Finance became disturbed. Ilsley became frustrated. Every cent of increase in the open market price for wheat was costing the federal Treasury $2.5 million. He wanted to stop the drain on the Treasury by closing the Winnipeg wheat market. Gardiner wouldn't agree and deliberately absented himself when efforts were made by Ilsley to discuss the subject in cabinet. In a rising market, delay was on the side of the western producers and Gardiner. Finally, after wheat prices had risen from about 77 cents for No. 1 Northern in October 1941 to $1.23 on 27 September 1943, Ilsley was able to persuade the Prime Minister to call a Cabinet meeting to face up to the issue.

We officials – from the Canadian Wheat Board and the departments of Agriculture, Finance, and Trade and Commerce – gathered in a suite of rooms in the Château Laurier to be ready for the decision. The National Liberal Federation was holding a meeting downstairs in the same hotel. After dinner we were told to vacate the sitting-room so that a cabinet meeting could be held there. We moved to the adjoining bedroom and, at midnight, MacKinnon emerged from the sitting-room to say that the decision had been made to close the market. The following morning, officials of the Wheat Board, who had attended our meeting and had then left on the overnight plane to Winnipeg, made the announcement on the Winnipeg Grain Exchange trading floor. A decision had been made by a group of ministers, but in fact there could be no government decision until the governor general had signed the necessary order under the authority of the War Measures Act. This signature was lacking. The president of the Winnipeg Grain Exchange – who had not questioned the validity of the announcement and had acted on it – was threatened with a lawsuit for having acted without authority in preventing trading, but the order, when it appeared had, of course, a retroactive effect and the issue died. That incident taught me a lesson I never forgot about the nature of the Canadian Constitution.

Until the Winnipeg wheat market was closed, the western farmer had the alternative of selling his wheat on the market or of delivering it to the Canadian Wheat Board, which acted like a cooperative, paying an initial price at time of delivery and the balance when the board had sold the wheat. When the Winnipeg market was closed, the farmer could sell only to the Canadian Wheat Board, which became, as the prairie wheat pool organizations had always advocated, the sole marketing agency for western wheat. In effect, it was a compulsory wheat pool making an initial payment to the producers on delivery and distributing any surplus from the sale of the wheat in the form of interim and final payments. It was said that the closing of the Winnipeg wheat market and the creation of the Canadian Wheat Board monopoly, which paid the same price to all farmers for the same grade at the same shipping point, removed one serious source of domestic discord on the Prairies, the discord that arose when the wife criticized her farmer husband because he misjudged the market and sold his wheat at a lower price than his neighbour. It wasn't the arguments of the wheat pool members, however, that led the government to make that crucial decision. It was the exigencies of wartime. What is significant is that there was no reversion at the end of the war to the former status of the Canadian Wheat Board as a voluntary marketing agency. Later, as C.D. Howe's deputy and, later still, as the minister responsible for the Canadian Wheat Board in my own right, I was to be closely involved with the operations of the board.

The closing of the Winnipeg wheat market and the establishment of the Canadian Wheat Board as the sole marketing agency for wheat concentrated decision making on wheat in Ottawa. At the end of the war in 1946, it enabled the government to enter into a long-term, four-year wheat agreement with Britain about which I had serious misgivings.

The story of that agreement is too long and complicated to present fully in these memoirs. Briefly, Gardiner wanted it and got his way, notwithstanding strong opposition from the Wheat Board and trade-policy officials in Ottawa, and even misgivings by Prime Minister Mac-kenzie King. When it was all over, a dispute arose as to whether the British government had fulfilled its obligations under a curious and celebrated 'have regard to' clause drafted by the British and accepted by Gardiner. The British government said it had. Gardiner contended that the Canadian producers were owed an additional amount over and above the prices stipulated in the contract. When the British refused to pay, the Canadian Government decided to assume the obligation and to pay $65 million to the Wheat Board – the unused portion of the wartime loan to the United Kingdom – for distribution to producers who had provided wheat to the British government under the contract.

Apart from opposing the agreement, my principal activity at the end, when I had moved to the Department of Trade and Commerce, was to draft, along with C.F. Wilson, the statement that Howe made in the House of Commons justifying the $65-million settlement, about which he was not enthusiastic. We thought that we had produced a balanced defence of the government's policy. After he had read our draft to the House of Commons, Howe decided to improvise and the careful balance we had struck was destroyed. When Howe returned to his office after making his speech in the House, he realized what he had done. 'I guess I should have stopped when the script stopped.'

The creation of a compulsory Wheat Board also facilitated negotiations for an international wheat agreement by providing a workable mechanism for Canadian participation. Although I had been associated with the private grain trade in Winnipeg before going to Ottawa, I came to the view that the fundamental changes in the Canadian wheat-marketing system that had taken place were not only inevitable but, on the whole, in the interests of the western producers who would otherwise have been alone and unprotected in meeting government-supported competition from exporters like the United States. Fortunately, the Canadian Wheat Board was led then and was to be led later by some particularly able chief commissioners, about whom I shall have more to say.

Tommy Douglas versus Ottawa

In 1944, the Liberal government of Saskatchewan was defeated by the CCF under the leadership of T.C. Douglas. One of the inducements to voters held out by Douglas was the forgiveness of the debts owed by Saskatchewan farmers for seed grain advanced to them during the years of drought and economic depression. When he came to power, Douglas proceeded to implement his promise. These seed-grain advances had originally been guaranteed by the federal and Saskatchewan governments. The question therefore arose as to who was to bear the cost of forgiveness – the federal or the Saskatchewan government?

Clark was of the view that the federal government should bear the cost, since there never was any real chance that the advances would be repaid by the farmers. Ilsley was uncertain. During the election campaign the former premier of Saskatchewan – W.J. Patterson – had asked the federal government to authorize him to match Douglas's promise of forgiveness, but had been refused. I was sent to Regina to discuss the situation with Patterson, Gardiner, and Gordon Taggart, former Saskatchewan minister of agriculture, who was to come to Ottawa as Donald Gordon's right-hand man on agriculture. They were adamant that the new CCF government should be held to its guarantee. I so reported and advised and Ilsley agreed.

The Government of Saskatchewan responded by offering in payment of the amount owing under the guarantee a demand note for some $14 million, this being the form of indebtedness that the Saskatchewan government had offered as security for other Depression- and drought-related debts owed by the province to Ottawa. Payment of those demand notes had never been demanded.

This time, however, the federal government interpreted the note literally and sent a Treasury official to the Royal Bank in Regina to demand $14 million. The startled manager, of course, had no such sum available and could not meet the demand. The federal government declared Saskatchewan to be in default and deducted the amount owing from the next payment due to Saskatchewan under the federal-provincial tax agreement. Saskatchewan took the matter to arbitration under the provisions of the tax agreement. Ottawa won the case and negotiated a settlement with Saskatchewan involving payments stretched over a long period of years.

This incident throws light on a number of facets of the Department of Finance in those years. Clark was by no means the hard-fisted Treasury stereotype. He sympathized with those who had suffered during the calamitous thirties, as he had suffered personally. Clark was working in New York when the Depression struck and found himself owing a substantial sum of money when property values collapsed; he was still paying off the debt when he became deputy minister of finance. He wanted to improve the position of debt-ridden governments like Saskatchewan, so that they could better discharge their responsibilities in the future. Nevertheless, he did not question my advice to the minister. The incident also illustrates vividly how difficult it is in practice for a non-partisan civil servant to draw the line between political and economic advice.

Revision of the Bank Act

I played a minor role in the 1944 decennial revision of the Bank Act, which, because of the war, took place a couple of years late, a revision that began the modernization of our banking institutions, that I continued as minister of finance in the 1965 revision, and that is still under way as I write these memoirs. I was assigned the negotiations with representatives of the chartered banks (James Muir of the Royal Bank and James Stewart of the Canadian Imperial Bank of Commerce, both to become presidents of their respective institutions) to induce them to make loans to farmers to finance the purchase of machinery and equipment. This involved extending the powers of the banks to take security under the Bank Act and new legislation to provide a limited federal guarantee against loss to the banks – the Farm Improvement Loans Act – the operation of which, after enactment, I supervised. The banks responded positively to the challenge. Farmers turned, many of them for the first time, to their local bank branch to finance their purchases of equipment. For a number of years, losses under the Farm Improvement Loans Act were absurdly small.

One of the central issues then was, and continues to be, the place of the chartered banks in the financial structure of Canada. In that 1944 revision, the banks were encouraged to extend their activities. At the same time, rivals to the banks outside federal control were beginning to appear, among them provincially incorporated trust companies, credit unions, and caisses populaires. These institutions were not called banks but increasingly performed banking services, including the acceptance of deposits and the making of loans. Should an attempt be made to bring them under the provisions of the Bank Act? My recollection is that the deputy minister of finance and the governor of the Bank of Canada, although tempted to do so, were not prepared to make such a recommendation to the minister. I have often wondered what would have happened if the attempt had been made in 1944 and had been successfully carried through. My feeling is that there would have been fewer failures of trust companies and caisses populaires if federal regulations had been in effect. It was not until many years later, when deposit-insurance guarantees became necessary because of the financial difficulties of some trust companies, that federal supervision began to be applied to such institutions in return for the guarantees.

Union with Newfoundland

Soon after the end of the war, the government had to decide whether to invite Newfoundland into the Canadian Confederation. Ilsley was not enthusiastic. He regarded Newfoundland as another poor Atlantic province that would impose an additional drain on Ottawa. He suggested to me that our high commissioner in Newfoundland, C.J. Burchell, and other Canadian officials, were exceeding their authority by encouraging talk of union. There was said to be on the files in External Affairs a memorandum on the subject on which O.D. Skelton had pencilled, 'Be careful, or the British will sell us Newfoundland.' Certainly the British government was ready to transfer the responsibility to Canada.

There was, however, strong support within the government for the idea of union. Louis St Laurent, minister of justice until he became prime minister on 15 November 1948, L.B. Pearson, secretary of state for external affairs, and Brooke Claxton, minister of national defence, were strong advocates. They were joined on the official level by Pickersgill in the Prime Minister's Office and Alex (Sandy) Skelton, who had been the powerful secretary of the Rowell-Sirois Commission and was the son of O.D. Skelton, regarded as the father of the modern Canadian civil service. External Affairs was fearful that Newfoundland might join the United States and dominate the entrance to the Gulf of St Lawrence; R.A. (Bert) MacKay worked hard for union. Prime Minister King was cautious, as usual.

I was assigned by Clark to study the economic and particularly the financial implications of the union. I persuaded Alan Hockin, who later had a distinguished career in the department before entering the banking business and academia, to come to Ottawa as secretary of the Interdepartmental Committee, of which I was chairman. In that capacity I met all the leading political figures in Newfoundland and, in the final stages of the negotiations worked closely with Joseph Smallwood, who became premier of Newfoundland, and F. Gordon Bradley, who became a minister in the St Laurent government.

In between the visit of the first delegation from Newfoundland in June 1947 and the opening of negotiations for the Terms of Union, I made my first visit to St John's, in company with Bert MacKay of External Affairs. On the day following our arrival there appeared in the St John's *Daily News*, in the column signed by 'The Wayfarer,' something

like the following: (I have not been able to find a copy of the original):
'There has arrived in St. John's Dr. R.A. MacKay of the Department of
External Affairs and Mr. Mitchell Sharp of the Department of Finance
in Canada. If Mackenzie King and Joe Smallwood are the undertakers
of Union with Canada, these are the undertakers' assistants.'

Throughout the negotiations it was evident to me and to all those
involved on the Canadian side that opinion in Newfoundland about
union with Canada was sharply divided. Without the skilful and vigorous
advocacy of Smallwood, the Canadian option would have had little
chance of acceptance. Smallwood's methods were effective; they were
not always above reproach. The Canadian ministers became very concerned when, every day following the presumably secret discussions
between the Canadian and Newfoundland delegations, there appeared
in the St John's press a full account of what had taken place. We called
in the journalist who was writing the stories and asked him bluntly
whether some official was leaking the information to him. We had to
know, because so much was at stake. No, there was no leak, he told us.
Every day, Smallwood gave him a full account of what was happening.
As I recall it, Smallwood didn't apologize or desist. His purpose was to
keep the negotiations with Canada on the front page in Newfoundland.
As it turned out, even with his advocacy, the margin in favour of union
with Canada in the second referendum of 1948 was very small indeed:
52 per cent voted in favour.

Prime Minister King had said during the debate in Parliament that he
would offer union only if a substantial majority of Newfoundlanders was
in favour. The results of the referendum obviously fell short of that
criterion. Pickersgill told me that, when King hesitated, he asked the
Prime Minister how often, when the Liberal Party had won an election
under his leadership, more than half of the voters had voted for Liberal
candidates. It had hapened only once, in 1940.

Negotiations of the financial terms of union were not of the conventional kind. We didn't bargain directly with the Newfoundland delegation, trying to ascertain what price had to be paid to induce them to
join. The members of the Canadian government had to make up their
collective mind as to what sort of terms were fair and reasonable and
compatible with the treatment of other Atlantic provinces and leave it
up to the Newfoundland delegation to decide whether they were justified in recommending union.

Term 29 of the Terms of Union was the key, because it held out hope
that the financial provisions could be revised if they were found to be
inadequate.

Which Reminds Me ...

Review of Financial Position

29. In view of the difficulty of predicting with sufficient accuracy the financial consequences to Newfoundland of becoming a province of Canada, the Government of Canada will appoint a Royal Commission within eight years from the date of Union to review the financial position of the Province of Newfoundland and to recommend the form and scale of additional financial assistance, if any, that may be required by the Government of the Province of Newfoundland to enable it to continue public services at the levels and standards reached subsequent to the date of Union, without resorting to taxation more burdensome, having regard to capacity to pay, than that obtaining generally in the region comprising the Maritime Provinces of Nova Scotia, New Brunswick, and Prince Edward Island.

MacKay and I drafted that particular term after discussing it at length with Bradley. Had Prime Minister Diefenbaker understood the sensitivity of the issue, he would never have cast doubt upon the Newfoundland interpretation as he did in 1959.

Before leaving office in 1957, the Liberal government had appointed a royal commission under the provisions of Term 29. It reported to the Diefenbaker government and recommended additional payments to Newfoundland that rose slightly each year for five years and then continued indefinitely at the level reached in the fifth year. In 1959, the Diefenbaker government responded with legislation that accepted the royal commission's recommendations for the five years but terminated the payments at the end of the fifth year.

Here is the exchange in the House of Commons between Diefenbaker and Pickersgill on 25 March 1959.

Pickersgill I should like to ask the Prime Minister whether I understood him correctly to say that the legislation which he announced the government intends to bring down to implement the recommendations of the McNair Commission contemplated the complete discharge of the obligation under section 29 of the terms of union by that legislation will expire on March 31, 1962.
Diefenbaker That is so ...
Pickersgill Every person in Newfoundland will regard this as another breach of a solemn contract.

Which most of them did, and for years thereafter voters took it out on the Conservative Party in Newfoundland.

Several years after union, I went to Newfoundland to try to work out an agreement on prices between the fishermen and the fish trade. While passing through Gander, I encountered Ches Crosbie, the one member of the Newfoundland delegation who had refused to endorse the Terms of Union. He was holding forth to a crowd in the railway station when I entered the building. As soon as he saw me, he turned his invective in my direction. 'There's the son of a bitch who negotiated the financial Terms of Union. I wouldn't sign them.' And so forth. Fortunately for me, he was distracted by a U.S. soldier in uniform, from the nearby American base. 'Here's a representative of the occupying power.'

On that trip, Premier Smallwood asked me to meet with him. The embezzlement of several hundreds of thousands of dollars by Alfred A. Valdmanis, a mysterious Latvian who was principal economic adviser to the premier, had just been uncovered. While I was in the premier's office, the RCMP phoned to assure him that no member of his cabinet was involved. I took advantage of the occasion to urge the premier to appoint a strong businessman to his cabinet. In earthy language Smallwood expressed his opinion of Water Street merchants and declined my suggestion. Amused by my shock at the Valdmanis affair, he went on to describe in detail another attempt to defraud the Newfoundland government, that, fortunately, was frustrated at the last minute just as the culprit was about to leave Newfoundland with his ill-gotten gains. Joey was incorrigible.

Douglas Abbott becomes minister of finance

Douglas Abbott became minister of finance in 1946. He was a very different minister from Ilsley. As Ilsley himself remarked, 'Abbott will never be a martyr.' He was in appearance and manner easygoing, a popular figure in his party. He did not like long-drawn-out discussions and was prepared to make decisions and accept the consequences. In debate in the House of Commons he was quick and forceful and avoided acrimony. Many observers, like myself, thought he had a good chance of becoming leader of the Liberal Party. But apparently that was not his ambition. He is reported to have said that he would rather write a memorable decision as a Supreme Court justice, which he became, than be prime minister of Canada.

The advent of Abbott as minister represented an enormous change in the climate of discussion in the Department of Finance. In the first place the war was over; in addition, Abbott was not a worrier, as Ilsley had been. In one respect, however, the procedure of decision making remained much the same. Abbott consulted his deputy minister and other senior civil servants regularly as a matter of course. He liked to have issues argued out in front of him, although not interminably, and he liked to be well briefed both for cabinet and for the House. He handled his briefs with dexterity and aplomb.

After the lifting of the overall price ceiling, the fear was of inflation, and for a time in the post-war period prices rose substantially. In the two worst years, 1947 and 1948, prices were 8.5 per cent and 12.4 per cent respectively above the year before. I prepared a speech for the minister warning about the dangers of inflation and urging the public to avoid inflationary behaviour. The speech got a good deal of media attention. To temper my sense of satisfaction, Abbott read me a letter from one of his uncles who wrote that, while it was a good speech, the minister was on the wrong track politically; provided that prices do not rise too quickly, most people like inflation because it means higher wages and higher profits. As I was to discover for myself when I had the responsibility as minister of finance, that was probably a correct assessment of popular attitudes. At any rate Canadians got what they apparently favoured. Since the end of the Second World War, consumer prices have risen by more than 400 per cent – that is, have more than quadrupled.

Decontrol of prices and rents

The end of the war did not bring an immediate end to price and rent controls in Canada. A policy of gradual decontrol was decided upon by the government. Donald Gordon became chief executive officer of the Canadian National Railways, and Kenneth W. Taylor succeeded him as chairman of the Wartime Prices and Trade Board.

Abbott asked James Sinclair, his parliamentary secretary, to handle the legislation to extend for the last time the Transitional Measures Act that had replaced the use of the War Measures Act. I arranged for the Department of Justice to draft the bill, which was given first reading in the Commons, and personally drafted the speech to be delivered by Sinclair on second reading. Unfortunately, I did not meet with Sinclair until the day that second reading was to take place. He read the bill and expressed concern about its basic thrust, which was to seek undiminished authority for another year. Why hadn't the unneeded powers been allowed to lapse? I explained that in the judgment of Justice officials and myself it was easier to obtain parliamentary approval for a simple one-year extension of the legislation than to obtain approval of a complicated revision. Sinclair disagreed. But by that time it was too late to do anything about it, since the bill had already been read for the first time.

I sat in the gallery to watch the proceedings. Sinclair read the speech and, as he predicted, Donald Fleming, the opposition spokesman on economic matters and my predecessor as MP for Eglinton, rose in high dudgeon to condemn this power-hungry government for seeking authority to reintroduce price controls and rationing and so forth. There were some other interventions and Sinclair rose to conclude the debate on second reading. I wondered what he would say. He began by disposing of the minor opposition speakers and then turned to Fleming. What an eloquent speech the member for Eglinton had delivered! Sinclair had made notes of some of the high-sounding phrases, which he read back to the House. Listening to those phrases had rung a bell, said Sinclair. So he had called for *Hansard,* and sure enough Fleming had delivered much the same speech a year before when the Transitional Measures Act had last been extended.

I descended from the gallery to the floor to sit before Sinclair as the speaker left the Chair and the House went into Committee of the Whole for clause-by-clause consideration, which was the general practice for all legislation in those days. (Nowadays legislation is referred at the report stage to a select committee.) Sinclair leaned over to whisper to me that Fleming was furious and would renew his attack with even greater vigour. How many powers included in the bill did we really need? When I replied that we needed only the first four, he suggested private prayers. As soon as the first clause was called, Fleming was on his feet, once again attacking the power-hungry government and challenging Sinclair to say that this clause was needed. When he had concluded, Sinclair leaned over and in a loud whisper that could be heard throughout the House, asked me if we needed this particular power and, if so, why. I replied in a whisper that couldn't be heard except by Sinclair, who thereupon rose to his feet and repeated what I had said. And so it went for the next three clauses. Our prayers were answered. Fleming became tired and gave up after clause four, and the rest of the bill was approved without further discussion.

As I have recounted, at the end of the war the Canadian government decided to remove price controls gradually. The U.S. government, on the other hand, decided in 1946 to remove all their price controls in one fell swoop. As a result the general level of prices in that country rose more quickly than in Canada.

The Bank of Canada recommended to the minister of finance that the Canadian dollar, which had been at 90 per cent of parity with the U.S. dollar since 1939, should be restored to full parity, partly as an anti-inflationary measure, since the prices of imports and exports would be restrained by the increase in the value of the Canadian dollar. I participated in the internal debate and was one of a small number of people who was aware of the decision to make the change, effective on 5 July, 1946, after the close of business.

By chance, in the morning of that day, I travelled by streetcar with a newspaper reporter who specialized in economic matters. He began speculating about the effects of the differing decontrol policies of the Canadian and U.S. governments and finally came out with the inevitable question: did I think that this would result in a change in the exchange rate? I thought rapidly. To say that I could not comment would have been a dead giveaway. To hesitate might be subject to a similar interpretation. So, aware of the catastrophic consequences of a leak, I lied brazenly. 'John,' I said, 'that's way outside my field of responsibility. You'd better talk to somebody who knows more about exchange rates.' That night, after the announcement had been made I got a call from that reporter. 'Damn you,' he said, 'you put me off completely. I was certain that if anything was about to happen you would know, so I didn't follow it up.' I apologized.

The decontrol of rents proved to be a particularly difficult issue. The government was very much aware of the devastating consequences upon construction and building maintenance in several European countries of indefinite retention of rent controls and was determined to get out of controls, cleanly and fully, at some point. The question was how, since rent controls were very popular among tenants not only of housing units but also of commercial properties in desirable locations, where rents were bound to rise sharply when controls were lifted.

In the absence of a national emergency like war, rent control falls clearly within provincial jurisdiction. Somehow, therefore, the provinces had to be faced with the necessity and opportunity of deciding whether they wanted to retain controls when federal jurisdiction lapsed.

David Mundell, then solicitor to the Treasury, and I recommended to Abbott that the government should state a case to the Supreme Court of Canada. Our advice was accepted and the court was asked to rule on the validity of the Wartime Leasehold Regulations. In 1950, the court gave its opinion, which, in essence, declared that federal rent controls were still valid but not indefinitely. Thereupon the government wrote to the provinces notifying them that all federal rent controls would be lifted approximately a year later. The provinces squirmed but, with a few minor exceptions, did not replace federal with provincial controls. The federal government got out cleanly and fully.

Varied assignments

Because of the overriding interest of the Department of Finance in all activities with an economic aspect – and that was virtually everything – Finance officials were given widely varying assignments. Looking back I marvel at our versatility or, some might say, our presumption.

Just before the opening of serious negotiations on the Terms of Union with Newfoundland, Clark asked me to help his good friend Professor Clifford Curtis of Queen's University, and then mayor of Kingston, to prepare the report of the Royal Commission on Prices, of which he was chairman. The hearings were over and Curtis had neither the time nor the resources to draft a report. Within a few days, the commission was presented with a series of chapter headings, and young economists, some of whom subsequently rose to the top of their profession, were found to help draft the contents. I wrote a couple of chapters myself. It wasn't an earth-shaking document, but reports of royal commissions seldom are.

I worked with the President of the Royal Insurance Company, who was on secondment from his company, on a system of War Risk Insurance for grain. While Ilsley was minister, I tried my best to devise an equitable form of taxation of cooperatives, a method that survived for a time. In 1945, I attended an organization meeting of the International Civil Aviation Organization (ICAO) in Montreal to advise on a system of internal income taxation as a means of minimizing the problems of equity arising from the presence in this international agency of foreign personnel who, unlike their Canadian colleagues, were not subject to Canadian income tax. In 1947, I went to London as the head of the Canadian delegation to a Commonwealth Telecommunications Conference hosted by Lord Reith, head of the BBC. The conference was consequent upon the dismemberment of the British Cable and Wireless organization, and out of it in due course emerged the Canadian Overseas Telecommunication Corporation, later transformed into Teleglobe.

Bryce and I, on one memorable occasion, negotiated with James G. Gardiner, the minister of agriculture, and drafted the first agricultural-price-support legislation, a sort of rural counterpart of unemployment insurance for industrial workers.

My introduction to the United Nations came while I was an official in the Department of Finance. I was asked to allow my name to be put forward for election to the Committee on Contributions, which recommended the percentage contribution of each member country to the upkeep of the organization. I was duly elected in 1949 and served for three years, latterly as vice-chairman. My name was put forward again in 1952 by the Canadian delegation for re-election to another three-year term, on the naïve assumption that members were elected for their personal qualifications to what was asserted to be a technical committee. Our delegation did not campaign on my behalf. The Czechoslovak delegation were politically realistic. They campaigned for their candidate as a representative of the Eastern European Bloc and won. By this time, C.D. Howe was my minister, and that experienced politician laughed when I told him of my first electoral defeat.

Post-war recruitment

Just as O.D. Skelton had recruited Clifford Clark as deputy minister of finance, so Clark had recruited the core of the senior bureaucrats in the department. Similarly, Graham Towers had selected his principal officials in the Bank of Canada. In both Finance and the bank they were drawn from private business and university faculties.

Few of these officials were career bureaucrats who had spent their working lives in government in Ottawa. When John Maynard Keynes came to Ottawa at the end of the war to negotiate a settlement of British government wartime debts, Clark gave a luncheon for him, to which he invited his senior departmental officials, the governor of the Bank of Canada, and his senior officials. I overheard Keynes ask Clark where these officials had come from. Clark went around the table: Towers came from the Royal Bank, Donald Gordon from the Bank of Nova Scotia, Rasminsky from the League of Nations Secretariat, Bryce (who had been one of Keynes's students) from the Sun Life Assurance Company, Sharp from the grain trade, and so on. Keynes's comment was that this could not happen in Britain. The senior public servants there had been recruited at university level, without outside experience. (Keynes was wrong, as it happened, and as his own career reveals.)

When the war came to an end, active recruitment for the Department of Finance had to take place. The Public Service Commission advertised openings at three levels, hoping to attract candidates from the returning veterans as well as civilians. The response was good and, after a preliminary screening to eliminate those who could not meet academic standards, a board was established to meet candidates who had survived.

Our standards were high and the examining board of similar quality, including Taylor, Deutsch, Bryce, Coyne, Eaton, and myself. We had not only to qualify candidates but to grade them. Out of this and subsequent examinations came Sidney Pollock, Simon Reisman, John Macdonald, Denis Hudon, and Edgar Gallant. All except Pollock, who unfortunately died prematurely of a brain tumour, were in due course to rise to become deputy ministers.

Those of us at senior levels considered it part of our responsibilities to encourage talent and the perpetuation of the ideal of public service at the top levels of the service.

During the war, there were no French Canadians in the senior ranks of the Department of Finance or of the Bank of Canada, except one of the deputy governors of the Bank, L.P. St Amour, who was concerned with administration rather than policy. When I arrived in Ottawa I did not notice the absence, which is in itself a commentary on the prevailing attitudes of the time, particularly among westerners like myself who had had no significant contacts with French Canadians at university or in business. The only Canadian economists I knew, or had heard about, were English-speaking.

No effort was made until the end of the war to attract French-Canadian economists to Ottawa. Nor, on the other hand, was there much enthusiasm on the part of Quebec economists to move to the capital. Language of work was a barrier; even more important was the reluctance of the wives to leave the congenial Quebec atmosphere of family and friends. Maurice Lamontagne, who was among the first to accept an invitation to enter federal government service at the end of the war, told me years later how difficult it had been to make the transition from the Faculty of Social Sciences at Laval University to Ottawa and how grateful he was for the patience and understanding of senior English-speaking bureaucrats with whom he worked.

Since those days, French Canadians have come to assume their rightful place in the senior levels of the public service, and French-Canadian ministers from Quebec – who, when I came to Ottawa, were usually assigned the portfolios of Justice, Secretary of State, Post Office, and Public Works (except, of course, for Mr St Laurent, who held the External Affairs portfolio after he was minister of justice) – have in recent years held every important policy-making portfolio in the cabinet. Pierre Trudeau set out to prove to the people of Quebec that their MPs could play a full part in the Government of Canada. He succeeded, partly because of help from English-speaking Canadians like myself who shared his views about Canadian unity.

Veterans' rehabilitation and old-age pensions

Clark took an active interest in the program for post-war rehabilitation of veterans. He felt that this program should be comprehensive and generous and he did not wait for proposals to be made by the Department of Veterans Affairs, as might have been expected of the deputy minister of finance. He took the initiative, and it became one of my responsibilities to help him in the interdepartmental discussions that led up to the preparation and presentation to Parliament of the legislation. Clark looked upon the rehabilitation of veterans as a significant part of Canada's post-war reconstruction. The returning veterans were to be given not just money but education and training and a stake in the modern Canada that was emerging from the war. It was to be one of the most fruitful investments ever made by the federal government.

This concern also helped, I believe, to motivate Clark in his sympathetic approach to social security. Persuaded by Beattie of the Bank of Canada, he advocated the introduction of family allowances and, notwithstanding the scepticism of Ilsley, persuaded Prime Minister King to support them. I recall Clark pointing out, among other things, the usefulness of family allowances as a means of helping to equalize the personal position of a single wage earner and a fellow worker with children, both of whom were paid the same base wage rate. Family allowances came into effect in 1944. Clark favoured the replacement of the means-test system of old-age pensions by a universal system, although he was concerned, as I was, that universal pensions that were not related to individual contributions might be difficult to keep under control. This proved to be the case.

When the Joint Parliamentary Committee on Old Age Pensions was established in 1950, Clark asked me to attend the committee and to represent the department in the discussions with the Department of Health and Welfare. George Davidson, the deputy minister of welfare, and I worked with the chairman of the committee, Jean Lesage, later a minister in the St Laurent government and premier of Quebec.

Privately, I advocated a two-tier system of old-age pensions, consisting of a basic universal pension supported out of general revenue and payable without a means test to everyone seventy years of age and over, plus a contributory pension related to individual contributions. I was ahead of my time. The committee was interested in only one thing – getting rid of the means test. So they recommended unanimously a universal old-age pension of forty dollars a month payable at age seventy without a means test, a measure that Parliament subsequently enacted into law. I was, however, in the government that – years later – presented the legislation establishing the second tier, namely the contributory Canada Pension Plan.

As the Old Age Security Bill was moving through Parliament, I met Paul Martin, the minister of health and welfare, in a corridor of the House of Commons and congratulated him. But Martin did not accept my congratulations. My priority, he told me, prophetically, is medical-care insurance.

After the universal pension was approved, an Old Age Security Fund was established in 1951 into which certain earmarked taxes – 2 per cent on corporate profits, 2 per cent on personal incomes (with a limit of sixty dollars), and 2 per cent sales tax – were deposited and out of which the universal old-age pension was paid. The idea was to make abundantly clear to everybody that the government has no income of its own but can only pay out with one hand such money as it takes in with the other by taxation.

In other words, the hope was that the existence of the fund and the taxes would curb the inevitable pressures to raise the pension and to lower the eligible age.

There is no evidence that this hope was realized. The amount of the pension was increased from time to time; the age of eligibility was gradually lowered from seventy to sixty-five. At first, the earmarked taxes were increased to meet the added cost. In 1971, they were abolished and replaced by equivalent amounts of general revenue. In 1975, the fund itself was abolished. In ten of the twenty-five years of its existence, the fund was in deficit.

*The Economic Policy Division
and federal-provincial relations*

In 1947, Bryce became assistant deputy minister of finance and secretary of the Treasury Board. John Deutsch, like me a westerner, though a graduate of Queen's (twenty-one years later he became principal of the university), joined the Department of Finance in 1946. He and I divided the economic policy field, Deutsch covering the international side (he was one of the founders of the GATT) and I the domestic side, although from time to time both of us strayed across the line. I became the head of the Economic Policy Division.

One result was the enlargement of the scope of the papers tabled at the time of the presentation by the minister of finance of his budget. Until then, these papers had contained only the tables of federal expenditures and revenues. In 1948, for the first time these governmental statistics were prefaced by an analysis of the economic situation in Canada and its relationship to fiscal policy. The first preface that I drafted was brief, some six pages. Year by year thereafter, the scope of the analysis has been enlarged until these supplementary budget papers comprise several booklets – illustrated by graphics in colour.

Federal-provincial relations fell within my responsibility as head of the Economic Policy Division, a responsibility I shared, of course, with the Taxation Division of the department. The 1942 tax-rental agreements with the provinces, by which the provinces temporarily withdrew from the fields of personal and corporate income taxes in return for rental payments, were due to expire in 1947. By giving the federal government the freedom it needed to raise income taxes to what were considered maximum tolerable levels, these agreements had contributed substantially to the success of the Canadian financial program in the Second World War. The confusion and overlapping between federal and provincial income taxes that had existed before the war disappeared for five years throughout the country.

In 1937, the Rowell-Sirois Commission had recommended that personal and corporate income taxes and succession duties should be utilized solely by the federal government as part of its approach to the economic reconstruction of Canada following the Great Depression. There was strong opposition from the governments of the big provinces. In 1942, they did, however, agree to withdraw temporarily from these fields in return for rental payments. In fact, they had no alternative, since they would not have dared to impose provincial income taxes on top of the high federal taxes.

The tax-rental agreements had contributed to the successful financing of the war. Clifford Clark believed strongly, as did his associates in the department and in the Bank of Canada, that their extension, with suitable modifications, would contribute to post-war reconstruction. Equipped with these revenue levers, the federal government would be better able to implement national fiscal policies to promote steady, non-inflationary growth throughout the country. Taxpayers would benefit from having to satisfy only one tax collector. The rental payments could be used to distribute more fairly among the provinces revenues from taxes imposed on corporations whose head offices were located in Ontario and Quebec and, more generally, to give much-needed help to the smaller and weaker provinces.

From August 1945 onward, Ilsley made a series of proposals in an effort to persuade the provinces to continue to rent the 'triple tax fields' of taxes on personal income, corporation income, and inheritance to the federal government. In the end, Quebec declined to renew its agreement on any terms, and Ontario insisted on the restoration of its right to impose corporation taxes. Later developments when I became minister of finance are discussed in chapter 6.

Housing

Clark always took a keen interest in housing policy. The Dominion Housing Act of 1935 was his personal creation, and he continued to favour using government guarantees of housing loans as the principal means of promoting house construction and of raising housing standards. During the later stages of the war it became necessary, however, for the government to take more direct action to provide housing for those employed in wartime industries, and a Crown corporation – Wartime Housing – was created for the purpose.

As the war drew to an end and veterans began returning to Civvy Street, housing became an urgent and complicated issue. For a few months I was chairman of an interdepartmental committee on the subject. The National Housing Act remained as a conventional vehicle for those wishing to build and own their homes. The new Veterans' Land Act provided housing for those returning veterans who preferred a rural or semi-rural life. Wartime Housing continued to provide a minimum type of urban rental accommodation. There was growing support for new ideas, such as rent geared to income and cooperative housing of one kind or another, and for town planning.

David Mansur, one of the organizers of Victory Bond campaigns during wartime and before the war an expert in the field of mortgage financing, persuaded Clark that new comprehensive housing legislation was desirable and that responsibility should be assigned to a new government corporation. Clark did the first draft of the legislation. He sent his draft to the deputy minister of justice, Fred Varcoe, for comments. When the comments arrived, Clark phoned Varcoe to thank him and to ask why Varcoe had not revised the preamble, which set out the purpose of the bill. Varcoe's explanation was brief and to the point: 'You can't draft BS.'

Mansur and I worked on the ministerial statement. In due course, on 2 January 1946, Parliament approved the creation of the Central Mortgage and Housing Corporation (CMHC) and Mansur became its first president. The deputy minister of finance was an ex-officio member of the board of directors. I attended board meetings as his representative.

My involvement in housing led me to work for a short period with William Anderson, a brilliant mathematician and actuary (and bridge player). Charles Goren, the international bridge expert, gave credit to Anderson for the probability calculations that underlay his bidding system. Mrs (Marjory) Anderson was for a time Goren's bridge partner. Clifford Clark asked Anderson, as head of the North American Life Assurance Company, to come to Ottawa for six months as an adviser on housing policy. Anderson's mind was fertile. He threw out ideas one on top of another, some practical, some not so practical, but all of them stimulating. A conversation with him was exhausting. At one point, he became interested in tax reform and elaborated a system of heavy consumer taxes and a flat income tax combined with universal demographic payments that would substitute for most social programs like family allowances, unemployment insurance, and old-age pensions and eliminate the disincentive effects of the graduated income tax. It was a brilliant effort but far too revolutionary to be acceptable to Canadian politicians of those days. Donald Macdonald, one of my colleagues in the Trudeau government, made similar proposals in the 1985 report of the Royal Commission on the Economic Union and Development Prospects for Canada, of which he was chairman, without much effect on policy, unless one regards the GST as the beginning of heavy consumer taxes.

My transfer at the end of 1950 from the Department of Finance to the Department of Trade and Commerce was related in a curious way to this connection with housing and the CMHC. Mansur had told me that he would like me to become vice-president of the CMHC and in due course succeed him as president. When cabinet was considering the appointment of General Hugh Young, who was then vice-president of CMHC, as deputy minister of public works, one of the cabinet ministers remarked that this would clear the way for Mansur to propose me as vice-president. Whereupon Howe is reported to have said that if Sharp was prepared to leave Finance there would be competition. A few days later, Max Mackenzie, Howe's deputy in Trade and Commerce, who was about to become deputy minister of the newly created Department of Defence Production, offered me the job of assistant deputy minister of trade and commerce. It was understood that when Mackenzie moved on, three months later, I was to become associate deputy alongside Fred Bull as deputy minister.

CHAPTER THREE

In the Department of
Trade and Commerce,
1950–1958

Learning to work with C.D. Howe

My move to Trade and Commerce took place at the beginning of 1951 in the midst of the Korean War. The day I reported for business as assistant deputy minister, Max Mackenzie, the deputy, was ill with chickenpox, and Fred Bull, who was to succeed him when Mackenzie moved to Defence Production, had fallen down the cement steps at the rear of No. 1 Temporary Building, where the department had its headquarters, and was temporarily out of action. Nominally, I was the senior official and in charge.

At that particular moment in time, however, the most important departmental official was Norbert Beaupré (known as Beaup), executive assistant to Mackenzie, because he was seeing Howe on a regular basis, representing the absent deputy. Beaupré came to visit me. Howe, he explained, wanted to participate in the debate on the reply to the Speech from the Throne when Parliament resumed. He wanted me to prepare a draft speech. At the same time, Beaupré handed me a thick book of notes about the activities of the Department of Trade and Commerce prepared by Jack Firestone, head of the Economics Branch.

I set to work and produced a draft forty-minute speech that included among other things a dissertation on price controls, for the administration of which I was to be responsible if and when they were introduced by the government during the Korean War. Fortunately, they never were. I sent the notes to Mackenzie at home for review. He thought they were satisfactory so I sent them along to Beaupré. Nothing happened for several days and I was about to ask him for the Minister's reaction when Beaupré appeared, carrying with him a long manuscript. The Minister had dictated it to his secretary. Beaupré thought it was dreadful. When I read it, so did I. The Minister couldn't possibly deliver a speech like that, we both agreed. I was uncertain how to proceed so I phoned Mackenzie, who gave me some excellent advice. He suggested that I retain the substance of my draft, but use as many as possible of Howe's phrases and structures from his dictated manuscript. This I did and Howe was delighted with the result. That was a good speech I had first prepared, he told me, but it wasn't his speech. Having grasped the essentials of Howe's vocabulary and style, never again did I have trouble in getting Howe to accept my drafts. He didn't always, however, follow them strictly, and his ad libs were not always consistent with my carefully balanced argumentation. I have to admit that the most interesting parts of Howe's speeches for the listener and the press were often the off-the-cuff portions, when Howe lifted his eyes from the text and expressed his thoughts directly to the audience.

My first encounter with Howe, some years before, had been disastrous. It had taken place at a meeting of ministers and officials when I was in the Department of Finance. Something that I said annoyed Howe, and he put me in my place with a blistering comment. Hence my surprise when Max Mackenzie, on Howe's instructions, invited me to join Trade and Commerce. I did not think I was the sort of official that Howe was naturally drawn to. Howe was a man of action. He didn't like arguments, and when his officials differed in front of him he told them to go away and return when they had settled their differences, unlike Ilsley and Abbott, my two previous ministers, who wanted to hear conflicting points of view before making decisions. Nevertheless, Howe and I made a good team, probably because we were essentially different and complementary in our approaches.

Cultural affairs were not of much interest to C.D. Howe. But they were to me. I took the occasion one morning during our customary meeting to put in a word in support of the proposal then under consideration in cabinet – this was shortly after the 1953 election – to create the Canada Council, using as a founding fund the windfall of succession duties on the estates of two wealthy Canadians, James Hamet Dunn and Isaac Walton Killam. Support for the arts and artists wasn't much of a vote getter, said the Minister. I agreed and urged therefore that the legislation be put through early in the new Parliament, well in advance of the next election. It was approved on 28 March 1957.

One day, Howe asked me, as a personal favour, to draft a speech for him, honouring Prime Minister St Laurent on his seventy-fifth birthday, which took place in 1957. I liked and admired the Prime Minister and wanted Howe to rise to the occasion. Hitherto my speeches for Howe had been clear and factual and, I hoped, persuasive. This time I sought to be inspirational, something new for me and my Minister.

In his *Louis St. Laurent: Canadian*, Dale Thomson described what happened:

> The Prime Minister's seventy-fifth birthday was made the occasion by the Liberals for a mammoth party in Quebec City. Supporters and admirers from as far as Yellowknife, Northwest Territories, and Twillingate, Newfoundland, gathered in the old city to pay tribute to the man whom one Conservative newspaper, the Vancouver *Province*, described as 'Mr. Canada'. C.D. Howe introduced him at a fourteen-hundred-seat banquet. 'I sometimes hear it said that Prime Minister St. Laurent carried on where Mackenzie King left off,' the normally dour minister commented. 'I have heard him referred to as a second Laurier. These are meant as tributes to our Prime Minister. But to me, he stands in the shade of no man, living or dead.' Caught by surprise at the eloquent tribute, the guests were silent for a moment, then rose to their feet as one man to endorse the testimony; tears filled St. Laurent's eyes ...'

Fred Bull and I reached an amicable division of responsibilities within the department. Bull, as the senior deputy minister, with his long and distinguished service as a trade commissioner, took charge of the trade-promotion side of departmental activities. As associate deputy – which I became when Bull became deputy – I took charge of the divisions involved in economic analysis and policy formulation, including the Dominion Bureau of Statistics, international trade relations, and those agencies concerned with the grain trade, namely the Canadian Wheat Board and the Board of Grain Commissioners. Every morning that we were all in Ottawa Fred Bull and I met with Howe at 9:00 a.m., a routine I was to adopt for meetings with my deputy ministers when, many years later, I became a minister.

We tried our best to keep Howe informed of current developments, but we were by no means Howe's only sources of information. He knew every significant businessman in Canada, many in the United States and Britain, and some on the continent of Europe. Occasionally, he may have called them. Mostly they called him to tell him of their plans and to get his reaction, even when no government approval was necessary. During the early 1950s, Howe was also minister of defence production, which gave him another window on Canadian industrial development.

Ludwig Erhard, economics minister of West Germany, and Howe were kindred spirits, builders and optimists. On one occasion, I travelled from Geneva to Bonn on behalf of my Minister to carry a message to his German counterpart.

These were the years when relations between business and the federal government were least hostile. Many of the business leaders had served as dollar-a-year men and in other capacities in government during the war. They knew the bureaucracy and how it worked. Most important of all, it was a period of economic expansion, encouraged by federal ministers like Howe, and given practical stimulation by tax incentives. Capital imports, particularly direct investments, were encouraged not only by Ottawa but by the provinces, which opened offices abroad principally to persuade foreign companies to establish branch plants in Canada. It wasn't until 1956 that Howe was persuaded, partly by me (see page 59), to express publicly his concerns about some of the consequences of foreign ownership and to advise foreign-owned companies to become Canadianized in their operations.

Howe and the Canadian Wheat Board

Almost from the beginning of his professional career in Canada, Howe, who had been born in the United States, had been associated with the Canadian grain trade, first as an engineer with the Board of Grain Commissioners, later, when he established his own company, as a builder of terminal grain elevators. With this background and as an MP representing Port Arthur at the head of the Great Lakes, through which a large portion of western grain moved to market, he was able, when he became minister of trade and commerce, to retain responsibility for the Canadian Wheat Board, notwithstanding the competing claim of Gardiner, the minister of agriculture.

The Wheat Board at that time, following its conversion in 1943 from a voluntary to a compulsory board, operated in effect as the agent of the western producers, taking delivery of wheat, and later of oats and barley, at initial prices fixed by the government each crop year, selling the grain, and distributing any balance to the producers in the form of interim and final payments.

The relation of the minister to the board was therefore a delicate one. As trustee for the farmers, the board made its own marketing decisions without ministerial direction. The government, on the other hand, determined the level of initial prices and paid any losses suffered by the board, if the average selling price plus costs turned out to be lower than the initial prices paid to the producers plus expenses.

Howe took an active interest in the board's activities, meeting regularly with the chief commissioner, who from 1937 until he resigned in
April 1958 (the same day I resigned from the public service) was George
McIvor, a man of great political as well as administrative talents. As one
of Howe's deputies, I usually attended these meetings, although Howe
was always careful, and so was I, to maintain the right of the board to
have direct access to the minister. Howe was as busy a minister as any
I have known, but he always seemed to find time to meet those of his
officials who needed his personal advice and judgment.

Although the Wheat Board made its own marketing decisions, the
government could be and was helpful in protecting and finding markets
for Canadian grain, both domestic and export. Apart from my activity
as an adviser to the minister on board matters, I found myself actively
involved in promoting grain sales, principally by the extension of credits
to countries behind the Iron Curtain and by the negotiation of a trade
agreement with Japan and with the Soviet Union. The idea of credit
sales was first suggested by Charles O. Swartz of Northern Sales in
Winnipeg, an aggressive grain exporter specializing in feed grains, who
foresaw an opportunity of breaking into the Polish market for barley.
The suggestion was not greeted enthusiastically in Ottawa. To give
buyers credit for a period of twelve months or so on grain that is milled
into flour or sold as feed within a matter of weeks after purchase is
unusual, to say the least. On the other hand, Canada had not succeeded
in selling grain for cash to Poland, and the government of that country,
which valued its international reputation, was not likely to default. I
helped to work out the techniques, which varied somewhat from contract to contract but always involved a government guarantee of repay-
ment. Year after year, from that time forward and for many years,
Canadian grain was sold behind the Iron Curtain to Poland, on a credit
basis and without cost to the government; and not only to Poland, but
also to Yugoslavia, Czechoslovakia, and Hungary.

International wheat negotiations

I also took over from Charles Wilson, head of the Grain Division in the
Department of Trade and Commerce, responsibility for leading the
Canadian delegation to the international wheat negotiations in which
Canada as a main exporter took a prominent role. This was an instructive if, at times, frustrating experience. In principle there is widespread
agreement, at least among governments, that it is desirable to bring
about greater stability in agricultural commodity markets, which are
notoriously unstable. It is much more difficult to translate this desire

into workable machinery to limit the swings in prices. The conclusion I reached after participating for several years in international negotiations on wheat, – a view that was reinforced later with respect to sugar and coffee – is that whatever degree of improved stability is achieved by international commodity agreements for agricultural products rests in the main upon the ability and willingness of the main exporters of the commodity to hold the line, that is, to be prepared to sell for less than they might be able to obtain when the market is strong and to be prepared to hold stocks rather than to sell them when the market is weak. I saw very little evidence that importing countries individually or collectively were either willing or able to use their market power for similar purposes.

All commodity agreements differ from one another. The International Wheat Agreement, negotiated in 1953, involved both exporters and importers. In principle, the exporters undertook to supply wheat at a stated maximum if prices reached that level in the market; importers undertook to buy wheat at a stated minimum if prices reached that level in the market. The hope was that trading would take place between the agreed minimum and maximum levels.

To head a Canadian delegation to an international wheat conference was to be engaged in continuing negotiations, not only with wheat-importing countries and other wheat-exporting countries, but also with the members of the Canadian delegation, each element of which was anxious to demonstrate its support for the highest attainable prices and volumes of Canadian exports. Every proposal put forward by Canada and every Canadian response to other countries' proposals had to be cleared in advance both with the delegation and, of course, with the minister of trade and commerce, who would ultimately have to defend in the House of Commons any agreement reached at the conference, or, what might be equally significant, any failure to reach agreement. International commodity agreements had a fascination in those days for farmer-owned organizations like the wheat pools, led by men who believed fervently in the principles of marketing cooperation – notably J.H. Wesson of the Saskatchewan Wheat Pool and W.J. Parker of the Manitoba Wheat Pool. They represented a projection internationally of the view that Canadian producers deserved a remunerative price for an essential foodstuff like wheat.

Howe and the Liberal leadership

People are inclined to say that C.D. Howe wasn't much of a politician, by which they mean, I suppose, that he didn't fit their idea of the conventional politician. Certainly he wasn't a spellbinder as a speaker, and his performance in the House of Commons wasn't such as to give great confidence to government House leaders.

When judged by his ability to survive, however, Howe was a most successful politician. He won five successive election campaigns in his constituency at the Head of the Lake and was in the cabinet for twenty-two years, under Mackenzie King and Louis St Laurent.

One day he asked me whether I thought he should run for the leadership of the party if St Laurent retired. Apparently, someone had encouraged him to try. I didn't think he was serious in seeking my opinion, since he and St Laurent had some sort of understanding about retiring together. In any event, I didn't consider myself one of his political advisers. So I said very little.

I am not at all sure what constitutes good political leadership at the highest level – as a leader of a national party in Canada. Canadian party leaders, successful and unsuccessful, have been a mixed lot. Moreover, the most talented and popular party leaders of our two principal parties, the Liberals and Conservatives, have not always been the most successful as prime ministers.

In Canada, as in most other parliamentary democracies, governments usually defeat themselves. They are seldom if ever defeated by opposition parties that convince the public that they have superior policies or superior leadership. Consequently, a more valid test of political leadership, although one difficult to apply, is the ability to give cohesion and enthusiasm to one's party, particularly when it is out of office, so that it can take over the reins of office when the government falters, as it is bound to do sooner or later.

By that test, Howe would not have been a good party leader, although he undoubtedly added strength to the party by his performance in office. (His thought processes were remarkably clear and so was his ad hoc speaking in the House of Commons.) Howe was a doer, not a thinker in the sense of being interested in political philosophy. The distinction between Liberal and Conservative approaches to policy did not interest him very much, and while he would never have embraced socialism, he was more involved in state enterprise and more prepared to intervene in the private sphere than most socialist ministers would have dared to be had they come to office.

On 17 June 1955, the St Laurent government, on the recommendation of L.B. Pearson, the secretary of state for external affairs – and, I am told, when Howe was absent – appointed Walter Gordon as the head of a commission to investigate and report on Canada's economic prospects. Howe regarded the appointment of the commission as an enquiry into his activities as the minister mainly responsible for Canada's industrial policy. He strongly resented it and said so to his friends.

The Gordon Commission report did not, in my view, have much of an effect on future Canadian economic policy, although it contains some excellent studies, such as that by Professor Jack Young of the cost of the Canadian tariff, probably the best analysis ever made of the regional impact of Canadian tariff policy. The report did not prescribe the sort of economic nationalism that Gordon himself advocated in his later speeches, books, and pamphlets. It did not damage Howe's reputation as a nation builder. It did impose a heavy burden on Douglas LePan, who, under heavy pressure from Pearson, agreed to be secretary of the commission and who was the principal draftsman of its main report.

The Korean War

In the 'war book' prepared at the time of the Korean War, I was designated to be in charge of price controls and rationing if that became necessary. This gave me the opportunity to sit in on the discussions relating to other matters, such as preparations for a nuclear attack. The prevailing doctrine in the 1950s was the evacuation of cities on warning of an imminent nuclear attack. The Minister of National Defence was to give the order for evacuation, which, in itself, was bound to result in many casualties. What if the minister of national defence were unavailable or drunk or otherwise unable to function? I asked. The answers to these questions were not very reassuring. I remember expressing my misgivings to Howe, whose reaction was scathing. I was wasting my time: there would be no policy of evacuating cities. His prediction turned out to be correct.

I spoke to Donald Gordon, who had been the chairman of the Wartime Prices and Trade Board during the Second World War, about the possibility of reintroducing price controls. He warned me that price controls other than the application of an overall price ceiling would be extremely difficult to enforce and would probably be ineffective. Fortunately, I never had to discharge the functions assigned to me in the 'war book' of the 1950s. Many years later, in 1975, I was a member of a government that did introduce a system of price controls, short of a price ceiling, administered by Jean-Luc Pepin. That decision raised a political storm because in the 1974 election Robert Stanfield, as leader of the Progressive Conservative Party, had proposed price controls to curb rising prices and the idea had been scornfully rejected by Trudeau. I, too, was opposed publicly to the introduction of price controls in early 1974, because at that time the principal causes of rising prices were external, and we had virtually no control over them. In 1975, it became clear that there were also forces at work within Canada that were leading to larger-than-necessary price and wage increases. The deputy minister of finance called on me and urged me to support immediate action, a most unusual thing for a civil servant to do. Donald Gordon was right about the difficulty of administering that kind of policy. Nevertheless, unlike Donald Gordon, I concluded that the effort was worthwhile. Prices did continue to rise after price controls were introduced in 1975, but the rate of increase was moderated, which was the purpose.

Price controls were not reintroduced during the Korean War, but controls on consumer credits were, and an innovative approach was taken to try to restrain private capital investment as a means of reducing inflationary pressures. Although these were essentially financial measures, responsibility for administration was turned over to the Department of Trade and Commerce and came under my direct supervision.

Accelerated capital-cost allowances had been one of the principal instruments for encouraging capital expenditures during the post-war period. To be able to write off a new plant and equipment quickly against taxable income was an effective incentive to expansion. Would the deferral of capital-cost allowances be equally effective in causing business corporations to postpone expansion of capacity for consumer goods, thus making room for expansion of production related to the Korean War effort? We tried and probably accomplished something. It proved to be extremely difficult in practice to distinguish between urgent and postponable investments, and decisions in many cases became arbitrary. I sympathized with members of the cabinet and of Parliament who had to explain to voters that, because of the fear of inflation, the government wanted to discourage the building of a new factory in their constituencies. When the country is engaged in an all-out war effort, the priorities are clear; not so clear, however, when the war requires only partial mobilization of resources.

Visit to the Soviet Union, 1955

In 1955, Lester B. Pearson, then secretary of state for external affairs, was invited to visit the Soviet Union. He was reluctant to accept unless there was some purpose other than to be the living symbol of the thawing of the cold war. What about negotiating an agreement of some kind while he was there? We officials looked over the situation and recommended a try for a trade agreement. The problem confronting us was that while the traditional exchange of most-favoured-nation treatment between our two countries would give the Soviet Union access to the Canadian market on the same terms as were accorded to imports from the United States, most-favoured-nation treatment for our exports to the Soviet Union meant very little, since all imports into that country were purchased by state trading agencies, which might or might not practise discrimination. We therefore recommended that, as a balancing item, the Soviets should be asked to undertake to buy a quantity of Canadian wheat each year for a period of several years, thus assuring us of a continuation of Canadian wheat sales, which had been made occasionally in the past for delivery at the Pacific Coast port of Vladivostok. When I told him of the plan, Howe was sceptical.

Off we went to Moscow on 1 October 1955 – Mr and Mrs Pearson, John W. Holmes, an assistant under-secretary of state for external affairs, George Ignatieff and Raymond Crépault, also from External Affairs, and myself, on the C-5, then the official plane for such purposes. (I joined the plane in Paris.) When we arrived at the Moscow airport we were instructed to go immediately to the Bolshoi to see the ballet *Don Quixote.* During the four intermissions, we had dinner, with V.M. Molotov as our host, and with the inevitable toasts. To everyone's relief, when Pearson asked Molotov whether 'bottoms up' was to be the rule, Molotov replied, 'As you please,' which enabled us the better to enjoy the ballet and the conversation in the intervals between the acts.

The following day, trade negotiations began. Pearson made the opening statement. I conducted the negotiations, ably assisted by Ignatieff, who, being the son of Count Ignatieff who had served in the Tsar's government before the Bolshevik Revolution, understood fully what was being said by the Soviet officials and could check the official interpreter, who was Soviet. We reached agreement in principle that a trade agreement would be desirable, and it was arranged that the negotiations should resume in Ottawa early in 1956.

Before our departure from Moscow, our ambassador gave a dinner to which he invited leading members of the Soviet government and at which Pearson spoke. Canada, he said, is not a big country; we have lots of geography but not many people – but we occupy a strategic position in the world, situated as we are between the two superpowers, the

United States on the south and the Soviet Union on the north, and subject to pressures from both sides. L.M. Kaganovitch, one of the big five Soviet leaders, interrupted – 'As far as we are concerned, friendly pressure.' Pearson's response was quick: 'The strongest pressure I know is friendly pressure.'

At the end of six days (on four of the six evenings that I was there I went to the Bolshoi to see ballet and opera), I left to return to Ottawa, while Pearson and the rest of the party went to the Crimea and then on around the world in the C-5. As I descended the ramp in Montreal, a TV reporter took some pictures and asked some innocuous questions about the trip. Much to my surprise, my wife, Daisy, greeted me in the airport in Montreal. She had motored from Ottawa early that morning with strict instructions from Howe to whisk me off to the Laurentians for the weekend and to deliver me at his office in Ottawa Monday morning without talking to anyone. I explained that I had already given a TV interview but that I had said nothing of significance.

We followed instructions and at nine o'clock sharp on Monday, 17 October, Howe asked to see me. I reported and expressed the view, which turned out to be accurate, that there would be a trade agreement between Canada and the Soviet Union, with substantial benefits for Canada and particularly for the western grain producers.

A few minutes later, Prime Minister St Laurent asked to see me. I gave him the same report. Had I reported to Mr Howe? he asked me, and when I assured him I had, he asked me about Howe's reaction. I replied that I thought the Minister was relieved. 'I am sure he was,' said the Prime Minister. 'At cabinet the other day he asked me what I thought was going on in Moscow. I replied that Pearson was an experienced diplomat and that you knew your business. I am sure they are carrying out our instructions. To which Mr. Howe replied: "I hope so. That fellow Sharp is so damned enthusiastic."'

The first Canada-Soviet trade agreement

In the early months of 1956, the negotiations were resumed in Ottawa. S.A. Borisov, a deputy trade minister, led the Soviet delegation. I led the Canadian team. The central question was, of course, the exchange of most-favoured-nation treatment. As a bargaining ploy, since I knew that my request would be refused, I asked the Soviets to agree to a clause forbidding Soviet state trading enterprises from discriminating against Canada when buying imported goods. They could not agree, Borisov said, because to include such a prohibition would imply that state trading enterprises sometimes engaged in discrimination, which, he said, they never did. Finally, after the point had been well made and we had established our claim for something over and above the exchange of most-favoured-nation treatment, I enquired of Borisov what principles governed the activities of Soviet state trading enterprises. 'They buy as cheaply as possible and sell as dearly as possible and distribute the profits.' 'It sounds to me,' I commented, 'like private enterprise.' 'Where else do you think we learned – on the moon?' Borisov asked. On 26 May 1956, the first Canada-U.S.S.R. Trade Agreement came into force. The Soviet Union agreed to purchase 1.2 million to 1.5 million tonnes of wheat within the next three years, marking the commencement of continuous Soviet purchases of Canadian grain, which were to grow to enormous proportions in the years when I was minister of trade and commerce. This happened at a most fortuitous time, when we were so concerned about the effects on Canadian wheat markets of U.S. giveaways under 'Public Law 480', which provided for agricultural export subsidies. Thereafter, friends told me, my sceptical minister referred to me as the most skilled negotiator in the government service.

Eighteen years later, in 1974, as secretary of state for external affairs, I was invited to the Soviet Union by Aleksei Kosygin, the prime minister. It had been the intention that I should meet with him in Moscow. When I arrived in that city, I was informed that we were to meet instead in Pitsunda, a Black Sea resort in the Republic of Georgia. The evening I arrived with my party was free of any duties, so we had dinner with some Soviet officials in a restaurant catering to the working-class residents of the resort hotels. On this as on my previous visit to the Soviet Union in 1955, I had spent most of my time in Moscow, which is not a city renowned for its gaiety. So I was not prepared for Georgia. Imagine my astonishment when the waitresses in Pitsunda were peroxide blondes wearing miniskirts and the music on the jukebox was from the Broadway musical *Hair*. Perhaps someone was aware that it had been composed by a Canadian, Galt MacDermot, the son of a retired Canadian diplomat, Terence MacDermot.

On this trip there were conversations about world affairs and Canada-Soviet relations but no serious negotiations. I therefore had the opportunity, in addition to the visit to Pitsunda, to tour Leningrad, listen to a concert by one of its great symphony orchestras, view the art of the Hermitage, and visit Kiev in the Ukraine.

Visit to Japan, 1956

When he went to the Soviet Union, Pearson took with him a Canadian painting to present to Molotov and some samples of Canadian grain to present to the Soviet minister of agriculture. Much to our embarrassment, just before leaving Moscow, each member of the Canadian party received gifts that made the Canadian painting and grain samples appear paltry by comparison. The following year I accompanied Howe on an official visit to Tokyo and, forewarned by our Soviet experience, I arranged for gifts more appropriate to the occasion, ranging from a splendid presentation package of National Film Board scientific films for the Emperor of Japan, to Eskimo carvings for Japanese officials who looked after the local arrangements for our visit. I visited the Hudson Bay store in Winnipeg to buy the carvings and acquired a dozen or so for $100. Today, some of the carvings I acquired at that time would individually be worth at least $100. Our Japanese hosts were delighted by the artistry of the carvings, so much so that Japan began, not long after our visit, to turn out cheaper replicas for sale to Canadians!

That visit to Japan in 1956 furnished me with an anecdote that I later used in the general election of 1962 when contesting the Eglinton constituency with Donald Fleming, then minister of finance in the Diefenbaker government. In that election, Fleming was thought by many voters in Eglinton to be a strong, able minister in an otherwise weak government; it was believed that he was not responsible for the disasters that occurred and should therefore be supported. My task was to try to convince those voters that Fleming, as a senior minister, could not escape responsibility.

So I told this story about our visit to Japan in 1956. Howe accepted an invitation from the Japanese government to go fishing. Since there are no wilderness areas in Japan we were taken to a fish hatchery, given rods with baited hooks, dressed in high rubber boots, and placed in a stream connected to the hatchery, Howe first, myself second, and T.C. (Tommy) Davis, our ambassador to Japan, third. At an appropriate moment the gate to the fish hatchery was opened and some fish swam by. Howe caught one but I didn't. I was disappointed. Howe consoled me: 'Mitch, I don't know whether it's worse to say you went to a fish hatchery and caught a fish or that you went to a fish hatchery and didn't catch a fish.'

On the way to Japan, we stopped in Chicago and Milwaukee to enable Howe to deliver a speech, which I had drafted, that in many ways was historic. It marked the first time the minister saw fit publicly to urge American-owned corporations to act as good Canadian corporate citizens:

> ... I have a word of advice to those who plan to establish branch plants in Canada or who are already operating them.

Remember that these branch plants are in Canada, not in a state of the Union.

They may be closer than branch plants in California or New Mexico but they are still in a different country.

We are just as pro-Canadian as you are pro-American.

We believe in the Canadian way of life, just as you believe in the American way of life.

You will be more successful in doing business in Canada, therefore, if you Canadianize your branch plant operations as far as possible.

Until then, his message to them had been to participate in Canadian post-war expansion.

I shared Howe's view that the emphasis in that post-war period should be on industrialization, which required both foreign capital and foreign know-how. It seemed to me, however, that the minister was creating the impression that he not only welcomed foreign capital but also the control over the Canadian subsidiary that usually accompanied ownership. The Chicago and Milwaukee speeches helped to redress the balance. I never thought, however, that Howe was comfortable lecturing foreign investors about their responsibilities to their host country. He wanted modern factories and modern technologies. That was his priority – and mine. Who owned those modern facilities didn't matter as much as having them located in Canada and subject to Canadian laws rather than having them serve the Canadian market from the United States or elsewhere.

The GATT

I went to Geneva in January 1955, to assume the leadership of the Canadian delegation to the General Agreement on Tariffs and Trade (GATT), of which there were then twenty or so signatories.* For me, it

---

*For me that trip to Geneva is memorable because it was in Geneva that I met for the first time Jeannette Dugal, secretary of the Canadian delegation to the GATT, who, many years later, was to become my secretary and, in 1976, my wife, following the death of Daisy, my first wife. In her prime a scholarship student, a pharmacist, a technician in several scientific fields, Lady Stick of the Science Faculty at University of Manitoba, and a natural athlete – probably the best woman ice-hockey player of her generation and a Manitoba junior tennis champion – in the middle 1960s, Daisy was diagnosed as having Alzheimer's disease. Gradually, over a period of some eight years, she lost the use of her faculties and died in 1975.

was an educational trip. I had some responsibility within the department with respect to trade policy but I was occasionally baffled by the experts, whose terminology was often unfamiliar to me.

In those days, Canada was not only a strong supporter of the GATT, as befitted one of the founding members, but in international trade meetings we took a rather sanctimonious view of our own behaviour. Canada obeyed the rules; other countries should do likewise. We were seldom challenged because in fact we did honour our obligations. But, without doubt, we were smug.

That our 'holier-than-thou' attitude did not go unnoticed was brought to my attention and to the attention of the Canadian delegation by a witty and talented Australian.

At that time, the German Federal Republic maintained some trade restrictions that had been put into effect during the period of post-war reconstruction. The Australian delegation proposed that Germany should be granted a blanket exemption from the GATT rules for a limited time. Canada was not opposed to giving Germany time to remove the remaining restrictions, but favoured a procedure whereby that country would be requested to justify each remaining restriction. We didn't like blanket exemptions.

Allan Westerman, head of the Australian delegation, presided when the matter came under discussion. Each country expressed its view. Westerman summed up in a brilliant *tour de force* with biting and at times hilariously funny comments about each of the speakers – except me. My relief was short-lived. Finally, he came to his concluding comments about his own country, which began, 'Unlike Canada, Australia is not without sin.'

The TransCanada Pipeline

I went back to Geneva in January 1956 for a few weeks. On my return to Canada, I called my friend Bob Beattie, deputy governor of the Bank of Canada, to find out what had been going on in my absence. I was puzzled when he said that my absence had been costly. He went on to explain why. Howe was on the verge of resignation because of disagreement about the financing of the proposed trans-Canada natural gas pipeline. Things were in a mess. When I protested that I didn't know anything about pipelines, Beattie said that might be so, but I was the only person who might have been able to get through to Howe.

For a few days I hesitated, but then decided to take the plunge. When I raised the subject, Howe reacted very negatively. He was angry and frustrated. He had proposed a government guarantee of the bonds of the TransCanada PipeLines Company so that the company could raise sufficient money to build a gas pipeline across Canada. Coyne, the governor of the Bank of Canada, had countered by proposing that TransCanada sell debentures convertible into common shares to a government agency so that, in return for the financing, the government could, if it wished, exercise the convertible feature of the debentures and thus become a shareholder in the company and participate in the profits. Howe thought the idea preposterous and was contemplating resignation because he felt his advice was no longer being accepted by the Government.

I asked Bob Bryce, then secretary to the cabinet, and Ken Taylor, the deputy minister of finance, if they would be prepared to join with me in reviewing with the chief executives of TransCanada the nature of the financing problem to see if we could come up with some acceptable solution. They agreed, so I put the idea before Howe. He was far from enthusiastic. As he put it, 'Go ahead, things couldn't be worse.'

The three of us spent a couple of days in conversation with the president of TransCanada, Nathan Tanner, and Charles Coates, general manager, after which we met to consider, in the light of what we had learned, what might be done to get the project under way. We quickly came to realize that we were faced with the traditional problem that had faced the builders of transcontinental railway lines in Canada – namely the long stretch of barren, sparsely populated, non-revenue-producing country between the Prairies, where the grain and now the natural gas were to be found, and the industrial heartland.

During the discussion, Taylor mentioned that at one time he had proposed that the Canadian transcontinental railways should jointly own and use a single line between Winnipeg and Sudbury rather than two separate lines. This led me to suggest that perhaps that was the solution to the TransCanada problem – a government-built and -owned pipeline between Winnipeg and Sudbury to be leased to TransCanada at a rent based on throughput of gas that would, within a reasonable period, as volume increased, return the cost of the line, plus interest and perhaps a profit to the Government when it was sold to TransCanada. 'A bridge in time,' I called it.

We put the idea on paper and reported to Howe that we had met with TransCanada and were now in a position to make a recommendation. Did he want us to prepare a memorandum to cabinet for his signature? What was the recommendation? he wanted to know. I outlined it. I have forgotten the exact words of Howe's reaction, but they were to the effect that we officials were as usual living in an ivory tower, divorced from reality. I was angry. After reiterating my view that this was the right solution I more or less stomped out of his office, declaring that I didn't want to have anything more to do with pipelines.

Later that day Howe phoned me. He had discussed the idea with Prime Minister St Laurent, who liked it. Would I prepare a memorandum to cabinet for his signature?

TransCanada also was prepared to go along and at first believed that relief from raising money for the line between Winnipeg and Sudbury would be sufficient to enable the company to finance the balance of the line. The market was not receptive, however, and it became necessary for the government to include in the legislation authority to advance to TransCanada $80 million to finance construction from Alberta to Winnipeg. As security for this advance, the government took a mortgage on the entire line, so that, if TransCanada defaulted, the pipeline would become government-owned.

To reach Winnipeg before freeze-up, construction would have to begin in June. Steel to build the pipe was scarce. In order to ensure a supply for this vast project, TransCanada had entered into an option that expired on June 6. This became the deadline.

The legislation was prepared and submitted to the House of Commons forthwith. There were twelve sitting days before the deadline of 6 June, and Howe made it clear to me that the government was prepared to use closure to expedite a parliamentary decision. The officials and ministers concerned with the legislation had, perforce, to try to learn about closure. One thing became clear to us and that was that there were no experts, there was only confusion. Each morning when I met Howe I asked him if he knew how to apply closure, particularly when the House was in Committee of the Whole. His stock answer was that he was not in charge of House business; that was the responsibility of the government House leader, Walter Harris. One morning when I arrived in his office, however, he had seven slips of paper spread out on his desk, each containing the terms of a motion. He now knew what had to be done. There were seven clauses in the bill. When each clause was called in Committee of the Whole, he would move that further debate on the clause be postponed. When debate had been postponed on each of the seven clauses, a general discussion on any or all seven clauses would be in order and a motion could then be made at an appropriate time to close debate in the committee. That was also my understanding of the procedure. I assumed that this procedure would be explained to the House in advance by the House leader or by himself. No,

Howe said, there would be no advance explanation. I predicted disaster.

The debate began. Closure was applied at the resolution stage and on second reading. The House was in an uproar. There was virtually no debate on the substance of the bill. The issue was closure, which had not been applied for many years. Up to that point it looked as if the government, notwithstanding the objection to closure, was making steady progress towards its objective.

When the House went into Committee of the Whole, there was no explanation of the procedure. Howe did what he said he would do. On his motion, debate on the first two clauses was postponed. It took the House a few minutes to react to this unusual procedure. On the third clause, all hell broke loose. It looked to members of the opposition as if there was to be no debate in committee. It was a sad business, which had devastating effects on the government in the 1957 general election and on the speaker of the House, René Beaudoin, who, at one point in the debate, reversed himself. Howe was blamed. The pipeline debate reinforced the adverse public image of Howe created the previous year during the debate on the Defence Production Act. Since I was not in cabinet, I do not know who made the decision not to explain to the House in advance the procedure in committee, an explanation that might have forestalled the worst of the troubles.

I sat in the officials' gallery every day that the TransCanada legislation was debated except on so-called Black Friday. I predicted what would happen that day and was afraid I would be sick to the stomach if I observed the sorry spectacle.

The bill was eventually approved and within the deadline. The Trans-Canada Pipeline was built and became a profitable enterprise. The advance was repaid promptly, and the Crown section between Winnipeg and Sudbury was bought by TransCanada at a price that returned to the government the full cost plus interest (at that time around 3.5 per cent). I argued unsuccessfully with both Howe and the premier of Ontario, Leslie Frost, who was prepared to participate (but didn't actually participate) in the financing of the Crown section, that Trans-Canada should be charged at least commercial non-governmental rates of interest, since that is what TransCanada would have paid in the market if they had financed the line themselves. Neither Howe nor Frost wanted to add anything unnecessarily to the cost of moving natural gas between Alberta and Ontario.

On 29 May 1963, seven years later, when I had become minister of trade and commerce, I had the satisfaction of receiving from David

Golden, the president of the Crown corporation, a cheque for some $108 million, in full payment of the government investment. It is seldom in public affairs that things work out so well, at least from a financial and development point of view, if not for those politicians who suffered in the 1957 election from the débâcle in the House of Commons. That débâcle arose not from the legislation but from the clumsy application of closure during the debate in the House.

During and following the pipeline affair, Doug Fraser, who later became a member of the National Energy Board, Jack Davis, who later became a minister in the Canadian and the British Columbia governments, and I tried to convince Howe that the time had come to establish a national energy board to deal in a more structured way with the questions of exports of energy and pipeline proposals, which were then being handled by him personally on an ad hoc basis. Before he left office his opposition to the idea may have weakened. When I first raised the subject with him his reply was short and to the point. 'What in the hell would a national energy board do that I'm not doing now?'

Cuban sugar

During my official life, I have travelled abroad to many places and for many purposes. Nearly all the trips were hurried, overly busy, and generally exhausting. This was not true, however, of a trip I made to Cuba in 1953. My mission was to ascertain if the Cuban government, then headed by Batista, wished to renew an agreement with Canada whereby, notwithstanding the preference for Commonwealth sugar, we undertook to buy 75,000 tons of Cuban sugar annually and in return Cuba undertook not to discriminate against imports of fish, potatoes, and other traditional items from Canada. We were blackmailed into that agreement and anxious to get out of it, but not at the expense of traditional exports from the Altantic provinces to Cuba.

I had been the head of the Canadian delegation to the International Sugar Conference earlier that year at which the British government had agreed to enter into an international sugar agreement for the purpose, *inter alia*, of supporting the price of sugar, with one important proviso, namely that no signatory importing country would be party to a bilateral agreement to buy agreed quantities of sugar from a signatory exporting country. This provision was aimed at the Canada-Cuba agreement. Cuba, therefore, had to choose between having an international sugar agreement – British participation being essential – or continuing its bilateral deal with Canada. My instructions were simply to ascertain the decision of the Cubans and to ensure that, if the bilateral deal came to an end and Canadian refiners stopped buying Cuban sugar because it did not enjoy the Commonwealth preferential tariff, there would be no discrimination against imports from Canada.

When I arrived, I met with the Cubans and stated the Canadian position. Twelve days later, I was asked to meet again. The Cubans informed me that they had opted for the international agreement and the bilateral agreement with Canada would therefore be cancelled. I thanked them and said that I wanted to be sure that if, as a result, Canada did not buy any Cuban sugar, I could assure my government that there would be no retaliation against imports from Canada. The reply was that it would be helpful (I think that was the word they used) if Canada nevertheless continued to buy some Cuban sugar. When I enquired how much sugar, they said it was contrary to the International Sugar Agreement for them to talk about quantities. I pursued this merry-go-round of continuing blackmail a couple of times and the meeting adjourned. The following day we met again, by which time the Cubans had concluded that they had to make a clear choice and gave the necessary assurance. I returned to Ottawa having spent nearly two weeks loafing and enjoying myself and about three hours on government business.

The Japanese trade agreement

It became my responsibility to negotiate Canada's first post-war trade agreement with Japan, which was then beginning to emerge as an industrial power. In 1953, when the negotiations began, Canadian exports to Japan amounted to $139 million and our imports from that country to $13.8 million, a ratio of ten to one in our favour. Our attitude during those negotiations was motivated principally by a desire to bring Japan within the most-favoured-nation group of countries with whom we traded and within the discipline of the GATT. My right hand during those negotiations was Simon Reisman from the Department of Finance. He had joined that department in response to my job offer and was beginning, even then, to show the competence, toughness, and outspokenness that characterized his distinguished career in the public service. The leader of the Japanese delegation was Shinichi Kondo, then a commercial attaché at the Japanese Embassy, who was later to reappear in Ottawa as Japanese ambassador. The agreement became effective on 7 June 1954, and Japan entered the GATT in September of the following year. Although the balance of trade was very much in our favour, we were concerned even then about Japanese imports, and the signing of the most-favoured-nation treaty was accompanied by undertakings by Japan to restrain exports to Canada of certain sensitive items, such as textiles. There was also an exchange of letters in which Japan undertook to buy increasing quantities of Canadian wheat.

The Brussels World Fair

While I was associate deputy minister of trade and commerce I had some experience with exhibitions that proved useful later when I was federal minister responsible for Expo 67. In order to assist in the re-establishment of trading links disturbed by the war, the Government of Canada held an annual international trade fair in Toronto from 1948 to 1955, for the benefit of exporters to Canada. These came under my supervision when I moved to Trade and Commerce at the beginning of 1951.

When Canada accepted the invitation to participate in the Brussels World Fair in 1958, Glenn Bannerman, who had organized the Toronto fair, became the commissioner general for the Canadian pavilion and I became the chairman of the Interdepartmental Committee to which Bannerman reported. The members of the committee were, in the main, deputy ministers and other senior officials, a pretty hard-boiled lot. At one point we had to decide the content of the art exhibit to be housed in the Canadian pavilion. We asked Donald Buchanan, the second man in the National Art Gallery, to assemble a team of art experts and to make recommendations. In due course he did so, identifying not works to be shown but artists to be represented, defined as living Canadian artists who had made an impact on the contemporary world of art, or something to that effect. The list circulated around the table. To most of the Interdepartmental Committee they were unknown names. There were comments to the effect that most Canadians wouldn't think these were leading Canadian artists. I asked Buchanan if his group of art experts would take the responsibility for the list. He assured us they would and added that the last time Canada had exhibited at an international show was in Wembley in the United Kingdom in 1926. There were loud outcries in Canada about the unknown artists to be exhibited. Who were those Canadian artists unknown in 1926? Members of the Group of Seven: Franklin Carmichael, Lawren Harris, A.Y. Jackson, Franz Johnston, Arthur Lismer, J.E.H. Macdonald, and F.H. Varley. As chairman of the Interdepartmental Committee I expressed the hope that fifty years or so down the road Canadians would recognize the similar perspicacity of Donald Buchanan and his colleagues in their choice of Canadian artists to be exhibited at the World Fair in 1958.

Some thirty-five years later, in the course of preparing these memoirs, I obtained from the National Gallery a list of the Canadian painters whose works had been exhibited in Brussels in 1958. Today no one would question the selection. Many of these Canadian painters have become the modern equivalent of the Group of Seven and better known internationally: Paul-Emile Borduas, Jean-Paul Riopelle, Harold Town, William Ronald, B.C. Binning, Fernand Leduc, Fernand Toupin, Jean-Paul Mousseau, Edmund Alleyn, Jack Shadbolt, Oscar Cahén, Bruno Bobak, Jacques de Tonnancour, Gentile Tondino, Jean Dallaire, Jack Humphrey, Marian Scott.

Howe is defeated and Churchill becomes minister

On 10 June 1957, the Liberal government was defeated in a general election. Howe was defeated in Port Arthur by Douglas Fisher of the CCF. We civil servants prepared for the transition. As deputy minister (I had succeeded Fred Bull when he was appointed ambassador to Japan), I gathered together the heads of divisions of the Department of Trade and Commerce and told them that our tradition of political neutrality was now to be tested and that I expected them to work as loyally for the new Progressive Conservative government as we had worked for the outgoing Liberal government and that I had no doubt they would do so.

Howe was still the minister until his resignation became effective, although he was no longer an MP. I liked and admired Howe and knew that his defeat in Port Arthur had deeply wounded him. So I went to the airport to meet him when he returned to Ottawa, a fact duly noted and reported by the media. It was a gesture I have never regretted, although it may have contributed to the suspicion in the Progressive Conservative Party that I was not politically neutral.

After leaving Parliament, Howe was not active politically, although he did not hesitate to express his views in private about the way the Liberal Party was conducting itself. Not surprisingly, he did not like the Kingston Conference. Nevertheless, the fact that I organized that conference did not affect our personal relationship. We met from time to time and at one point he asked me to join him in a partnership, which I declined because I had been vice-president of Brazilian Traction for such a short time.

I do not recall having met my new minister, Gordon Churchill, before he arrived at the old No. 1 Temporary Building on Wellington Street to take over his office. I had, of course, seen him in the House of Commons. I had made all the necessary preparations for his arrival and reception, but somehow, and for reasons I didn't understand then, the atmosphere was less than cordial when we met; it was cold. Friends of Churchill have told me that they thought he and I should have got along well.

In retrospect, what I think interfered with the development of a satisfactory relationship was my feeling that Churchill shared the reservations that Diefenbaker undoubtedly held about my political neutrality and hoped I would eventually leave, which I did. Indeed, from time to time, when I demonstrated by my advice that I could be helpful in the development of the new government's policy, he was not only grateful, but appeared mildly surprised.

Perhaps I had been spoiled by working with a succession of experienced and powerful ministers – Ilsley, Abbott, and Howe – who understood the functions of senior civil servants, knew how to use them, and did use them. I expected Churchill to trust me as they had trusted me. Churchill and I never quarrelled. There was no bad blood between us, and in the end we parted amicably, if without regret on either side. During that first Diefenbaker administration we met regularly. I prepared draft speeches and statements for him. I did my best to ensure that his foreign travels were successful. My departmental officials cooperated loyally.

Much to the surprise of myself and other senior civil servants, the new government took seriously and tried to implement some policies they had advocated while in opposition that to those of us who had had long experience in government were simply based on ignorance of the facts.

One of these was the idea of strengthening Commonwealth trade by restoring Commonwealth trade preferences; another was the closely related idea that it would be desirable to shift trade from the United States to the United Kingdom.

On taking office, the new government made plans for two major events with implications for trade policy. One was a meeting of the Canada–United States Joint Cabinet Committee on Trade and Economic Affairs scheduled for 7–8 October 1957. These consultations had been inaugurated by the St Laurent administration in 1953 and had taken place on previous occasions. The other was the hosting of a Commonwealth economic conference at Mont Tremblant in the Laurentian mountains of Quebec.

The ministers of Finance, Trade and Commerce, and External Affairs and their departmental officials met to prepare for the Commonwealth conference and in particular to discuss what initiatives Canada could take to strengthen Commonwealth ties. What about restoring Commonwealth preferences? The advice of the officials was that this idea would receive very little, if any, support from other members of the Commonwealth. Britain's objective was to try to get into the European Economic Community. Australia and New Zealand were trading off Commonwealth preferences for access to the EEC. The new Canadian ministers were taken aback. What then could Canada propose? The officials responded with some practical suggestions in the field, including support for education, that in due course were acted upon and that helped to give substance to the subsequent Commonwealth conference and did in fact help to strengthen the Commonwealth.

For the meeting with the Americans, the government decided to make it plain to their Washington counterparts that Canada was determined, by direct trade action, to reduce its economic dependence upon the United States. The officials did their best to warn the new ministers that this approach was likely to provoke an equally blunt response. But they were not deterred.

So off we went to Washington – Fleming, Churchill, Doug Harkness, the minister of agriculture, Sidney Smith, who had just been appointed secretary of state for external affairs, and their deputy ministers and other senior advisers. For a time there was some uncertainty as to how we should travel – all in one plane, which might crash, depriving Canada of all these top ministers and officials, or separately? The ministers decided to take a chance. As we approached Washington, the plane was buffeted by a severe storm. Finally, we landed and the ministers and officials, rather shaken, lined up for disembarking in strict order of protocol. This put Sidney Smith last among the ministers and just ahead of the officials. He turned to us and said: 'I can see the headline in the *Washington Post* tomorrow – Canadian ministers finally get feet on ground.' Lou Rasminsky, then deputy governor of the Bank of Canada, taking care that the minister could not overhear, muttered, 'Sub-heading, officials relieved.'

When the meeting began, Fleming, as the leader of the Canadian ministers, made the pitch about Canada not wanting to put all its eggs in one basket and being determined to diversify its trade. John Foster Dulles, the U.S. secretary of state, who led the American group, replied with vigour and some sarcasm to the effect that the reason that Canada did so much trade with the United States was that Americans paid cash for Canadian imports and produced the kinds of goods that Canadians wanted and that if it hadn't been for the generosity of the United States in helping to rebuild Europe under the Marshall Plan, Canada would not have been able to sell much across the Atlantic. This exchange did little to advance Canadian economic interests or Canada-U.S. relations.

This general approach to trade diversification of the Diefenbaker administration was given public exposure by the Prime Minister after his return from a meeting in London in 1957 when he told a press conference that the government intended to achieve a diversion of 15 per cent of our imports from the United States to the United Kingdom. Officials were not consulted in advance. We did make the examination afterwards, questioned the feasibility of the objective, and drew attention to the implications for industry in Canada of measures designed to achieve that objective.

Subsequently, at the Commonwealth conference in Mont Tremblant, the British government indicated to the Canadian government that imports of British goods into Canada could be facilitated by a free-trade arrangement between Canada and the United Kingdom. The Canadian ministers, aware of the implications for certain Canadian industries such as textiles, denied that any proposal to this effect had been made by the British, which in a formal sense was probably true. I learned subsequently that the British, feeling pessimistic about Europe, were quite serious in proposing free trade with Canada and felt rebuffed by our negative response.

The 'hidden report'

Two incidents during that minority Diefenbaker government had a significant effect on my career. One was the revelation by Diefenbaker of the so-called hidden report.

In the mid-1950s, primary responsibility for economic analysis and forecasting had been assumed by the Economics Branch of the Department of Trade and Commerce, although the Department of Finance and the Bank of Canada formed their own views, which were not always consonant. During the preparation of the annual budget, it became customary for the deputy minister of trade and commerce to sign and submit to the Privy Council Office for distribution to all ministers a document prepared in the Economics Branch analysing current economic conditions and indicating the outlook for the coming year.

I did so during the preparation of the 1957 budget, which was presented by the minister of finance, Walter Harris, on 14 March. Following the general election of 10 June 1957, a Progressive Conservative minority government took over.

During September 1957, in the course of one of our regular consultations, Churchill said that he understood that before the presentation of the 1957 budget I had prepared a report on the economic outlook for the current year and he would like to see it. I phoned back to my office for copies, which arrived in a few minutes, and I handed one to him and one to his parliamentary secretary, Tom Bell, who was also attending the meeting.

The Liberal opposition had been blaming the new Progressive Conservative government for rising unemployment. When Churchill and Bell read the outlook document they saw that, while the Liberals were still in office, I had presented a report predicting rising unemployment during 1957. They realized that they had a complete and highly embarrassing reply to these charges.

There had been no hesitation on my part in revealing the content of the outlook report to the new government. The new minister had every right to see it. When Churchill seemed prepared to reveal publicly the contents of the document, however, I protested. I pointed out that the report was marked 'secret' on the cover and each page was marked 'confidential.'

'Surely it is no longer secret? What harm would there be in making its content public now? It certainly didn't harm you, since your forecast had been accurate.' So Churchill argued.

To this line of argument I replied by asking a blunt question. Did the government intend to publish the outlook report that the department would be asked to prepare in advance of the 1958 budget? If the intention was to publish, at any time – simultaneously or later – we civil servants would ask the government what they wanted to put in the report so as to avoid possible public disagreement between public servants and their political masters. If, on the other hand, the government wanted the considered and frank views of their advisers, they would maintain confidentiality.

I went on to ask if the government intended to release the contents of any other papers prepared by their civil servants for the new government since they had taken office. When asked for an example, I referred to the report prepared for the government on the implications of the 15 per cent shift in imports from the United States to the United Kingdom advocated by Prime Minister Diefenbaker, a report that was highly critical of Diefenbaker's idea.

There was no reply to that question, and the discussion between Churchill and me came to an end. I thought I had convinced him that the outlook report should not be published, and perhaps I did convince him. As a precaution, I phoned Bryce, who was then secretary to the cabinet, to acquaint him with the discussion.

I heard nothing more until 20 January 1958, when Bryce phoned me to say that Prime Minister Diefenbaker intended to quote from the outlook report in his speech in reply to Pearson that day, and would undoubtedly be asked to table it in the House of Commons. Could I therefore have delivered to him in his office copies for that purpose. I delivered them personally, covers intact.

As Bryce had expected, Diefenbaker quoted from the report and was required to table it (Sessional Paper No. 227). He did so without the cover containing the word 'secret,' which had obviously been torn off. This must have happened after I delivered it to the East Block. When challenged on this point by the opposition, some of whom had meanwhile found their own intact copies, which they had received when in office, Diefenbaker replied that he had tabled the report as he received it.

Diefenbaker not only used the 1957 outlook report on that House of Commons occasion to humiliate Pearson, he flourished it throughout the 1958 election campaign with telling effect. For the first time my name began to appear prominently in the press – as the author of the 'hidden report.' As I was to remark later, Diefenbaker turned me into a national figure without any effort on my part.

Although that particular report subsequently attained great notoriety, it did not apparently have much of an effect contemporaneously upon the Harris budgetary decisions in 1957. The implication of the analysis of the economic outlook in our report was that the budgetary approach should be expansionary, to offset the tendency towards rising unemployment. Harris was not persuaded either by the 'hidden report' or by a letter along the same lines that Howe wrote to him – which I helped to draft. Advised by his departmental officials, Harris opted for a cautious approach, both on taxes, which he did not reduce, and by limiting the increase in the universal old-age pension to six dollars, from forty to forty-six dollars per month, thereby earning himself the title of 'six-buck Harris' in the 1957 election campaign.

The Liberal government was defeated in that election. The new Conservative government promptly reduced taxes and raised the old-age pension to fifty-five dollars, exactly what Harris had refused to do. As a student of relations between civil servants and ministers, I have asked myself the question: were his Finance Department officials wise in the advice they gave Harris? Wouldn't it have served the public interest better – apart altogether from the political interests of Harris – for them to have advised him, notwithstanding their legitimate concerns about inflation, to be moderately expansive, by suggesting some tax reductions and a somewhat more generous attitude towards the aged?

I do not know the answer, but the Harris 1957 budget dilemma illustrates a thesis I have repeatedly defended, that senior civil servants have a responsibility when giving economic advice to take into account their assessment of the political consequences of what they propose.

The handling of the 'hidden report' was one of two incidents that led me to resign from the public service. It also led me to wonder why Diefenbaker took the responsibility for releasing the report, when he could easily have transferred the responsibility for the release to the opposition Liberals. It would have served his purposes equally well to have said that he knew from the records available to the government when they took office that the Liberal government had been warned by its own officials about rising unemployment and had done nothing about it and, when the opposition, under this kind of goading, asked for proof, he could have produced the report. He couldn't have called it a 'hidden report,' which it wasn't, and he could have tabled it with cover intact, marked 'secret,' since members of the former government would have taken responsibility for publication.

Some curious events

The second incident was a curious and complicated one that reinforced my feeling of lack of confidence in me on Churchill's part, although here again I cannot be sure as to who was responsible for what happened.

One day in September of 1957, I received a telephone call to the effect that a Dutch-Indonesian businessman had arrived in Vancouver on his way to Washington to try to persuade the U.S. government to participate in an arrangement for the sale of wheat on credit. He had been persuaded by some Vancouver friends that he should first put the proposition before the Canadian government. The idea was a complicated three-cornered deal, involving Canada, the Netherlands, and Indonesia.

It didn't appear to me that there were any advantages to Canada in the deal, and I informed Churchill of my views. He didn't disagree and asked me to be present when the Dutch-Indonesian gentleman called on him. When the meeting took place, Churchill appeared reluctant to pour cold water on the proposition so I pointed out that, whatever its merits, there was no legislative authority for the government to enter into it. Churchill quickly agreed and the interview came to an end.

I thought that was the end of the matter, particularly since Churchill was about to leave the country. The next day, however, I learned to my surprise that William McNamara, assistant chief commissioner of the Canadian Wheat Board, was on his way to Ottawa from Winnipeg to see James Macdonnell, the acting minister of trade and commerce. When McNamara did not get in touch, I phoned George McIvor, the chief commissioner, to ask him what was going on. He replied that he had told McNamara to get in touch with me immediately on his arrival. The morning was well under way when I received a phone call from Mac-donnell to the effect that he had met with McNamara and some other advisers, who agreed with me that the Dutch-Indonesian proposal had no merit. He called again later, first to say that a cabinet committee had come to the same conclusion and, in due course, that the cabinet too had turned it down.

I shall always be grateful to Macdonnell for his courtesy to me during those difficult months when he was often my acting minister. As became him as a gentleman and a loyal member of the government, he urged me to give the benefit of the doubt to Churchill.

McNamara finally got in touch at the end of the day. His instructions from the minister's office had been explicit – he was to see Macdonnell and no one else. He hadn't intended to follow those instructions. Unfortunately, after his overnight flight from Winnipeg, he had slept in and hadn't had time or the opportunity to give me a call without being observed. We agreed that, come hell or high water, we would never let anything like this happen again. Fortunately, no harm had been done.

Again I thought that was the end of the story. Again I was wrong. During the 1958 election campaign I received a call from McNamara. While he was in Vancouver, Churchill had met one of those who had been interested in the original proposal and had urged him to bring forward another proposal that might be acceptable to the government. He had asked McNamara to send a message to our trade commissioner in the Netherlands inviting a delegation to go to Ottawa for further consultations. I arranged to transmit the invitation. Accordingly, within a few days, there arrived a prestigious delegation, including some of our best flour-mill customers led by Mr Henri Johan de Koster, whom I was many years later to know and work with when he became minister of defence in the government of the Netherlands.

I arranged for the presence of senior officials from all the interested departments to meet with the Netherlands delegation. We finally worked out a deal that fell within the ambit of our legislative authority. It did, of course, require cabinet approval, which would be difficult since nearly all the ministers were out of Ottawa campaigning. Donald Fleming, the minister of finance, was, however, in his office, and A.F.W. (Wynne) Plumptre, assistant deputy minister of finance, undertook to obtain his reaction. Fleming's answer was clear. It was improper to consider any such proposal when the cabinet was not available. I got in touch with Churchill, who didn't question Fleming's decision to terminate the negotiations and asked me to let the delegation down as easily as possible. I had the unpleasant responsibility of telling our guests that we had brought them across the Atlantic on a wild-goose chase. We gave them a bang-up lunch to demonstrate our goodwill. I dashed off a memorandum to Churchill reflecting my frustration.

This sequence of events looks now like a comedy of errors. At the time, it simply added to my feeling that I should leave the public service of Canada, a feeling that was reinforced by indirect advice from one of my friends in cabinet that Diefenbaker would never trust me. Arnold Heeney, a Winnipeg-born friend who had been secretary to the cabinet as well as under-secretary of state for external affairs and a distinguished ambassador, and other senior officials with whom I discussed my plans to resign, tried to persuade me to accept a transfer to a less conspicuous post, such as an ambassadorial appointment. I was not interested.

Resignation

Just before the date of the 1958 election I wrote to Churchill saying that when he returned to Ottawa I wished to speak to him about my personal future. I did so because I did not wish him to think that I was withholding my resignation plans until the results of the election were known.

The resulting meeting was brief and to the point. I told him that I had received an offer from Brazilian Traction, Light and Power Company. I had received offers from other organizations on earlier occasions but had turned them down without consideration because on those occasions I had no intention of retiring from the public service. This time I had not done so. The offer remained open. Should I accept? The answer was an unqualified yes. I thanked Churchill and added that I had not decided whether to accept the Brazilian Traction offer or to consider alternative offers. Therefore, I would appreciate it if, when he was speaking to the press about my resignation, he did not mention where I was going. He followed my advice, the result of which was a headline in the newspapers that I was looking for a job, which was not quite what I intended. The news item did bring forth a number of offers, but none of them appealed to me as much as that from Brazilian Traction, which I accepted. For company reasons, my employment with Brazilian began a month later, and the announcement of my appointment as a vice-president did not appear until that time. Technically, I was unemployed for a month, the only time in my life that I could claim that status, which I tried to do, unsuccessfully, when applying for a passport in preparation for a trip to Portugal.

Relations with the media

There was no television when I first arrived in Ottawa during the war, and the radio, as I recall it, was not depended upon as a major news source. In the 1940s, that role was still fulfilled by newspapers. The Parliamentary Press Gallery was full of reporters competing with one another for spot news and the inside dope on national political news. I was on the beat for columnists seeking factual background material, among them Grant Dexter, Bruce Hutchison, Blair Fraser, and Kenneth Wilson.

As officials, we were not forbidden to talk to the press, either by the minister or by our seniors. It was assumed that we understood our responsibilities and would be discreet. Moreover, in those days, newspapermen like Dexter, Hutchison, Fraser, and Wilson valued their access to officials and did not betray confidences when they were given information 'off the record.' They expected to be writing stories for a long time to come. They expected that the officials who could help them would also be around for a long time.

This relationship between officials and the press also reflected the relationship of the press with politicians, particularly ministers. It was very different then from what it became when, many years later, in the midst of the TV age, I attained ministerial rank. Before TV, the leading newspapermen cultivated close relations with ministers, particularly those whose newspapers, like the *Winnipeg Free Press*, supported the Liberal Party. In return for sympathetic – or at least fair – treatment of political events, ministers provided inside information to newspapermen.

In those days the media did not consider themselves the opposition to the government. That role was left to the political opposition in Parliament. Newspapers provided news and commentary, much of it very well informed even when partisan, because of a reasonably good working relationship between politicians and the press. Few, if any, top newspapermen practised investigative, antagonistic journalism as we now know it.

One day, very early in my career in the Department of Finance, I arrived at my East Block office about 9:00 a.m. The door was ajar because the spring lock was defective. I stood in the hall talking for a few minutes with a colleague about something that had happened in cabinet. Much to my alarm, when I pushed the door open to enter my office, I found Grant Dexter waiting to see me. He must have overhead the conversation on the outside. Before I could ask him to protect me by forgetting what he had overheard, he asked me a question that set my mind at rest. He had been given contradictory accounts by two ministers – Gardiner and Crerar – of what had gone on in cabinet the previous day. Whom should he believe? Dexter was better informed than I about cabinet proceedings.

When I left Ottawa in 1958, I remember thinking that nothing that was likely to happen in the future would provide stimulation and satisfaction of the kind I had experienced as a senior civil servant, working under ministers like J.L. Ilsley, D.C. Abbott, and C.D. Howe, and alongside brilliant and dedicated colleagues like Clifford Clark, Bob Bryce, Graham Towers, Norman Robertson, Hector Mackinnon (formerly head of the Tariff Board and a senior official in the Wartime Prices and Trade Board), Bill Mackintosh, Donald Gordon, Bob Beattie, Lou Rasminsky, Jim Coyne, Arnold Heeney, Alex (Sandy) Skelton, Ken Taylor, John Deutsch, Jack Pickersgill, David Mansur, Max Mackenzie, Fred Bull, George Davidson. And, in a way, I was correct in my prediction. Nothing that happened later, even when I entered politics and became a minister, gave me as much satisfaction as that period of sixteen years when I was fortunate enough to be at the centre of decision making in the Government of Canada. First of all, I was young and idealistic enough to stand the strain of long hours and intense pressure. Second, during that sixteen-year period Canada developed rapidly. In the post-war period standards of living rose at an unprecedented rate and without serious interruption. Third, the favourable economic environment enabled the federal government to undertake and finance social programs and federal-provincial arrangements that transformed for the better the structure of Canadian society from coast to coast and brought Newfoundland into the federation. Finally, there was an underlying consensus in those years (which began to disappear in the middle 1950s) about the direction of economic and social policy, enabling the politicians and their senior public-service advisers to work together with a remarkable degree of harmony.

In the Department of Trade and Commerce

Reflections on the role of the mandarins

Which leads me to reflect on the role of senior civil servants – the mandarins – in the governing of Canada, a role that is not well understood and often resented.

On the one hand are those Canadians convinced that civil servants, like the fountains of Trafalgar Square, play from ten to four.

On the other hand is the portrayal of senior civil servants, in the highly entertaining TV series 'Yes, Minister,' and 'Yes, Prime Minister,' as loyal but devious officials who manipulate their naïve minister.

To begin, let me recall an incident during the 1968 general election campaign when an impertinent young man asked me what qualifications I had to be secretary of state for external affairs, an office to which I had just been appointed. I replied that my essential qualification was that I had been elected to Parliament.

Perhaps my international negotiating experience helped to persuade Mr Trudeau to move me from Finance to External. However, I doubt that relevant experience had much to do with it or counts for much in the appointment of most ministers. Generally speaking, ministers take office with very little relevant experience or expertise. Their constituents elected them as MPs, not as ministers.

On taking office, a new minister of finance in a new government, for example, has the task of translating election pledges into a budget. Imagine the helplessness of the minister who did not have at his side experienced officials who had worked on previous budgets, to inform him of the government's financial position and prospects, the financial implications of election promises, the consequences of alternative taxation policies, and, finally, to put it all together in the form of a proposed budget speech that would make sense.

Ministers should be professionals in politics; regional leaders of their party. Rarely, and only by chance, are they professionals in government, at least at the beginning of their careers. The exception was the Pearson government, which at the outset included eight ministers who had been senior civil servants. Ministers jeopardize their future if they neglect politics in favour of acquiring technical expertise. Fortunately, there are some talented amateurs among ministers with whom it is a joy to serve as a colleague or as a non-partisan adviser. J.L. Ilsley told me that a constituent had said to him how wonderful it must be to be a minister, able to call in the deputy minister and tell him what to do. Ilsley replied that it wasn't like that at all. When he had a problem he asked the deputy minister for advice. The deputy offered several alternative courses of action. Ilsley then made his decision and the deputy minister carried it out.

There are in Canada many people more expert in financial matters than the minister of finance, whoever he or she may be, and many who know more about international affairs than the secretary of state for external affairs. Under the U.S. constitution, the president can appoint an acknowledged authority like Henry Kissinger to be secretary of state. If Mr Kissinger were a Canadian and coveted the External portfolio, he would have to get himself elected to Parliament as a member of the winning political party and hope that the prime minister didn't regard him as a rival and appoint him as minister of finance!

Consequently, it is essential under our parliamentary system of responsible government that there be available to ministers first-class policy advice in the fields of their responsibilities.

This kind of advice can come from the permanent public service or from individuals from outside the service hired for the purpose. There are some who contend that ministers should be advised by those who share their political views and are committed to the same policy goals. Political advice is one thing. Ministers are provided with funds to hire staff that do the things and proffer the kind of political advice they need to get re-elected. Professional advice on government policy is quite another matter.

There are some who fear that the senior public service advisers, the 'mandarins,' collectively have their own agenda, which may not be the agenda of the government. In our service, there is a consensus among senior public servants in Ottawa. They do have a view of the country derived from their experience as advisers and administrators. I am sure I speak for the overwhelming majority of them when I say that they believe that the federal government should have the powers to enable it to discharge its responsibilities. They believe that Canadians, wherever they live, should be able to enjoy a minimum level of social security. By training, and in their own self-interest, they want to see Canada remain united. This is an agenda that would not conflict with the agenda of any government that took office in Ottawa.

Some uncertainty about the loyalty of the senior public servants is not unreasonable for politicians who have never been in office as ministers. Those who have been in office know from experience that the Canadian tradition in the public service is to serve the government whatever its ideology or its programs. They do not share the fears of the inexperienced politicians. To which I would add this – that Canadian senior public servants who have been around for some years are not likely to be surprised by the innovations proposed by an incoming government. Their instinct will be to ensure that the innovations are thoroughly explored and, if they survive that exploration, are in such a form that they have the best possible chance of achieving their purpose. On many occasions, I participated in that process.

Those who offer professional advice should be not only familiar with the policies advocated by their ministers and the options available to the government, but also prepared, when the decisions have been made, to see that they are implemented. Ministers are likely to find advisers with these qualifications in the public service among officials who were appointed on merit and have risen to senior positions within departments and agencies and know from experience both the pitfalls and possibilities of alternative courses of action.

At the top of the public-service ladder are the deputy ministers, a misleading title, since it suggests that they can deputize for ministers in their political responsibilities, which is not the case. They are the public-service heads of departments, appointed by Order in Council on the recommendation of the prime minister. Among other things this gives the PM control over the machinery of government, although, if the PM is wise, the appointment of a deputy minister should have the whole-hearted support of the minister. I know of cases where the deputy minister threatened to appeal to the PM when his minister asked him to do something that he felt was unethical.

At the time of writing this book, a high proportion of deputy ministers had been promoted from the ranks of the non-partisan public service, and even those who were appointed from outside had merit to commend them. It is reassuring that there has been so little patronage in the appointment of mandarins.

The impartiality and versatility of the public service is tested when the government changes. For a variety of reasons, a few of us left when the Diefenbaker government was re-elected in 1958 with a majority in the House of Commons. On the whole, and in spite of Prime Minister Diefenbaker's obvious suspicion of the 'Pearsonalities' among the civil servants, the structure was not impaired during the Diefenbaker years, as we found when we took office in 1963. It is ironic that Diefenbaker came to depend so much on two mandarins from the Liberal era, R.B. Bryce, the secretary to the cabinet, and Basil Robinson, assigned to him from the Department of External Affairs. There was a very small turn-over of deputy ministers at the time of subsequent changes of government in 1979, 1984, and 1988.

Sometimes talented individuals can be found on the outside who make excellent heads of departments. Their appointment is not only not resented, it is welcomed by their peers and their departmental subordinates, subject to this proviso: not too many such appointments. The best and the brightest cannot be expected to stay in the service if they are denied the opportunity of rising to the top.

To work well, the relationship between ministers and their top professional advisers should be one of mutual confidence. The mandarins cannot perform well unless they have direct and regular contact with the minister. I have worked on both ends of the team. I was granted daily interviews with my minister when I was deputy and insisted on meeting daily with my deputy ministers when I became a minister. It is a mistake on the part of a minister to interpose one of his or her political staff as a conduit for the deputy's views or his own views to the deputy.

The top officials in the major policy departments are key players in the Canadian system of government. It is essential that they be well informed with well developed views about public policy and, if possible, a wide acquaintanceship with the movers and shakers in the private sector. Politically neutral they should be. Politically ignorant they cannot afford to be. The ministers I served wanted to know the views of their non-partisan advisers on all aspects of the matters under discussion. When I became a minister I expected my deputy ministers to be frank and open in the expression of their views. Top officials worth their salt should be prepared to tell the minister, politely, of course, that his or her pet ideas are for the birds.

The public service of Canada numbers in the hundreds of thousands and engages in a wide variety of activities, most of them of an administrative character. It is a responsibility of government to ensure that these activities are organized as efficiently and economically as possible. Managerial efficiency and economy in the public service, important as they may be, do not, however, guarantee that ministers have available to them the policy advice they need to make the right decisions.

Good judgment and constructive imagination are the most valuable qualities in an adviser. Unfortunately, these admirable qualities are difficult to teach and are not always to be found in the most efficient administrators. Some of the most influential advisers that I knew were poor administrators and admitted it. Being wise, they turned administration over to others in the department who were better equipped.

In those far-off days of 1942 when I entered the public service of Canada it was small in numbers. The senior civil servants knew one another, met frequently, and talked shop non-stop. For some years following post-war recruitment, the numbers were still manageable, and it remained possible to identify relatively easily the mandarins of the future. Those at the top considered it part of their responsibility to bring along potential successors.

Nowadays, that is not so easy. There are twice as many departments, more than twice as many ministers, and several times as many civil servants, many of whom live outside the nation's capital. Although top officials gather in committees and socially, morale is not as high as it was when there was greater consensus as to national objectives, the economy was expanding, and government finances were in good order. To be a top adviser to a minister today is not the high adventure it was in the fifties and the sixties.

Notwithstanding these difficulties and discouragements, the calibre of the top officials in the public service of Canada remains high. Unfortunately, their talents are not being as fully utilized and developed as they were when I was involved and the ministers and their top public-service advisers worked together as a team in the formulation and execution of policy.

Are they paid enough? When I left the public service to join Brazilian Traction my salary doubled. If I had stayed with the company or returned to it later as I was invited to do, my salary would have soared. I returned to Ottawa as a politician and took a big drop in income. Why? One reason was that government service gives me great personal satisfaction.

Because of the satisfaction and the excitement of public service at senior levels, the salaries of top officials do not have to match those in private business. They must, however, be high enough so that when top officials meet with business types their attitude and their judgment are not affected by feelings of unfairness or inferiority. It was ridiculous that the salary of the governor of the Bank of Canada, responsible for protecting the value of the Canadian currency, should, during my time in office, have been so much below the salaries of the presidents of the chartered banks, who looked to the governor for guidance.

It is true that although salaries of the top officials are below what they could earn in private business, there is greater security in the public service. But it is only a matter of degree. Technically, deputy ministers have no security of tenure. They can be dismissed at any time. Arrangements are usually made to ease the transition. But I have never heard of 'golden handshakes' to match those that eased the pain of management changes in the private sector.

Ministers are temporary heads of departments who come and go as the prime minister and the voters decide. Continuity is provided by the civil servants who run the departments. This is the theory and usually the practice. In the 1970s and 1980s there were periods when deputy ministers seemed to change as rapidly as ministers, with the result that instead of there being an amateur in government as minister and an experienced deputy as professional, two amateurs have been in charge.

This doesn't matter too much in departments concerned mainly with administration. It shouldn't happen in major departments like Finance, External Affairs, Trade and Commerce, Health and Welfare, Energy, Mines and Resources, and Environment, where the decisions are so crucial to the country as a whole and where the minister is so dependent on the experience and judgment of departmental advisers.

One final reflection: Senior public servants are never going to be popular and should as far as possible stay out of the limelight. Nor is their contribution, however great, going to be acknowledged by the politicians, who have to accept the blame for mistakes and will take full credit for the successes.

Which is as it should be.

CHAPTER FOUR

In Private Business, 1958–1963

Vice-president of Brazilian Traction

When I arrived to take up my responsibilities as vice-president of Brazilian Traction, Carey Fox was chairman of the board, Henry Borden was president, and Grant Glassco was executive vice-president.

Carey Fox became a friend and a counsellor, a man of great integrity whose business ethics were impeccable and who understood the true meaning of charity. He was very proud that towards the end of his life he financed research that led to effective treatment for German measles. Borden and Glassco were leading Conservatives. Borden was a close personal friend of Sidney Smith, former president of the universities of Manitoba and Toronto, who became secretary of state for external affairs shortly before I left the public service. As chairman of the Wartime Industries Control Board, Borden had worked closely with Howe.

My years with Brazilian Traction taught me much, not only about corporate business but, perhaps more significantly, about foreign ownership. Until I joined that company, I had been concerned as a government official about foreign ownership of Canadian companies. Now, I was to experience for the first time the problems of a Canadian-owned company operating in a foreign country, Brazil. The 'Light,' as the company was popularly known in Brazil, was attacked by local nationalists as the Canadian octopus, the tool of American imperialism.

We were a natural target of the Brazilian nationalists if only because, at the time I joined Brazilian Traction, we were probably the largest company in Latin America, with more than 50,000 employees, and we operated public utilities – tramways (known as '*bondes*' in Portuguese because they had been financed by the issue of bonds), electricity, gas, and telephones – all subject to government regulation. At the same time, it was widely recognized that the Light was a good employer, with Brazilians in the top management and directorship of the subsidiaries, and providing security and working conditions for its employees that were not exceeded by any other major company, domestic or foreign-owned. We always had a long list of job applicants.

At one time, before the era of inflation, Brazilian Traction had been a profitable enterprise, its shares highly regarded on the stock markets, particularly in Britain. By 1958, when I joined the company, profitability had fallen drastically, mainly because in the inflationary environment that existed in Brazil (in those years the rate of inflation sometimes exceeded 50 per cent annually) costs had risen and were rising more quickly than the regulators were prepared to adjust rates to consumers. Under these circumstances, there was little incentive for the company to extend services. One day, the English-language newspaper in Rio de Janeiro reported that a resident was having a cocktail party to celebrate the tenth anniversary of his application for a telephone.

I spent weeks and months at a time in Brazil and learned a good deal of Portuguese during my four years or so with the company. To a Canadian, Brazil was full of ambiguities and contradictions: cities of skyscrapers like Rio de Janeiro and São Paulo, surrounded by shanty-towns – *favelas* – of abject poverty; a multiracial society on the streets and the beaches of Copacabana, but with few blacks in high places.

Most of my attention was devoted to the telephone side of the business. I came to the conclusion that it was virtually impossible to run the telephone system efficiently and to turn a legitimate profit so long as it was fragmented by individual municipal franchises. I therefore recommended that the company should try to convince the Brazilian federal government to take over the telephone service as a federal operation and to buy our assets. Soon after I left the company to enter politics, my recommendation came to fruition and began the process whereby the company eventually disposed of all its public utilities and invested a high proportion of the proceeds outside Brazil. I sometimes wonder how things would have developed if I had accepted the invitation of the directors (made while I was minister of finance) to resign from the government and become president of the company. At the time I was not tempted, and I have never regretted my decision to stay with politics.

Henry Borden, the president, was appointed chairman of a Royal Commission on Sources of Energy on 15 October 1957; Grant Glassco, the executive vice-president, was appointed chairman of a Royal Commission on the Public Service on 16 September 1960. From time to time, both of them discussed their enquiries and alternative policies with me. Borden confirmed the pattern of petroleum trade that had been developing, which was to import petroleum mostly from Venezuela to meet the requirements of eastern Canada and to export surplus petroleum from the Prairies to the United States, and recommended the establishment of a national energy board. The gist of Glassco's report on the public service was to give deputy ministers greater authority in the management of their departments. In general, I found both the Glassco and Borden Commission reports to be useful and supported their implementation when a few years later I became a minister.

During my years with Brazilian Traction I thought that the Progressive Conservative Party would have been more successful in office if it had been able to persuade Borden and Glassco to be more actively involved in politics. Glassco, in particular, would have made an outstanding MP and minister. He had broad views on public policy and was a most persuasive advocate of his ideas.

The Donwood Foundation

During this period of residence in Toronto I was approached by Dr Gordon Bell to help him raise capital for a private hospital for the treatment of addictions. During the war he had been involved in this kind of treatment and was already in charge of a small clinic of nine beds. Although a bit mystified as to why he had selected me, I agreed to become chairman of the board of the Donwood Foundation and held the position until I had to resign when I joined the cabinet in 1963. Today, Donwood is a very large Toronto hospital with a record of great success in the treatment of addictions – particularly, but not exclusively, of alcoholism. During one of his informal lectures to the board of directors, Dr Bell told us that alcoholism was not the only serious addiction and mentioned one patient who was addicted to drinking milk, hid bottles everywhere, resisted treatment, and died!

When, years later, I was minister of finance, Bell asked me to attend one of his annual meetings to speak to patients, former patients, and their families. It is customary at such meetings, when introducing the guest speaker, to raise the audience's expectations of the forthcoming address. I have often suffered through this well-intentioned silliness. In his introduction, Bell referred to the great debt he and Donwood and its patients owed to my chairmanship of the board. I found this excessive since, after all, my chairmanship had lasted such a relatively short time. Then came the explanation, which is the reason I include reference to Donwood in these memoirs.

When he began to explore the idea of establishing a hospital for the treatment of addiction, Bell said, he went to the United States to talk to his counterparts and was greatly discouraged by what he learned. Those he spoke to said that they had not been successful in their fund-raising because businessmen they approached to head campaigns felt that, if they accepted, the public would think they were themselves alcoholics or were former alcoholics who had taken the cure.

When he returned to Canada, Bell went on, he spoke to a friend who suggested to him that he should ask Mitchell Sharp to take the lead. No one would think of him as an alcoholic. When he accepted, other businessmen who were approached were encouraged by Mitchell Sharp's example and agreed to serve on the board.

Mitchell Sharp – sober citizen; never thought to put that in my CV!

The Kingston Conference

Having been associated with government over a period of sixteen years, I followed federal affairs closely after I moved to Toronto. Until L.B. Pearson, leader of the Liberal Party and leader of the opposition in the House of Commons, called me on the telephone to ask me to organize a thinkers' conference, however, I took no part in political activities, partisan or otherwise. I did not join the local constituency organization of the Liberal Party. I did not attend political gatherings of any kind. I did not try to raise money for the party or its candidates. Indeed, one of the reasons why Pearson asked me to organize a thinkers' conference was that, while I was known to have liberal views, I was not a member of the party and could therefore attract to a conference people who would hesitate to accept an invitation from the leader of the Liberal Party of Canada.

I accepted Pearson's invitation not because I looked upon this as a first step to a political career (I had no such thoughts at that time), but simply because I thought the country was being misgoverned and that Pearson would make a better prime minister than Diefenbaker.

During my years in the civil service I met Pearson a number of times as a colleague, and later when he became a minister I worked closely with him, particularly during the negotiations for the trade agreement with the Soviet Union. I shared his love of Canada and admired his careful diplomatic approach to serious issues, both foreign and domestic, his intelligence, and his quick wit. I didn't always agree with him and sometimes felt that, in his desire to avoid taking a position on difficult issues, he created the impression that he agreed with the last person who spoke to him. But I had no doubt that overall he had the qualities that were needed to lead Canada at that time.

Plans for the conference were worked out in the evenings at my Toronto home, 4 Highbourne Road. Among those who gathered with me were Michael Mackenzie, a chartered accountant in the Clarkson, Gordon firm, who became vice-chairman of the Kingston Conference, William Wilder of Wood Gundy, and R.M. McIntosh, then with the Bank of Nova Scotia: all were young and enthusiastic. The secretary of the conference was Nancy Burpee, my secretary at Brazilian Traction. David Ferguson was responsible for physical arrangements.

Pearson had originally thought of a small conference of about fifty thinkers. So great was the demand to participate that we had difficulty holding attendance at the Kingston Conference down to about two hundred, each one of whom (except the principal speakers) paid $25 for the privilege of attending, plus room and board at Queen's University. I asked a few prominent Canadians to be sponsors and, for the privilege, to ante up $1,000 each to help cover expenses. At the end of the conference, I was able to offer to return $400 to each of them. One rule we enforced rigidly: no member of Parliament was to be on the program as speaker, except Jack Pickersgill, who was one of those asked to sum up their impressions of the conference at the closing session. Before the opening of the conference, Pearson gave those who attended a dinner at which he spoke.

Our original intention had been to exclude the media, other than newspapermen who were on the program as speakers. In the end, we had to compromise, permitting the media to attend the sessions and to report what was said by the principal speakers and, without attribution, the gist of the resulting discussion. It was a wise compromise. The conference was well covered by the media who, as is natural with them, gave the greatest prominence to speakers who criticized the Liberal Party. Conservatives were delighted and were puzzled by the willingness of the Liberals to open themselves to such public criticism. They failed to see that by so doing the Liberals demonstrated to the public their willingness to listen to their critics and their intention to make a fresh start after the electoral disaster of 1958 ended twenty-two continuous years in office.

As chairman, I was responsible in the main for the program and for the list of speakers. As for the list of invitees, I was only casually acquainted at that stage with what might be termed the Liberal intelligentsia throughout the country, or the people who might become candidates in the next election, so I deferred to Walter Gordon and to others in the party. As it turned out, the choices were excellent. Not only was the debate of a high order, but among the participants were a substantial number of men and women who offered themselves as Liberal candidates for the first time in 1962 and 1963 and later, including Walter Gordon, Judy LaMarsh, C.M. (Bud) Drury, John Turner, Maurice Lamontagne, Jean Marchand, Gérard Pelletier, Maurice and Jeanne Sauvé, Tom Kent, Pauline Jewett, Gordon Blair, Jack Davis, Alastair Gillespie, Otto Lang, and myself.

There were some distinguished French Canadians among the speakers and participants, including Jean Marchand, leader of the Canadian Confederation of Catholic Labour, Maurice Lamontagne, assistant dean of the Faculty of Social Sciences at Ottawa University, Gérard Pelletier, editor of *La Presse*, André Laurendeau, who later co-chaired with Davidson Dunton the Royal Commission on Bilingualism and Biculturalism, and Claude Morin, later a senior civil servant in the Quebec government and still later a leading member of the Parti Québécois. Nevertheless, one could not have judged from the Kingston Conference that the main support for the Liberal Party in the years to come would be found in the province of Quebec. The Quiet Revolution was under way in Quebec, but it was not until the election of Pierre Trudeau (who was not at Kingston) to the leadership of the party that Quebec Liberals took the place in the councils of the federal party that their numbers and intelligence merited.

Looking back at the program for the Kingston Conference in September 1960, what strikes one is that thirty years ago the matters about which Canadians were then concerned are very much the same as those about which they are concerned today, although, of course, much has happened in the meantime. Here is the list: 'Defence'; 'How Independent Can We Be?'; 'External Economic Policy'; 'Growth, Stability and the Problem of Unemployment'; 'Towards a Philosophy of Social Security'; 'Programs of Social Security, Old Age Security, Unemployment Insurance, Medical and Hospital Care'; 'The Aims of Organized Labour'; 'Agriculture'; 'Policies and Plans for Urban Development and Land Use'; 'The Development of Canadian Values and Our Cultural Heritage.' The agenda of the Kingston Conference, including the names of speakers and commentators, appears in Appendix 1.

The Kingston Conference opened on the morning of Tuesday, 6 September, and came to an end in the afternoon of Saturday, 10 September, five full days, in itself a remarkable event. The days were crammed with the presentation of papers, and the discussion continued long into the evening after dinner. We planned the conference on the assumption that people would come and would be prepared to stay for five full days. We were naïve and inexperienced, but we were right. They did come, and a high proportion of them did stay to the end.

The closing event on Saturday afternoon was in itself worth the price of admission. Three prominent Canadians summed up their impressions of the conference: Davidson Dunton, a liberally minded but non-partisan man of long experience in public affairs, including an appointment as president of the CBC; Jack Pickersgill, an articulate Liberal politician who had once been an academic; and Frank Underhill, a controversial but much-loved and highly respected academic who had once been a socialist.

Frank Underhill displayed his talent for invective, employing it not only against Canadian Liberal governments, the Liberal Party, and the Kingston Conference, but also against his former colleagues in the CCF. These were his concluding words: 'But you see where this leaves me. I feel like Huckleberry Finn. I have no home to go to. And like Huck, that irredeemable individualist, I reckon I got to light out for the territory. For the past twenty-five years or so I been floating down the political Mississippi on the CCF path. And now, this week, my Aunt Sally Sharp, she's caught up with me, and she's wanting to adopt me in a good Liberal home, and civilize me, and I can't stand it. I been there before.'

When I rose to thank him, I wept tears of laughter as well as of affection.

Davidson Dunton, then the president of Carleton University, followed with a perceptive appraisal of the conference:

I suggest that liberal thinking needs sharper ideas about what it will leave to the market place, to individual decision and action, and in what fields it will take, or provide for, collective action ... it would be hard for any LMP (liberally minded person) to go away from here and casually, or by mistake, argue for higher tariffs, or not work on every possible and practical occasion for tariff reform and reduction of tariffs.

... There were the references by those who spoke in the social security debates to thinking about the people concerned and finding out what they wanted and why they wanted it; the urgings not to start with a plan just because it looked like a logical structure, but to go to the people and study their particular concerns.

91

The importance of human factors seemed to come out, too, in other places as well as in the debates on social measures. It kept being referred to at other times by economists and business people who said that our capital doesn't just consist of material things ... human beings, know-how, knowledge, ability, skill, all those things are a vital part of capital for growth.'

Finally, I introduced Jack Pickersgill. 'Perhaps,' I said, 'if Professor Underhill is one *enfant terrible*, Mr Pickersgill is the other.'

He objected to Frank Underhill's description of the St Laurent government, of which Pickersgill had been a member, as managerial and to Tom Kent's criticism of it as conservative, a period of digestion. 'Look at what we accomplished,' he went on:

We abandoned the notion that in peacetime we kept our armed forces at home, we abandoned the notion that we had no share of responsibility for keeping the peace of the world, we joined in the North Atlantic Alliance and ... we sent troops to Europe who've been maintained there at vast expense ever since ... When the Korean business arose Canadian troops were sent overseas to take our share of our international responsibilities and to fight. The Colombo Plan was very largely a Canadian initiative and to a very great extent the initiative of Mr. Pearson himself. There was also the completion of Confederation ... the St. Lawrence Seaway, the Canso Causeway, and locating a great military camp at Gagetown, not for strategic reasons, but to build up the economy of New Brunswick ... equalization of provincial revenues, the Massey commission, the Federal grants to the Universities, the Canada Council, the new Old Age Security system, hospital insurance, the establishment of nationally operated television. These new and different things were done with general consent by this Liberal Government that has been described as merely managerial ...

What has impressed me in retrospect about the Kingston Conference is that it turned out to be so successful politically, even though that was not what Pearson originally had in mind. He wanted it known, of course, that as leader he was open to fresh ideas which he could adopt and adapt. I don't think he had contemplated either such a big conference or the publicity that it generated. The media paid attention because of the calibre of the speakers and the clash of ideas and opinions. It wasn't just another gathering of the faithful – a Liberal love-in – at which the speakers praised their party and its leader. In fact, there was none of that. Nor did I conceive it as a conference to help draft a platform for the Liberal Party, which may originally have been in Pearson's mind. For that purpose I was the wrong chairman since I was not at that time a member of the Liberal Party. Certainly I did not select the speakers with that in mind. Kingston didn't draft a platform for the Liberal Party, but it did have a significant effect upon future Liberal policies, mostly because of the people who were there and who later did formulate policy.

Tom Kent, who wrote one of the most brilliant essays for the conference, had a legitimate grievance against me for agreeing at the last moment to change the rules about press coverage. His essay was prepared for consideration by a small group of well-intentioned and intelligent advisers and not for publication. The ideas he put forward, particularly the suggestion of a tax on advertising, caused a sensation and dogged Tom for years. I doubt, however, that in the long run that bit of unintended publicity did him any harm, politically or otherwise. To judge from what he has written about those years, his most serious complaint about Kingston was the conversion of the original idea of a closed thinkers' conference to advise the leader of the Liberal Party to a more open forum for the exchange of ideas, in the presence of Pearson and other prominent Liberals.

Entry into politics

As a civil servant, my various offices had always been close to the Centre Block of the Parliament Buildings, and I used to think how wonderful it must be to have the right to enter that magnificent building and take a seat in the House of Commons. That was the extent of my political ambitions. It never occurred to me during those long years as an adviser to governments to stand for Parliament. I looked upon politicians as a different breed of people, motivated quite differently from myself. Nor did any of the politicians with whom I worked suggest that I should enter politics.

After I had left the public service – for that matter, even after the Kingston Conference or after attending my first Liberal Party policy Conference in 1960 – I did not take seriously the idea of entering politics. Somehow, it didn't fit with my own evaluation of my personal qualities. I couldn't imagine myself performing like Paul Martin, or Paul Hellyer, who was the first Liberal to win a seat after the 1958 catastrophe, or Pickersgill, who had made the transition directly from the public service to politics. When Pearson phoned me one day towards the end of 1961 to say that he would like me to run for Parliament as a Liberal candidate in the next general election, it took me some time to react. I became more reconciled to the idea when he added that if

I were not prepared to be a candidate he would like me to be the chairman of the Liberal Party. That I didn't want to be.

When I told my wife about Pearson's invitation, she was far from enthusiastic, more or less saying, 'If you decide to enter politics you'd better get yourself another wife.' To which I replied that she was better equipped to enter public life than I was. Knowing Daisy's idealism, I then went on to say that perhaps she was right; why give up a good job with good prospects to take on the uncertainties of politics? This was a ploy on my part that worked. Her attitude changed. Don't put money first; do what you think is right.

The relinquishment of a career in business did not concern me too much. True, I had an interesting job with a salary well above an MP's or minister's remuneration and with good prospects for advancement. I had also become a director of some medium-sized enterprises – Montreal Shipping and Toromont, among others – and could look forward to invitations to join other prestigious boards.

I liked my associates at Brazilian Traction – Carey Fox, Henry Borden, and Grant Glassco – all men with a great breadth of interests outside business. I cannot say, however, that I looked forward to having to join the clubs and to engage in the social activities that seemed to be an inseparable part of belonging to the business establishment. I found that I missed Ottawa – not the physical climate, which is deplorable, but the continuous discussion of national and international affairs. On the whole, politicians and senior civil servants are more stimulating company than businessmen. So, I opted for politics.

I informed Borden and Glassco of my intentions to seek the Liberal nomination somewhere, so that the company could decide whether to require my resignation or to grant me leave of absence if I succeeded in becoming a Liberal candidate. I explained to them that I did not want to be influenced in my decision to enter or not to enter politics by their decision about my future with the company. I was prepared to take the risks. In due course, the board of directors decided that they did not wish a vice-president of Brazilian Traction on leave of absence to be running against the minister of finance. Borden told me privately that the decision might have been different if Diefenbaker had not been prime minister. So I submitted my resignation.

The choice of Eglinton and the 1962 campaign

I told Pearson that I was prepared to run in the next election. But where? When my willingness to run became known I received calls from several Toronto constituencies, inviting me to stand for nomination. At that stage, I did not receive an invitation from Eglinton, probably because the constituency organization, which had woefully few paid-up members, thought I would not agree to run in what was regarded as one of the safest Tory seats in the country.

What caused me to look closely at Eglinton was its sitting member, Donald Fleming, minister of finance. If I were to be a candidate, I wanted to have an opponent with whom I could debate government policy. During those nine months or so of Tory minority government following the 1957 election, I had worked in interdepartmental committees chaired by Fleming. We got along quite well, so there was no personal animosity in my wish to oppose him during the election.

Before making a final decision, however, I asked some friends who lived in Eglinton to do informal soundings and, much to our gratification, this constituency seemed to be good fighting ground, as it turned out to be.

No sooner had I let Pearson know that Eglinton was my choice than I had a call from Keith Davey, whose parental home was in Eglinton, and a visit from David Anderson, who at one time had contested the provincial seat of Eglinton, the boundaries of which were then almost identical with the federal seat. Anderson became my closest political associate, a great bear of a man of enormous enthusiasm and intense loyalty. In the organizational stages of my first Eglinton campaign, he was reprimanded by some of the other members of the team for calling me 'sir.' Thereafter he called me 'Mitchell' in public and 'sir' in private.

First, I had to win the nomination in Eglinton. My opponent was a young research doctor, Russell Taylor, also, curiously, like myself a graduate of the University of Manitoba. That nomination contest proved to be a blessing in disguise because it required the putting together of an organization well in advance of the election. Membership in the Eglinton riding association rose quickly from a handful to several hundred. The core of my campaign organization began to take shape. By good fortune, my first piece of campaign literature – a simple announcement of my nomination – was received by the voters the same week that the 1962 election was called. The designer of all my campaign literature, including that first piece, was Paul Break, an unorthodox but brilliant publicist. When he joined my campaign he said he thought he could sell me and added that he hoped I did not mind being treated like a box of soap flakes. My signs and literature were arresting and different. He forbade me to do anything so obvious as exhorting the voters through lawn signs to 'vote for Mitchell Sharp.' All that appeared on those signs was a square photo of my eyes, nose, and mouth (arresting if not flattering), my name, my party, the date of the election, and an X. Break's designs were so attractive that at one school in the constituency a teacher told me that all but one of the children in her class wore my campaign buttons.

We used sample surveys, not so much for the purpose of ascertaining the views of constituents on the issues of the day, although we included questions of that kind in our survey, but to measure name recognition and general attitudes towards my candidature. The results at the beginning of the campaign were very helpful. In areas where I was best known support was highest. So we intensified activities in areas where I was not well known. When asked the question 'Who is likely to win?,' a very high proportion said Fleming. This was to be expected. Fleming had won the 1958 election by a margin of 18,000 votes. When asked the question 'Whom would you like to see win?,' the results were very different, close to an equal split between Fleming and Sharp. Our sampling towards the end of the campaign confirmed the closeness of the contest.

Much to my surprise, I found I liked campaigning and meeting people. Only rarely were they rude. I stood at bus stops in my constituency from 7:30 a.m. to 9:30 a.m., along with a campaign worker, greeting passengers before they stepped on to the bus. This form of campaigning is ideal because the candidate has time to introduce himself and pass along a piece of literature. The voter, on the other hand, doesn't have time (unless he or she is prepared to miss the bus) to engage the candidate in a long discussion. In the course of a campaign, one can meet thousands of one's constituents in this way and with less expenditure of time and energy than calling door to door.

Public meetings have to be held, if only to demonstrate to voters that the candidate is willing to meet them in public. Such meetings do not constitute effective local campaigning, however. They are media events. Most of those who attend public meetings organized by a candidate are already supporters. During the 1962 and 1963 election campaigns, Paul Break arranged for a talented CBC-TV artist, George Feyer, to entertain the crowd with spontaneous drawings projected on a screen.

Coffee parties

The so-called coffee party – a gathering of neighbours – turned out to be an excellent way to meet and convince Eglinton residents to vote for me. In the course of the 1962 and 1963 campaigns, I attended something like one hundred such parties, with an average attendance of about twenty-five. Eglinton, as then constituted, was ideal for this approach to campaigning. There were plenty of houses that could accommodate twenty or thirty people, and the hosts and hostesses were accustomed to entertaining their neighbours.

When the Conservatives learned about the effectiveness of our coffee parties, they organized some for Donald Fleming, but the technique didn't suit Fleming as well as it did me. The president of the Liberal Women's Association in Eglinton told me that she was invited to a coffee party being given by her neighbour for Fleming. When the minister arrived there were only three women in the room. Nevertheless, he delivered a fifteen-minute speech, standing.

Public policy was my main interest. But I also had to learn about raising money for election campaigns. Fortunately, my supporters in Eglinton understood clearly my attitude towards fund-raising. They knew that I wasn't prepared to make deals or give favours in return for contributions. I took the same attitude when I was a candidate for the leadership of the Liberal Party in 1968. So a finance committee was formed that operated separately from the campaign committee and from my agent.

The committee deposited its collections in a special account and made money available from it to meet expenses. When the campaign was completed I sent contributors simple letters of thanks, prepared by the finance committee, that made no mention of the amounts contributed.

My agent was required to file with the election authorities a statement showing the amounts of money spent and a list of contributors. The 1962 campaign was his first experience as an agent, so he read the law carefully and did his best to comply. He had no difficulty with the expenditure side of the statement. As to the contributions, he had heard that there was a finance committee and that it had an account with a trust company. So he phoned the manager and asked to see it. The manager assumed that my agent was a member of the finance committee and complied. The account concealed as much as it revealed, because most of the deposits were in the names of members of the finance committee who had collected cash from many contributors and had deposited it in their own names. But there were a few cheques that did identify contributors.

My agent presented his statement to me for signature. Because I didn't want to know too much about the contributors, I signed without reading the list.

Donald Fleming paid twenty-five cents to obtain a copy and found the names of some of his friends among the list of contributors of substantial amounts. I was told he called them and protested.

I reappointed the same agent for the next general election in 1963 because I knew he would benefit from his experience. Thereafter I had no more problems of that kind. Most of the contributors were listed as anonymous. When contributions to political parties and candidates became tax deductible in 1974, they also, of course, became public.

Eglinton at the centre

As I had hoped, the contest between the minister of finance and myself became one of the focal points of the 1962 campaign, and my literature and in my remarks on the public platform I addressed the main issues, particularly those that related to the responsibilities of the minister of finance. All this was widely reported in the media throughout Canada.

John Diefenbaker helped me enormously to become a national figure. He attacked me as one of those new Liberal recruits (the others were Walter Gordon, Bud Drury, Tom Kent, and Maurice Lamontagne) who had 'in the war years and in the post-war period treated Parliament with the utmost contempt ...' Reporters told me that this was one of the 'Chief's' favourite lines. He lovingly repeated this preposterous assertion all across Canada, apparently without recognizing how counter-productive it was. I shall always be grateful.

I was fortunate that there gathered around me a large group of dedicated workers who got enormous pleasure out of that 1962 campaign, led by Robert Wright, David Anderson, Michael McCabe, who later became my executive assistant, Gordon Farquharson, Paul Break, and Pierre Genest. I teased Genest by referring to him as the leader of the French-Canadian Bar in English-speaking Eglinton. Looking back, they were a distinguished lot, those hundreds of Eglinton workers, many of whom subsequently rose to the top in business, the professions, and academia. I also had remarkably efficient and enthusiastic managers of all six of my campaigns: Robert Wright in 1962, Burke Doran in 1963, Burke Doran and Stephen Borins in 1965, Stephen Borins in 1968, Hugh Rennie in 1972, and Anna Young in 1974.

The population of Eglinton during my incumbency as MP included a remarkable number of university graduates, professionals, and academics. This was brought to my attention in the early 1970s when I was invited to a meeting in a church basement in Eglinton constituency to protest the alleged lack of support by the federal government for research. The room was crowded, and before the meeting began I asked the chairman where the audience came from, from the whole of Toronto or only from Eglinton? The chairman put the question. 'How many of you live in this neighbourhood?' Almost every hand went up. Then he turned to me. 'Mr. Sharp we did a count in Eglinton. You have some four hundred academics, scientists and similar professionals in your constituency.'

Plenty of campaign literature and signs were available from Liberal Party headquarters, but I didn't use them much in Eglinton in the 1962 election. My problem was to try to defeat Donald Fleming, minister of finance. My pamphlets, prepared by Paul Break, were directed to that objective. Party literature that condemned the Diefenbaker government and described what a Liberal government would do if elected was not sufficient to persuade Eglinton voters to vote for me rather than for Fleming, a politician of distinction who had represented that constituency in federal and local politics for umpteen years.

Partisanship is not my forte. The trouble with having been a senior civil servant is that I knew from experience how difficult it would be to carry through successfully the Liberal Party platform. I even admitted the difficulties when I met voters privately and publicly. I sympathized with Pearson who, like myself, had been a senior public servant and found it difficult to be partisan and to be utterly confident that his promises as Liberal leader could be fulfilled. Nor do I think, I may add, that the Liberals would have done any better in any of the elections under Pearson's leadership if he had demonstrated more conviction in his public appearances. Indeed, Pearson was most effective when he was natural, humorous, and rather tentative.

In any event, by the time I had fought a half-dozen election campaigns I came to the conclusion that most voters are cynical about the declared policies and platforms of political parties and mark their ballots in the polling booth for other reasons.

Very early in that first campaign, I received a telephone call from a man who did not identify himself other than to say that he was a voter in Eglinton and was trying to make up his mind about supporting me. 'What is your attitude towards the CBC?' he asked me. I could not tell from the way he asked the question what his own attitude might be. So I decided not to equivocate but to answer honestly and to defend the CBC vigorously: without the CBC, I said, there would be very few orchestras, or theatres, or playwrights in Canada. Much to my relief and delight he said that he would vote for me; he was a freelance producer for the CBC.

During that first campaign another voter, a man of Eastern European origin who had just become a Canadian citizen, told me he was confused because he couldn't see much difference between the Liberal and Conservative parties. There is not much difference, I agreed. By the time any national party has reconciled the differing views of its members from the various regions of Canada, they are likely to arrive at very similar conclusions about policy. The Liberal Party should be the party of reform, the Conservatives the party of consolidation. But John Diefenbaker is a populist, not a conservative, so the situation is very confused. I told my constituent that he would have to make up his mind which party appeared to hold out the best hope of better government and, of course, I favoured the Liberal Party.

In that 1962 election the *Globe and Mail* supported the Conservatives, and Donald Fleming in Eglinton, as it had supported the Tory party through thick and thin for more than twenty years. Nevertheless, I was satisfied that the *Globe and Mail* took my candidature seriously when it devoted a leading editorial to my campaign close to election day. It was entitled 'The Duke of Eglinton.' According to the writer I was like the grand old Duke of York who in the well-known rhyme, 'had 10,000 men. He marched them up to the top of the hill and marched them down again ... when they were up they were up, and when they were down, they were down, and when they were only half way up they were neither up nor down.' The Liberal candidate in Eglinton, said the *Globe*, took us up to the top of the hill to survey the wreckage of the Diefenbaker administration and then took us down again without saying what he or the Liberals would do to repair the damage.

Fleming had the editorial reprinted and distributed to every household in Eglinton, which, of course, concerned me and my organization. On my way by plane to Winnipeg I remembered that when I was a student in London I had come across a monument to the Grand Old Duke of York, which meant that he must have accomplished something to have merited such an honour. I telephoned Ottawa to ask that a historian do a little research. He found that the duke had been appointed commander-in-chief of the British Army to root out the bad administration of his predecessor. I said in my next speech that I didn't mind being compared with that worthy gentleman. It was a good reply, as the editor of the *Globe and Mail* told me some time later, but he didn't give it much publicity before the election.

On the day of the 1962 election, David Anderson asked me if I thought I would win. I predicted that I would lose by 500 votes, which turned out to be a pretty accurate forecast. The actual figure was 760.

It was a heart-breaking disappointment for many of my workers, but not for long. Within a year, there was another election when the Diefenbaker government collapsed, the outcome of which, in Eglinton at least, was never in doubt, so solidly was the foundation laid in 1962. It helped, too, that Fleming, for family reasons, decided not to run. My majority in 1963 was more than 8,000. This time the *Globe and Mail*, having had enough of Diefenbaker, endorsed the Liberal Party, including the Duke of Eglinton.

The U.N. Coffee Conference

Meanwhile, after the 1962 election, I was a defeated candidate without a job. I went to my summer cottage at Lake Simcoe to recuperate after the strenuous campaign, and to contemplate my future. Before I had time to do much worrying or planning, a telegram was delivered asking me to telephone the ambassador of the United States. Would I consider being the chairman of the United Nations Coffee Conference about to begin in New York. My first reaction was to express astonishment that the Diefenbaker government would sponsor me for that position. I was assured that the Canadian government had nothing to do with the offer. The Americans were acting on behalf of the coffee-producer and -consumer countries, which wanted an independent chairman with experience relating to international commodity agreements.

My wife thought I should have a longer rest, but I pointed out that offers of this kind were few and far between. So I agreed and went off to New York and Washington to meet representatives of the Latin American and African coffee-producing countries. Presumably I passed muster, because when the conference met in New York on 9 July 1962, I was unanimously elected chairman. It was an occasion I shall never forget because in my excitement as the newly elected chairman, I said to a vast international audience, by radio and TV, that it was my pleasure to open this United Nations *sugar* conference. (I take sugar in my coffee!)

I asked William Van Vliet, who was the head of the Canadian delegation to the conference, what his instructions were about my chairmanship. Was he to vote for, or against, or to abstain? Being a discreet public servant, he didn't reply!

Negotiations for the coffee agreement were prolonged and difficult. It didn't help that delegations often didn't arrive for hours after the time for a meeting indicated on the agenda, particularly the Latin Americans, whose concept of time, I sometimes think, is different from that of North Americans and Europeans. The chairman, however, had no choice but to be in his chair awaiting their arrival.

For the first time, I encountered black French-speaking officials from former French colonies in Africa. I was impressed by the quality of their French speech and remarked on this to a member of the secretariat. The French government, he told me, took pains to educate those colonial officials to speak French and to appreciate the values of French culture and tradition. They didn't prepare them as well as the British prepared their colonials for independence and self-government. It was only later, when I was a minister and involved with both La Francophonie and the Commonwealth, that I appreciated the perceptiveness of that comment.

Finally, we reached unanimous agreement in principle, and it became necessary to adjourn the conference for a month to give time for the lawyers to put the agreement into proper legal form. I had serious misgivings about what might happen during that month-long adjournment. Sure enough, the morning of 28 September, when the conference resumed, there appeared in the *New York Times* an article to the effect that Guatemala had decided not to sign, believing that it could enter later and negotiate a more favourable export quota and that other Latin American coffee producers might follow suit. It was too late for me to do anything about Guatemala. At the appointed time, I called the conference to order and asked if there was a motion to approve the text of the agreement, which had been drafted by the international panel of lawyers and circulated in advance. Adlai Stevenson, the U.S. ambassador to the United Nations, who had become the head of the United States delegation to the Coffee Conference for the purpose, called for the floor and made a speech and the necessary motion. Much to my surprise and delight, the motion was seconded by the delegate from Guatemala and approved unanimously.

After the formal signing, I went to Michael Blumenthal, who had been chairman of the U.S. delegation during the negotiations, and asked him what had led to this remarkable turn of events. He directed me to a Mr Robbins, an adviser to the U.S. delegation and the principal coffee buyer for General Foods. When he saw the item in the *Times*, Robbins told me, he contacted the Guatemalan delegate and told him that since the U.S. government was keen to have an international coffee agreement, General Foods did not intend to buy any coffee from a non-member country. Hence the quick conversion. The International Coffee Agreement operated for a long time because it was one of the few commodity agreements that has been strongly supported by the United States.

My observation is that commodity agreements can be useful in stabilizing prices on the international market, but their successful functioning depends not so much upon the terms of the agreement as upon the willingness of one or two of the principal producing countries to be prepared to act as a cushion, particularly to be prepared to hold supplies off the market when surpluses put pressure on prices. Brazil, which is by far the largest producer of coffee, performed that function within the International Coffee Agreement.

Political columnist

The Coffee Conference occupied me and provided income for some four or five months in 1962. Before I could decide whether I should establish an office and offer my services as a consultant, pending the resumption of my political career, I was asked to undertake a number of tasks for business firms and organizations and I joined the board of Canadian Pacific Investments. I was also asked by the editor of the *Financial Post*, Ron MacEachern, to write a weekly political column under a pseudonym, 'Rideau Hill,' derived from Rideau Hall and Parliament Hill. How long I would have been able to protect my cover I do not know because, before I could be unmasked, I entered Parliament and the cabinet in 1963 and had to retire as a journalist. It was amusing to be asked by friends and acquaintances what I thought about the views of Rideau Hill. The cover provided by my pseudonym was also useful when, in my column, I was critical of Pearson and his Liberal supporters in Parliament, whom I hoped to join in due course.

CHAPTER FIVE

Minister of Trade and Commerce, 1963–1965

Former civil servants become ministers

On 22 April 1963, I joined the Privy Council and became minister of trade and commerce in Prime Minister Pearson's cabinet. In the early 1960s, the minister of trade and commerce had responsibility for trade promotion, for the Trade Commissioner Service, for economic research, for the Bureau of Statistics, for the regulation of weights and measures, for trade negotiations under the GATT, for the National Energy Board, the Canadian Wheat Board, the Board of Grain Commissioners, and Eldorado Nuclear Limited, and for federal participation in Expo 67. Insofar as the federal government promoted industry, the prime mover was the Department of Trade and Commerce. The establishment of the Department of Industry, which I had publicly advocated before and during the 1962 election, came later, and later still the reincorporation of that department into the department of Industry, Trade and Commerce. The trade commissioners were proud of their separate identity and as such had the support of the business community. Individually, of course, they did not mind being appointed as ambassadors and thus joining External Affairs.

I had hoped for this post. It was my old department, the ministry I knew best. I had been deputy minister, and this gave me a certain advantage as I contemplated my new job.

Not that being permanent head of a department necessarily equips one to be its political head. The respective functions are quite different. The advantage of having been the deputy is that as minister one knows how to obtain the best results from officials. As I told a reporter at the time, I did not intend, as minister, to run the department. That was the job of the deputy; I had done it once and didn't want to do it again. It was my function as minister to set policy, make decisions, defend them in Parliament, deal with the caucus, try to get re-elected in Eglinton and help the Liberals survive as the government.

In that first Pearson cabinet there were eight of us who at one time had been senior civil servants, several as deputy ministers – Pearson, Jack Pickersgill, C.M. (Bud) Drury, Guy Favreau, René Tremblay (a deputy minister in the Quebec government), Hédard Robichaud, Maurice Lamontagne, and myself. There was also Walter Gordon, who had done work for the St Laurent government and had been head of the Royal Commission on Canada's Economic Prospects. The presence in the cabinet of this large number of former senior officials undoubtedly helped in the transfer of power, but it was also used by Diefenbaker and some other Tories to support their claim that during the long Liberal reign the civil service had been politicized and that many of the senior officials were what Diefenbaker called Pearsonites or Pearsonalities.

It was not particularly healthy for the political process in Canada that this happened, and I doubt very much that it will happen again. Diefenbaker was himself mainly responsible for my own entry into politics, because his doubts about my impartiality led me to decide to leave the public service and four years later predisposed me to accept Pearson's invitation to become a Liberal candidate. As I used to reply when asked why I entered politics: 'Diefenbaker pushed me, Pearson pulled me.' It is pertinent to observe that Pearson resigned from the public service in 1948 for the purpose of entering politics, as did Pickersgill in 1953. The other former civil servants like myself had resigned many years earlier, for one reason or another, and had gone into private business before entering politics in 1962 and 1963. What we had in common was our friendship and admiration for Pearson, our former colleague – and our disagreement with the way Diefenbaker was leading Canada.

The transition in 1963 from minority Progressive Conservative government to minority Liberal government was accomplished with comparative ease, thanks to the presence in the new government of former ministers – Pearson, Paul Martin, Lionel Chevrier, Paul Hellyer, and Jack Pickersgill – and former senior civil servants, two of them with cabinet experience.

It was a cabinet of considerable talent and with a variety of views, many of them strongly held. On the main points of policy there was a consensus: we were ready to introduce legislation to change radically the structure of social security in Canada. We were determined to restore Canada's reputation in international political and economic circles as a leader in the search for peace, security, prosperity, and the elimination of poverty in the Third World. We gave high priority to establishing sound relations with the United States. Quebec had to be better represented in the formulation and administration of policy. Such differences as there were among ministers related to the timing and implementation of those policies. Debate in Pearson's two governments was often tough and forthright, like the debate between Walter Gordon and me on economic nationalism. Some of the impromptu performances by Judy LaMarsh, the only woman in the cabinet, were memorable. One I remember when LaMarsh, frustrated because she didn't get her way, pushed her papers across the table and left the room abruptly, telling her colleagues to go to hell. It was dramatic. In fact, she left because she had to catch a plane. The colleague I trusted most was Bud Drury, because of his intelligence and integrity.

In 1963, Guy Favreau, Maurice Lamontagne, René Tremblay, and Maurice Sauvé gave intellectual quality to the French-speaking ministers from Quebec, which was to be further enhanced after the 1965 election, when Marchand entered the Cabinet, followed in 1967 by Trudeau. A very considerable change from the Diefenbaker years, when Quebec felt its interests were neglected.

At the end of the Pearson regime, rivalries among the potential successors emerged, as was to be expected. For the most part, however, these rivalries were not of an ideological character and did not affect the decision-making process in cabinet, although they did on one occasion in the House of Commons have a direct effect upon my personal aspirations, as I describe on pages 159–60.

Behind the scenes in the Prime Minister's Office was Tom Kent, who, as I have described, played a prominent role in the Kingston Conference, and together with Allan MacEachen and others had given direction to policy when Pearson was opposition leader. Tom continued to be influential when Pearson became prime minister. I had met Kent when he was with the *Economist* magazine in the 1950s and came to know him better when he became editor of the *Winnipeg Free Press.* Whatever his activity, he was strong-minded, thoughtful, and expressed himself with clarity and vigour. I did not always agree with him; indeed I sometimes took an opposite position, just as from time to time I opposed the protectionist views of Walter Gordon, whom Kent greatly admired.

At the outset Pearson met with the deputy ministers and assured them of the government's confidence in their integrity. I inherited James

Roberts as my deputy minister. He had been an appointee of the Diefenbaker government from outside the public service, but, on my recommendation, Pearson retained him. He served me well and in 1964 was appointed ambassador to Switzerland. He was replaced as deputy minister of trade and commerce by J.H. (Jake) Warren, who had risen through the ranks of the public service in the departments of Finance, External Affairs, and Trade and Commerce and went on to even greater accomplishments in government and in private business.

How Pearson ran his cabinet

In 1963, the Pearson cabinet was relatively small by modern standards – twenty-six ministers, including the PM. We could all sit around the oval table in the beautiful old East Block cabinet Room, where John A. Macdonald and his colleagues once gathered. Documentation for Pearson Cabinet meetings was relatively small by later standards, and procedure was also much less formal than it was to become. Pearson tried to enforce the rule that no business not on the agenda could be introduced by a minister, but there were some ministers, like Pickersgill, who were very adept at circumventing that rule. Most proposals by ministers were made directly to cabinet. There were few cabinet committees, although more were created during the two Pearson administrations, including, near the end, the Committee on Priorities and Planning. The usual procedure was for the cabinet or the prime minister to refer issues to committees only when they could not be decided in cabinet in the first instance.

Cabinet met Thursday morning when Pearson was prime minister and sometimes adjourned for lunch. More often we ate sandwiches at the cabinet table so that we could continue doing business until we had to gather in the House of Commons for the opening of the session at 2:00 p.m. In those days, the House sat from 2:00 p.m. to 6:00 p.m. and from 8:00 p.m. to 10:00 p.m. (there was no evening session on Wednesday), except on Friday, when it opened at 11:00 a.m. and did not sit in the evening.

The number of ministers grew until we could not be accommodated in the East Block Cabinet Room. We met instead on the third floor of the Centre Block, down the hall from the Prime Minister's Office, in an austere and ugly room.

In cabinet, the prime minister decides the consensus. If he chooses, he can ignore the views of his colleagues. I remember only one instance when Pearson did so; the circumstances were most unusual. One of the recognized prerogatives of the prime minister is to nominate senators;

he brings their names before cabinet but does not seek approval; he assumes approval. It happened that on one occasion Pearson had to be absent and asked the senior minister, Paul Martin, to preside and to announce the names of proposed senators. If Pearson had presided there might have been some muttered grumbles. Without Pearson in the chair, the grumbles erupted into vigorous criticism. Martin withdrew the item and we turned to other business. At the next meeting Pearson strode into the cabinet room, obviously annoyed, announcing, even before he sat down, that the senators had been appointed.

Pearson's sense of humour and boyishness served him well in cabinet. He could dissipate tensions by a witty off-hand comment or an anecdote, or he could comment on professional baseball teams and players, on which he was an acknowledged expert. During Centennial Year, 1967, Pearson opened a cabinet meeting by telling us, tongue-in-cheek, that he had decided to have a medal struck to celebrate Canada's one hundredth birthday. On one side of the medal would be the customary portrait of the Queen. On the other a nude male figure similar to the design for Terre des Hommes at Expo 67 in Montreal; legs apart and arms reaching out on either side to touch the rim of the medal. For prudish reasons, Pearson added, he had decided to place a maple leaf on the nude male body. Judy Lamarsh spoke up – no, three maple leaves would be better. George McIlraith who was not famous for his wit, offered the crowning suggestion – three maple leaves on a single stem.

Pearson also employed his diplomatic skills most effectively in the Liberal Party caucus, which met Wednesday mornings when Parliament was in session. The ministers, with the PM at the centre, sat at a long table facing the non-ministerial Liberal members of both the Commons and the Senate. This was a time for the back-benchers to state their grievances and for the ministers to reply and to inform the MPs of their policies and plans. The atmosphere is informal and the exchange of views often candid, even angry. At the end, the PM often had the task of calming the troubled waters, restoring goodwill and party morale.

Each prime minister under whom I served had his own style in cabinet. From what I was told, Mackenzie King gave his ministers plenty of scope to present their proposals and their views and was reluctant to intervene when there were disputes. That was part of his technique of maintaining control over his talented and in many cases powerful regional ministers. His successor, Louis St Laurent, had a radically different approach. Bryce told me that when he was cabinet secretary he reviewed the agenda with the Prime Minister before cabinet meetings.

'I did my best to prepare myself, but almost invariably the Prime Minister thought of matters that I had overlooked,' Bryce told me. In cabinet, St Laurent took the lead, outlined the pros and cons of each item on the agenda, gave his own views, and asked for comments.

Pearson's pragmatism and diplomacy were reflected in his handling of the cabinet and the caucus; he was reluctant to take a clear position when there was dissent, hoping to be able to mediate. Only twice in my thirteen years as a minister did I threaten to resign; both occasions arose when I was minister of finance and for the same reason, namely, that I did not feel that the prime minister supported me on matters that were directly my responsibility. In our system of government, the Prime Minister has a duty, when all attempts at mediation have been exhausted, to come to the support of a minister in the field of his responsibility; otherwise, the minister may feel that he has lost the confidence of the prime minister and should offer his resignation. The converse is, of course, that the minister has a duty to heed the views of his colleagues and to try to meet their concerns; otherwise, he does not justify the confidence of the prime minister.

Pearson did not dominate the political scene. He was the acknowledged and unchallenged leader and prime minister, held in respect and affection by his colleagues, but there was also a Pearson team, composed of men and women who were political leaders in their own right and who had regional and national constituencies of their own. This did not always convey a sense of Liberal Party solidarity. It did, however, convey the diversity of Canada, particularly its regional characteristics. It also made for a healthy public debate on national issues, such as the debate on economic nationalism between Walter Gordon and myself, and the development of leadership potential, which became evident when Pearson stepped down in 1968.

Far too much importance is attributed to party unity in Canada. For a country like ours, it is unrealistic to assume that each of the national parties is unified on every issue. This is one of the reasons why, for so many people, debates in Parliament are a charade, concealing as much as they reveal about the real issues and the opposing views. I would like to see the day when, during Question Period in the House of Commons, the prime minister is as much concerned about questions from his own party as from members of the opposition parties.

Parliamentary secretaries

Prime Minister Pearson regarded the appointment of parliamentary secretaries as recognition of merit. (Prime Minister Trudeau introduced a system of appointment that was based not so much on merit as on giving as many MPs as possible the experience of office and a share of the extra pay that is provided for parliamentary secretaries.) The Pearson appointees had reason to hope they might some day become cabinet ministers, and nearly all those who served as parliamentary secretaries between 1963 and the election of 1968 did so.

Parliamentary secretaries perform certain functions for ministers that are inherent in their title, such as supervising the preparation of replies to written questions; keeping in touch with developments in Parliament of significance to their departments; if prepared in advance, answering oral questions in the Commons; if unprepared, taking note of oral questions. I treated my parliamentary secretaries as if they were ministers-in-training, by, for example, inviting them to attend morning meetings with my deputy minister. I used them to represent me at meetings throughout the country and particularly in Quebec, since, with one or two exceptions, all my parliamentary secretaries were francophone. When Pierre de Bané, who was my parliamentary secretary from 1972 to 1974, did not accept the invitation to my morning meetings, I chided him for not taking advantage of the opportunity to learn how to be a minister. To which he replied that he was not interested in becoming a minister. Later, obviously, he changed his mind.

My first parliamentary secretary was Jean-Luc Pepin. Perhaps I taught him something about government; he taught me much about French Canadians and French Canada. Like many French-speaking intellectuals, Pepin is logical and methodical, although he prides himself on having adopted the pragmatism of English-speaking Canadians. In his days as my parliamentary secretary, he was a strong advocate of cooperative federalism, a position that was later reflected in the Robarts-Pepin Report of the Task Force on Canadian Unity. Although I respected Pepin's views, I did not entirely share them. I found Trudeau's approach more convincing. Pepin performed his functions as my parliamentary secretary with intelligence and aplomb in both official languages and, in 1965, earned a place in cabinet, which he adorned.

He was succeeded by Jean Chrétien, who became my parliamentary secretary shortly after I became minister of finance, before he could speak English with much fluency. In his book, *Straight from the Heart*, he tells this story:

> The first day of my appointment Mitchell invited me into a meeting where there were nothing but big shots: the Governor of the Bank of

Canada, the Deputy Governor, the Deputy Minister of Finance, and so on. For an hour and a half they discussed bond issues and tariff rates and balance of payments, and I listened with wonder and awe. Finance was still a very mysterious thing for me. After the meeting Mitchell came up to me and said, 'Jean, what you have heard today is very secret. You must not say a word to anybody about it.'

'Don't be worried, Mitchell,' I said. 'I didn't understand a bloody thing.'

From the outset, Chrétien made a strong impression on me. Although his English left much to be desired, there was no mistaking his meaning. His mind moved quickly and smoothly and his political instincts were, if not infallible, very reliable. I liked his forthright and practical approach. What impressed me most was his ability to convey to audiences his feeling for Canada – from sea to sea. Soon after he became my parliamentary secretary I invited him to address a public meeting in my constituency, Eglinton, and witnessed for the first time the reaction of typical English-speaking Canadians to this young French Canadian from Shawinigan. They loved him. They gave him a standing ovation.

I became Jean Chrétien's champion. I had the satisfaction of observing his accomplishments as he moved up the ladder from ministry to ministry (he became the first French-Canadian minister of finance from Quebec), his effective participation in the separatism referendum in Quebec, and his vital role in the patriation of the Constitution in 1982 and the approval of the Canadian Charter of Rights and Freedoms.

He invited me to visit the village of St Tite in his constituency of St Maurice. In anticipation, I prepared short speeches in French to deliver when I was presented to local dignitaries. Things went well enough, I thought. But Chrétien had other plans. He invited me to a bean supper in the country and gave me a couple of drinks of caribou, a French-Canadian beverage with a high alcoholic content. My memory of subsequent events is not too clear. Chrétien claims I stood on a table and delivered an impromptu speech in French, without notes.

How to use ministerial staff

During the years that I was a civil servant, the number of exempt staff – ministerial staff appointed by the minister and not subject to the appointment rules of the Public Service Commission – was small. Ilsley was content with a secretary, an assistant secretary, and a messenger. Abbott had a male executive assistant as well as secretarial staff and a messenger. Howe had a male executive assistant, a couple of secretaries, and a messenger. Even prime ministers King and St Laurent had only a handful of people in their offices, nearly all of whom (like Pickersgill, who served both King and St Laurent) had originally been selected by the Public Service Commission for departmental jobs. In those days, there were no constituency offices or constituency staff paid by the government. By and large, ministers depended upon their departments for policy advice, except prime ministers, who had no departments to serve them other than the Privy Council Office, the principal function of which is to service the cabinet.

Consequently, the ministers I served dealt directly with their deputy ministers and other senior civil servants. Politically appointed ministerial assistants did not intervene between Ilsley, Abbott, Howe, Churchill, and me in the decision-making process. When I became a minister I followed the same practice, although by the end of my time in cabinet I had both executive and special assistants and, like everyone else, a constituency office to help me serve my constituents and get re-elected Mine was run by Mrs Peter (Cathy) Campbell, who did a first-rate job.

Michael McCabe was my executive assistant while I was minister of trade and commerce and also of finance. Richard Kroft took over when I moved to External Affairs, followed by Jon Church, and, after I became president of the Privy Council, by David Paget. All of them served me well and later followed successful careers that undoubtedly benefited from their experience as ministerial aides in Ottawa.

I deplore the expansion that has taken place in the years since I left office in the number and the compensation of the staffs in ministers' offices. It is a poor use of tax revenues and in my opinion does nothing to improve either the making of ministerial decisions or the efficiency of government operations.

Agenda for a minority government

The 1963 Speech from the Throne at the opening of Parliament on 16 May was reasonably brief and straightforward. The excessive argumentation to which I take objection (see page 234) was to come later, as both federal and provincial governments learned to exploit the Throne Speech as a vehicle of government propaganda. I admit with sorrow that our own 1965 Speech from the Throne was twice as long as the 1963 speech and for no good reason.

The two speeches, in 1963 and 1965, contained an ambitious agenda for a government that enjoyed the support of less than half the members of the House of Commons (129 out of 265 in 1963, and 131 out of 265 in 1965). In addition to the customary statements about the pursuit of peace and security and of national unity and about plans to promote economic expansion and increased trade, our government announced its intention to introduce legislation or resolutions on the following matters:

1963

– establishment of the Department of Industry, the municipal development and loan fund, the Canada Development Corporation, the Economic Council of Canada, the Canada Pension Plan
– establishment of a twelve-mile limit offshore for the use of Canadian fisheries
– development of the Columbia River
– increased federal responsibility for technical training
– increased federal support for the Atlantic region

1965

– establishment of the Company of Young Canadians, the Canada Assistance Plan, Medicare, the Canada Dairy Commission, the Indian Claims Commission, the Science Council of Canada, and (again) the Canada Development Corporation
– approval of the Automotive Agreement with the United States
– reform of the procedures of the House of Commons
– approval of 'O Canada' as the national anthem
– travel assistance to workers seeking new jobs
– special help to the family farm
– amendments to the Bank Act, the Bank of Canada Act, and several other statutes.

By the time the 1965 election was called more had been accomplished than realistically we had expected. By 1968, when Pearson stepped down as prime minister after five years of minority government, the list of major innovative legislation – which, in addition to the agenda announced in the Throne speeches, included the approval of a Canadian flag and of student loans – would have done credit to a government ten years in office with firm control over the House of Commons.

We accomplished much. But things didn't always turn out as expected or intended. Here are two illuminating examples.

The Canada Development Corporation, a favourite project of Walter Gordon's, did not emerge from this process until 1971, although it was promised in two successive Throne speeches, in 1963 and again in 1965, and eventually was wound up.

The Economic Council of Canada, which was established early in the first session, had a different fate. Prime Minister Pearson himself introduced the legislation. The council, Pearson said, 'will be an effective instrument for creating in Canada ... an economic consensus ... economic understanding that we need if we are to make the most of our resources, achieve and maintain high levels of employment, make our economic growth adequate for the purpose and compete successfully as we must, in the new trading world.'

It was to be a 'central planning council' intended to coordinate all the planning that goes on in our economy. It might be able to avoid the proliferation of planning, said the Prime Minister.

This is what the Liberal Party had had in mind when, during the preceding election campaign, it had advocated the creation of the Economic Council. Although I had not helped to frame the party platform for that election, I, too, believed that there should be more planning – that is, more coordination among industry, labour, and government in the formulation and implementation of economic policy led by the federal government. I still do.

In fact, the Economic Council of Canada never was a central planning agency in the sense that Pearson used that phrase. It was never at any time at the centre of economic policy formation in Ottawa. The first chairman, John Deutsch, insisted upon an arm's-length relationship with the government. The council performed a different role, the role of an independent critic, adviser, and economic analyst.

I recall that first report of the council in December 1964. Among other things, the council said: 'Part of our task is obviously to reduce the existing level of unemployment which, although lower than a few years ago, is still inappropriately and unacceptably higher than the 3 percent level which we believe to be a realistic medium-term goal for the Canadian economy, although not an ultimate goal for the longer run ...' This was strange advice at a time of rising employment and expansion.

I took the view, and so did my departmental advisers, that because of Canadian climate and geography and the existence of transitional unemployment as workers moved from one job to another, a 3 per cent level of unemployment was very difficult to attain and maintain and led people to support and advocate inflationary macro-economic policies. Later, as minister of finance, I had to cope with just such inflationary pressures when unemployment fell below 4 per cent. The Economic

Council itself was later to adjust its recommended goals to more attainable levels.

The moral is that institutions created by the government do not always conform to expectations or intentions. Indeed, in my experience, they seldom do. Some of them disappear. Others, like the Economic Council, learn to adapt themselves to changing circumstances or have to be changed. The council survived for nearly thirty years.

The Gordon budget

That first Speech from the Throne did not include the phrase 'sixty days of decision' that spokesmen for the Liberal Party had promised during the election campaign. Among the strategists, the original version had been 'one hundred days of decision,' but the longer period was abandoned when someone (John English says it was Mrs Pearson) pointed out that Napoleon's campaign of a hundred days ended at Waterloo.

'Sixty days of decision' was a ringing slogan for determined action. In practice what it meant was the promise of an early budget, since it is in the budget that a government announces its comprehensive economic agenda.

We took office on 22 April 1963. On 13 June Walter Gordon, the minister of finance, presented his first budget. As was customary, the minister did not inform his colleagues in cabinet, except, of course, the prime minister, of the detailed proposals for tax changes to be contained in the budget until the day before its presentation in the House of Commons.

Consequently, there was very little opportunity for other members of cabinet to consider the specifics or to comment on them. I do not recall that I made any critical comments, nor do I recall that any of my colleagues did so. We did not foresee the storm that would break so suddenly over the government and the minister when his proposals became known. The centrepiece of the budget was a 'take-over tax' of 30 per cent, to apply to foreign purchases of Canadian companies. This responded to one of Gordon's favourite themes, the return of the Canadian economy to Canadian control.

Inside his own department Gordon fared no better. Some years later, when I became minister of finance, officials told me in response to my enquiries that they had warned the minister against the proposed taxes, but he had nevertheless gone ahead.

Needless to say, the budget proved upsetting to the stock markets.

Eric Kierans, who later entered Parliament and the Trudeau cabinet, termed the take-over tax complete and utter nonense: 'the financial capitals of the world have had enough from Canada.'

But the attack on the minister of finance came to centre not so much on the proposed 30 per cent tax on foreign take-overs, which was withdrawn, as on the hiring by him of three advisers from outside the public service, MP O'Connell, G.R. Conway, and D.C.H. Stanley, all of whom I knew personally.

I offered to speak in the House in defence of the minister, but Pearson thought that if any minister was to do that it should be the prime minister himself. At the last minute, on 24 June, Pearson changed his mind about participating in the debate on a motion of the opposition criticizing the minister for, in effect, breaking the principle of budget secrecy by hiring the three outside advisers. The first paragraph of the motion read as follows: 'this House regrets that the Minister of Finance by failing to maintain the constitutional practice of the essential secrecy of the Budget has seriously weakened public confidence.'

Since Diefenbaker had not spoken, Pearson felt he should not speak. He now accepted my offer to defend Gordon; would I speak that evening?

I protested that I was not prepared. Pearson offered me his speaking notes, drafted by Tom Kent. So, full of foreboding because of my lack of adequate preparation, I went down to the floor of the House, read through the notes, and, some forty-five minutes later, was recognized by the speaker. My speech centred on the point that the Diefenbaker government had revealed confidential material to hundreds of financial people sworn to secrecy, like Gordon's three advisers. In the middle of my speech it occurred to me to attack Diefenbaker directly by challenging him to make a forthright charge that Gordon had breached the principle of budget secrecy, rather than hide behind what I termed this sleazy, ambiguous motion. I am not good at histrionics. But that evening I issued the challenge to Diefenbaker three times, each time offering to sit down, the Liberal members behind me banging desks and shouting across the aisle. It was my maiden speech in the House of Commons and my most effective. Never again was I applauded as I was that evening.

Gordon had to withdraw some of his contentious budget proposals and offered to resign. Pearson called me to ask whether I would be prepared to replace him as minister of finance if he accepted Gordon's resignation. I replied that I would, although I did not seek the portfolio. However, the Prime Minister decided not to accept Gordon's resignation at that time. So I stayed where I was.

Trade promotion and trade policy

The minister of trade and commerce was expected to promote Canadian exports and to formulate and negotiate trade policies and agreements advantageous to Canadian producers.

My predecessor in office, George Hees, made his reputation as a trade promoter. I used to look with wonder and awe from the outside at the energy he put into his campaigns to sell Canadian products abroad. I am not sure how much was accomplished, but George deserved the credit he got for the enthusiasm of his efforts. That was not my style and I did not try to emulate him.

Exports increased when Hees was a flamboyant trade minister. They also increased and about as rapidly, when I was a less flamboyant trade minister.

Soon after assuming office as minister of trade and commerce I was invited to a meeting in London of Commonwealth trade ministers. In those days, the British government attached a great deal of importance to trade with Commonwealth countries – much more than we did – partly because of uncertainty about the future of trade with the European Community. The United Kingdom, which had taken the lead in organizing the European Free Trade Agreement, applied for EEC membership in 1961; it finally succeeded twelve years later in 1973. Unlike the Diefenbaker government, never at any time did we attempt to dissuade the British government from its purpose.

The Queen received the Commonwealth trade ministers at Buckingham Palace, and Prime Minister Macmillan had a cocktail party for us at 10 Downing Street. When I was presented to the Prime Minister, he first enquired about Mike (our Prime Minister's nickname) and then referred to an article in Lord Beaverbrook's London *Daily Express* that criticized me for putting the world ahead of the Commonwealth in matters of trade. Macmillan told me not to worry, to be attacked by the Beaver was an assurance of my future success. Nor did he overlook Mr Diefenbaker: What an extraordinary politician, his cabinet collapsing around him and he managed to win ninety-five seats! The British PM had a remarkable understanding of Canadian politics.

When I was an official I represented Canada from time to time at meetings of the contracting parties to the General Agreement on Tariffs and Trade in Geneva. Within a few months after taking office as minister of trade and commerce in 1963, I went to Geneva to represent Canada at the opening of the Kennedy Round of trade negotiations under the GATT. This was the sixth in a series of GATT negotiations.

For an organization that promotes free trade and fights protectionism,

GATT has a curious language. During negotiations, countries that offer reductions in their tariffs are said to make concessions, as if tariffs were beneficial to them and their economies are worse off when they are removed. There is no admission that countries might be better off if they made unilateral tariff cuts. I know, of course, the argument that even if unilateral cuts are beneficial, multilateral cuts are even more beneficial and help in the adjustment to increased competition. So I endorse the GATT procedure of exchanging 'concessions,' even if the language tends to support the views of the protectionists.

At the outset of these post-war multilateral negotiations, the average level of Canadian tariffs against imports was lower than the level in the United States and in many European countries. By 1979, with the end of the Tokyo Round, which followed the Kennedy Round, Canada had one of the highest levels of protection among the industrialized countries, although much lower than it had been at the end of the war.

One of the reasons: in the Kennedy Round Canada refused to accept the principle of across-the-board percentage cuts in tariffs, the general rule followed by most industrialized countries. We argued that because of the nature of our trade – the high proportion of foodstuffs and raw materials in our exports and of manufactured goods in our imports – across-the-board percentage cuts in our tariffs gave exporters to Canada much more valuable access to the Canadian market for manufactured goods than we gained from an equal percentage cut in the already low tariffs on foodstuffs and raw materials in countries to which we exported. We insisted upon equivalence of benefit, which meant that tariffs on our manufactured goods were not reduced as rapidly as those of the United States and Europe.

It was astute bargaining, led by Sydney Pierce – and good politics.

Looking back, it is a bit hypocritical for Canadian governments to argue, as they did from time to time, that we were leaders in the movement for freer international trade when in fact for a long time we lagged behind. It is one of the reasons, too, why our costs remained stubbornly high and why we have had difficulty in adjusting both to the Canada–United States Free Trade Agreement (which I opposed) and to the globalization of markets that proceeds apace.

Nuclear weapons

Governments of Canada have always had to struggle with an underlying ambivalence in Canada's policy in relation to nuclear weapons. During the war, we shared the anxiety of the Allies to develop the nuclear bomb ahead of the Germans. We refined uranium for the first bombs that were dropped over Hiroshima and Nagasaki and, for twenty years after the war, we supplied uranium to the United States and Britain for the manufacture of weapons in their arsenals. As a member of NATO, we supported the principle of deterrence, which means we relied upon nuclear weapons to deter the Soviet Union from attacking members of the Alliance, either conventionally or with nuclear weapons.

On the other hand, the government decided that Canada should not become a nuclear power, although we had the necessary resources and know-how. From June 1965 onward, we refused to export uranium for other than peaceful purposes. We signed the non-proliferation treaty on 23 July 1968 (and ratified it on 1 August 1969).

In the later 1950s and early 1960s, what was not clear was the Canadian government's attitude towards U.S.-owned and -controlled nuclear weapons on Canadian soil. The Diefenbaker government vacillated. As leader of the opposition, Pearson had expressed opposition to Bomarc missiles in Canada because they were nuclear-armed. As the 1962 election approached, some of us, as potential Liberal candidates, were concerned about Pearson's position. It seemed to imply that Canada would break its agreement with the United States that permitted the arming of the Bomarcs with nuclear weapons. We urged him to change his position, which he finally did – most reluctantly.

A larger issue was at stake. It made sense for Canada to avoid the possession of nuclear weapons. Otherwise, we could not in good conscience support nuclear non-proliferation. We have a responsibility as a uranium producer to conduct ourselves in such a way that we do not contribute to nuclear arsenals. However, it was posturing for Canadians to make a virtue out of the fact that, while living like other members of NATO under the U.S. nuclear umbrella, Canada did not itself permit any U.S. nuclear weapons to be located on Canadian soil. Such a position was particularly obnoxious to those European countries in the direct line of possible Soviet attack that did permit U.S.-controlled nuclear weapons to be located on their soil.

My first personal involvement as a minister in nuclear policy arose when, in the early 1960s, Stephen Roman of Denison Mines secured a contract to supply uranium to France. It was then our policy (although not clearly spelled out, as events were to demonstrate) not to export uranium except for peaceful purposes. I went to France in May 1965 to seek an undertaking from the French government that it would accept the surveillance of the International Atomic Energy Agency or the equivalent European agency to ensure that our uranium was not used to make bombs. The French government, represented by the secretary of state for scientific, atomic and space affairs, Mr Yvon Bourges, refused. Did we not trust the word of a NATO ally that Canadian uranium would be used only for peaceful purposes? To keep me humble, I have framed at home a copy of a cartoon by Macpherson of the *Toronto Star* that shows me, a diminutive figure, facing an overwhelming de Gaulle, who accuses me of hypocrisy – in French.

We did not approve the export, and the French purchased their uranium requirements elsewhere. We had then to announce that we were not discriminating against France because the same conditions would hereafter apply to exports of uranium to all countries, including the United States and Britain.

The Great Blackout

As an official I had urged C.D. Howe to establish a national energy board to regulate exports of energy and the building and operation of pipelines. I had discussed these ideas with Henry Borden when he was the chairman of the royal commission that recommended the establishment of an energy board. On becoming minister of trade and commerce, I became the responsible minister.

I thought I was familiar with the sort of problems that I would encounter. On 9 November 1965, I received a shock. On that day, there was a massive power failure covering Ontario and the eastern United States. It began shortly after 5:00 p.m. The outage lasted from a few minutes in some locations to more than half a day in others. It encompassed 80,000 square miles and directly affected an estimated thirty million people in the United States and Canada. It was the largest power failure in history. People got stuck in elevators in skyscrapers. Traffic lights stopped functioning. Whole areas went black. Oil and gas furnaces could not ignite without electricity.

The initial cause originated in the Ontario Hydro generating plants on the Niagara River. With the approval of the cabinet, I instructed the National Energy Board to investigate the circumstances. The president of the United States asked the Federal Power Commission to do the same. The commission invited the cooperation of the National Energy Board and Ontario Hydro.

The result was a thorough investigation and the adoption of measures to ensure that there could be no repetition.

The power failure illustrated dramatically the growing dependence of modern society upon a continuous supply of electricity. The chairman of the board, Ian Mackinnon, and I spent many hours worrying about the consequences of a breakdown in electricity supply on the everyday life of Canadians in the depth of winter. What if a saboteur managed to blow up vital interconnections? As I said at the time,

> In recent years the power industry has made tremendous strides forward in expanding and improving its services. Its product cannot economically be stored in the way that stocks of wheat, oil or copper may be held over for future use. Kilowatts must be produced at the same instant they are required for use ...
>
> We know enough to make me confident in emphasizing that the general lesson of this startling experience is not that we need fewer interconnections or less cooperation between electrical utilities within Canada and between those in Canada and those in the United States. This would be like claiming we should stop building bridges because one had collapsed. Rather the lesson is that we should seek to improve the security of our electrical supply by improving and strengthening our interconnections, and the technical arrangements through which the intent of such arrangements is put into practice. We must continue to strengthen one another in the common interest, and we must take every reasonable step to ensure that this mutual support is made as real, valuable, and reliable as human ingenuity can arrange. This, to the extent that it comes within the responsibility of the Government of Canada, we intend to do ...

And there has been no repetition of the Great Blackout.

Expo 67

As minister of trade and commerce, I inherited from George Hees ministerial responsibility for the federal side of Expo 67, which had been approved by the Diefenbaker government. I held it until I became minister of finance at the end of 1965, and Robert H. (Bob) Winters succeeded me as minister of trade and commerce. During the two years or so that I had responsibility – the building period – I had to obtain cabinet approval for the proposed expenditures. The division of cost was 50 per cent federal, 37.5 per cent Province of Quebec, and 12.5 per cent City of Montreal. In addition, the City of Montreal had to provide the site of Expo, which involved among other things the creation by fill of two artificial islands on the St Lawrence River at a cost of some $30 million.

Which Reminds Me ...

After Expo was over, Pickersgill told me that, when I presented the elaborate and expensive plans to cabinet, he thought I had a hole in my head. The net cost of Expo 67 was about $285 million, of which the Canadian government paid half. It seemed an immense amount. I had some concerns myself, but I came to the conclusion that, since Expo 67 would be the principal event of our Centennial Year, we should have as our goal a world-class show of which Canadians could be proud. In the end, some rough calculations indicated that the federal and Quebec governments recovered a high proportion, by some measure all, of their expenditures, through increased revenues from existing taxes of one kind or another that could be traced to the exhibition. The revenues of the City of Montreal benefited, but not so much as those of the federal and provincial governments. The city did acquire buildings and facilities that enabled it to continue Terre des Hommes as a Montreal festival for many years.

Without the energy and enthusiasm of Mayor Jean Drapeau, there would have been no Expo 67. It was the managerial talents of Pierre Dupuy, the commissioner general, Robert Shaw, the deputy commissioner General, Andrew Kniewasser, the general manager, Edward Churchill, responsible for design and construction, and their associates that made Expo 67 such a smashing success, (fifty-five million admissions over a six-month period). My counterparts on the trilateral corporation were Gérard D. Lévesque, Quebec minister of industry and commerce, and Lucien Saulnier, chairman of the executive committee of the Montreal City Council, tough, broad-minded, dedicated servants of the public, who shared my view that Expo 67 had to compare favourably with the best world fairs ever mounted anywhere. It did. For those few months in our Centennial Year, hundreds of thousands of people from across the country journeyed to Montreal, many of them for the first time, to celebrate the achievement of their country, Canada, of which Quebec is such a vigorous and talented community. I believe we also helped to ensure that no scandal would attach to the construction and operation of Expo. And none did.

Wheat sales

In September 1963, there appeared in my office S.A. Borisov, a deputy minister in the Soviet government, my Soviet counterpart during the trade-agreement negotiations in 1955–6, negotiations that had resulted in the first long-term undertaking by the Soviets to buy Canadian wheat (see page 58). Borisov told us that the Soviet Union had suffered a crop failure in the new lands in Siberia, was in urgent need of wheat, and had decided, because of the well-established relations between our two countries, to buy from Canada. The Soviet Union wanted to buy 5.3 million long tons of wheat, the largest quantity of Canadian wheat ever purchased at one time by any buyer, as well as 500,000 tons of flour. Overnight, the Soviet Union became the principal market for Canadian wheat and ever since has been either the largest or second-largest market, alternating with China.

Years before, when I was connected with the private grain trade, the Soviet Union had been an exporter of wheat, and China, although a big producer, neither an exporter nor an importer of any significance. The idea that these two countries would one day dominate world markets as buyers would at that time have been considered preposterous. What is equally remarkable is that, notwithstanding the greatly increased demand for wheat, traceable in large part to the growth in consumption and disappointing crops in the Soviet Union and China, world production has kept pace, some would say more than kept pace.

William McNamara was the chief commissioner of the Canadian Wheat Board when I became the responsible minister. Experienced, dedicated, sensitive to the problems of western farmers, and a first-rate salesman, he was a worthy successor to George McIvor. On 2 February 1961, he had made the first sale of Canadian wheat to China. In 1963, he handled that first big sale to the Soviet Union. I took the view that it was the job of the Canadian Wheat Board to sell Canadian wheat on behalf of the western producers and to deliver the proceeds to them in instalments as the sales were made. It was the job of the responsible minister and the government to do what they could to assist the board in selling, through government-to-government negotiations of favourable trade relations with customer countries, like the Canada-Soviet trade agreement in 1956, through credit arrangements where necessary, and by the personal intervention of ambassadors and trade commissioners in the field, acting on behalf of the board and the government.

Not Alvin Hamilton from Saskatchewan. As minister responsible for the Canadian Wheat Board under Diefenbaker, he took a good deal of personal credit for the first sales to China. In the House and on the public platform, I, on the contrary, gave full credit to the board as the farmers' agent when good sales were made. Judging by electoral results, however, Hamilton's tactics were superior to mine; although wheat sales soared after I became minister responsible for the Wheat Board in 1963, there was no addition to Liberal seats in the West in the 1965 election. The western voters apparently took the view that Hamilton and Diefenbaker as westerners fought the good fight and broke into new markets, notwithstanding the resistance of the eastern establishment, and that I, a Toronto minister, simply reaped the results of their pioneering efforts. It was silly, but in politics many silly things are accepted as facts.

There were no elected Liberal members of Parliament in Saskatchewan in either of Pearson's two minority governments. As a born westerner from Winnipeg and particularly as the minister responsible for the Canadian Wheat Board, I was designated by Pearson as the Saskatchewan minister in cabinet. This meant that I had to keep in touch with Premier Ross Thatcher and do what I could to persuade him to support federal government policies and to assist the party in electing federal members at general elections. Thatcher wasn't easy to like or to persuade. To put it mildly, Thatcher, although the head of the Liberal Party of Saskatchewan, was not enthusiastic about fighting Tories who supported him during provincial elections in Saskatchewan, or about helping to elect federal Liberals who would become rivals as spokesmen for the federal party in Saskatchewan and in the distribution of patronage. His relations with Otto Lang, the president of the federal Liberal Party in Saskatchewan, who aspired to become an MP and a cabinet minister, were abysmally low. It gave me special satisfaction when Lang managed a narrow win in Saskatoon in the 1968 election and succeeded me as the minister for Saskatchewan in the Trudeau Cabinet.

The Canadian flag

From the outset of his administration, Pearson had his heart set on the approval by Parliament of a Canadian flag. I frankly admit that it took me some time to become enthusiastic about the idea. Not that I was opposed; I simply looked on a Canadian flag as something that was bound to be highly controversial, and there was already enough controversy. I thought the flag could wait. Gradually, however, I became persuaded of the importance of the issue, and, when the debate took place on the resolution in the House of Commons to approve the design, I was the only English-speaking minister, other than the Prime minister, to participate. My father, who was a Canadian veteran of the First World War, wrote to me at the time to the effect that he had no opinion one way or another about the new flag but he wanted me to know that he had never fought under the Canadian Ensign and did not regard it as a suitable Canadian flag, as did John Diefenbaker. My father, like all Canadian troops in the First World War, had fought under the Union Jack.

When the House of Commons formed a committee to consider designs for the new flag, I received a call from Robert McMichael, who was in process of accumulating his monumental collection of Canadian art by the Group of Seven. A.Y. Jackson, who was one of the Group of Seven, had a flag design he wished to submit to the committee and through McMichael sought my assistance. I visited Kleinburg and there flying from the flagpole beside McMichael's log house, was a maple-leaf flag in red, white, and blue. The background was blue because, Jackson explained, Canada not only extends from sea to sea, there is water everywhere.

The parliamentary committee decided to recommend a design incorporating only the colours of red and white, which are Canada's official colours, rejecting the Pearson design and the Jackson design, both of which included the colour blue. In so deciding, they were greatly influenced by the views of John Matheson, MP, a member of the committee. Matheson was not only a vigorous and effective advocate of a distinctive Canadian flag, but by diligent study made himself an authority on the principles of heraldry and did much to ensure that the design that was finally accepted reflected Canada's history and traditions.

Some time later, after I had become minister of finance, I had the privilege and the responsibility of helping McMichael to establish a unique gallery in Kleinburg. He offered his collection and building to the National Gallery of Canada, which unfortunately could not establish a branch outside Ottawa. Consequently, McMichael donated his collection and his Kleinburg gallery to the Ontario government. I sponsored amendments in the next budget that authorized donations like his to provincial institutions as a deduction from federal income tax.

It is a tribute to Pearson's good judgment that, in retrospect, the approval of the Canadian flag stands out as one of the great accomplishments of his time in office. We became more of a nation, more unified, and more conscious of our separate identity the day the new flag in the two official Canadian colours, red and white, with a maple leaf in the centre, was hoisted on Parliament Hill. Like Diefenbaker, my eyes also filled with tears, not when the Ensign was lowered, but when the first truly Canadian flag flew in the breeze. At last, we had an unambiguous symbol of Canada.

I am not an economic nationalist in the accepted Canadian sense of that phrase. I confess, however, to being an ardent Canadian patriot and even to being somewhat sentimental on the subject. I want my fellow citizens to take pride in their country. I want foreigners to recognize us as a distinct society, even if we cannot call ourselves *nation* in the French sense of the word because of our bilingual and multicultural nature.

Which Reminds Me ...

The 1965 try for majority government

The minority Parliament elected in 1963 was a difficult one. We hadn't lost any votes in the House but we felt frustrated, and the opposition's exploitation of some so-called 'scandals' involving Maurice Lamontagne, René Tremblay, and Guy Favreau hadn't helped. It seemed to me that the longer we delayed in calling an election the fewer seats we would win. Walter Gordon was pressing Pearson hard to recommend dissolution to the governor general. Pearson called the cabinet together for the purpose of discussing the issue. In those days, we still met in the Cabinet Room in the East Block. Everyone was present, seated in order of seniority. Pearson explained the purpose of the meeting and then turned to Paul Martin, the most senior minister, sitting to his right, and asked for his opinion. Martin said he would prefer that the Prime Minister start at the other end of the table. Pearson did so, and one by one we expressed our views, a substantial majority, including myself, being in favour of going to the country. When Martin's turn came, he said he didn't have an opinion. I thought this was hilariously funny, given his obvious desire to be the last to speak. Martin was offended by my mirth. He told me that the reason he did not give an opinion was that he thought Pearson did not want to have an election and that Gordon was pressing him too hard; the Prime Minister should have been left to make up his own mind.

'Majority government' became the slogan for the Liberals in the 1965 election. We failed to persuade the voters and emerged with about the same number of seats as in 1963.

My opponent in Eglinton in the 1965 election was the formidable Dalton Camp, at the time president of the Progressive Conservative Party of Canada. As befitted the head of an advertising agency, his literature and signs were first rate, at least as good as mine. On the platform, he was less effective, so I was told, being more accustomed to the back rooms of an election campaign, discussing strategy. My supporters were very concerned, and for good reason, since Eglinton was a strong Conservative riding provincially and had until 1963 been thought of as a Conservative bastion federally. To add to the uncertainty, both Camp and I were less than enthusiastic about Diefenbaker, although for different reasons. In the end, thanks in part to superhuman efforts by my supporters to get out the vote, I emerged with a margin of some 1,800 votes over those cast for Camp.

CHAPTER SIX

Minister of Finance, 1965–1968

From Trade to Finance

When Walter Gordon resigned from the cabinet because of the outcome of the 1965 election, which he had pressed the Prime Minister to call, I became acting minister of finance and, on 18 December 1965, minister of finance. In some respects it was a home-coming. My deputy minister was my former colleague in the department, Robert Bryce, with whom I had worked for many years during and immediately following the war. Consequently, I did not have to take an introductory course in government finance, and although I did not pretend to be an economist of the calibre of my distinguished deputy minister, at least I understood the concepts and the language.

Bryce was the most influential and respected public servant in Ottawa. From 1954 to 1963, he had served as clerk of the Privy Council and secretary to the cabinet. He was one of the few civil servants whom Diefenbaker trusted. It is said that without Bryce and Basil Robinson, who was senior adviser from the Department of External Affairs assigned to the Office of the Prime Minister at that time, the machinery of government would have foundered under the weight of Diefenbaker's administrative ineptness. On 1 July 1963, Pearson, on Walter Gordon's recommendation, selected Bryce to succeed Kenneth Taylor as deputy minister of finance, following the disaster of Gordon's budget, for which, as I have said elsewhere, Taylor was not responsible.

Finance is said to be the graveyard of Canadian politicians. No minister of finance succeeded in becoming prime minister (although some prime ministers held both portfolios) except Charles Tupper and John

Turner, who held the top job for short periods at the end of their government's mandates. Nevertheless, with the exception of Larry Pennell, who preferred to become a judge, I have never heard of anyone who turned down the job when it was offered. Next to prime minister, it is the most challenging of all cabinet posts.

Although one unfortunate event during my occupancy of the portfolio diminished my chances of becoming leader of the Liberal Party and prime minister (even if that event had not occurred I do not think I could have won against Trudeau), I regard those two and a half years as minister of finance as the most interesting and rewarding of my political career.

I even managed to establish a Canadian tradition – unintentionally. My staff had been told – probably by a shoe manufacturer – that it was traditional for a minister of finance when presenting his first budget to wear a new pair of shoes. I fell for it. So did the press, which gave enormous publicity to my new shoes. About five years ago an investigative journalist, searching for the origins of the tradition that most of my successors followed, could not find that any of my predecessors as minister of finance had worn new shoes at budget time. Was it traditional? Perhaps not in 1965. It is now, after more than a quarter of a century.

The minister of finance is at the centre of policy making. Nearly everything that has to be decided by a government has financial implications. While it is the duty of the minister of finance to urge fiscal responsibility upon the cabinet, Parliament, and the public, and therefore to say no to some enthusiastic colleagues and attractive projects, the minister of finance can have more positive influence upon the direction of policy than other members of the cabinet simply because both his support and his opposition are so crucial.

For example, I felt it necessary in 1966 to insist upon a year's delay in the introduction of medicare. It was my ready acquiescence, on the other hand, that led to the speedy introduction of the Guaranteed Income Supplement to the universal Old Age Pension at about the same time.

In many respects, I was fortunate in the time I was minister of finance. The energy crisis did not erupt until several years later. Everyone, including myself, took cheap energy for granted. When I took office, most exchange rates, including that of the Canadian dollar, were fixed by law, our dollar at ninety-two and a half cents in terms of the U.S. dollar. Even after the Bretton Woods system of fixed rates collapsed in 1971, exchange rate movements were moderate. The volume of international financial transactions unrelated to trade, much of it highly speculative – so-called hot money – had not yet reached alarming proportions. Generally speaking, the governments of the industrialized countries, including the United States, raised sufficient or nearly sufficient revenues to cover expenditures. There were no huge deficits, no huge overhanging government debts like those that accumulated in the United States and Canada in the 1980s. Interest rates reflected confidence that inflation would not get out of hand. Unemployment, always worrisome, was at levels that would, by the later standards of the 1970s and 1980s, be considered quite tolerable.

Most significant of all was the belief in the industrialized countries among legislators, economists, and such of the general public as had informed views that, at a minimum, both the high unemployment that characterized the Great Depression and high inflation could be avoided by appropriate and timely fiscal and monetary policies. It was also assumed that cyclical economic fluctuations could be moderated by the same means, plus some jaw-boning from time to time, which, like other finance ministers elsewhere, I practised.

These optimistic beliefs in the efficacy of fiscal and monetary policy found support in the record of the economies of the industrialized countries since the end of the war – or so it seemed at the time. Never before had there been such a long period of steady economic growth and rapidly rising standards of living. From our present perspective we can see that worldwide forces more powerful than the fiscal and monetary policies of governments were also at work. It was natural, however, for governments in all countries to claim as much credit as possible, and most people at the time were apparently ready to accept that claim.

Although Canadian government expenditures grew steadily and substantially from year to year between 1965 and 1968, so did government revenues, reflecting rising personal and corporate incomes. As to the future, there was a widely shared assumption that increasing revenues would be sufficient, as they had been in the past, to enable the government to assume increasing financial responsibilities in the fields of social security, assistance to the needy provinces, external aid, support of the arts, and so forth, without having to resort to burdensome levels of taxation. All that was required, it appeared, was prudence, common sense, and good timing.

Keynesian budgeting

Before the Second World War, the declared purpose of the annual budgets of the Canadian minister of finance was to raise sufficient revenues to pay for expenditures, although there were some hints in the late 1930s, after President Franklin Roosevelt's New Deal, that it would not be inappropriate to borrow when the economy was slack and to pay off the public debt when times were good.

During the post-war period, by contrast, no Canadian minister of finance committed himself to a balanced budget as the sole purpose of his budgetary proposals. All accepted to some degree what can loosely be called Keynesian ideas that fiscal policy can be used to stimulate or restrain economic activity.

I took office as minister of finance at the end of 1965 in the midst of a period of rapid expansion and growing inflationary problems, which continued throughout my incumbency. In the three main budgets I presented to Parliament in the early months of 1966, 1967, and 1968, my principal theme was the necessity of moderating economic expansion so as to prolong it.

In my 1966 budget – my first budget – I said: '1966 presents a great challenge to Canadians. We have been successful during these past few years in stimulating the economy until it is now operating close to capacity. Are we now prepared to exercise the moderation – as well as the enterprise – needed to keep the economy operating at full capacity not only in 1966 but in the years to come? In other words can we now phase and prolong our prosperity?'

In my last budget in 1968 the words were somewhat different but the message was the same.

I budgeted for small deficits between federal revenues and expenditures, which meant significant surpluses in terms of the national accounts when additional non-budgetary revenues such as contributions under the Canada Pension Plan were taken into account.

In order to deal with charges that were incurred after the budgets had been presented, and to meet the cost of the new Guaranteed Income Supplement to the universal Old Age Pension, I presented a supplementary budget in late 1966. The governor of the Bank of Canada, Lou Rasminsky, supported the economic policy of the government by monetary restraint and by effective personal leadership. Occasionally, I had to persuade my colleagues that there were times when, in order to prolong prosperity, some of the government's highest priorities – such as medicare – had to be postponed.

This was fine-tuning of a kind never before practised by a Canadian minister of finance. To judge from the behaviour of the Canadian economy, it seemed to work. Unemployment fell as low as 3.5 per cent and, while I held the office, never exceeded 4.6 per cent of the labour force. The cost-of-living index rose 3.7 per cent between 1965 and 1966, by 3.6 per cent between 1966 and 1967, and by 4.1 per cent between 1967 and 1968. Interest rates reflected confidence that inflation was under control; the lowest interest rate on Treasury bills was 3.98 per cent and the highest 6.99 per cent. Borrowers never had to pay more than 8⅝ per cent on Central Mortgage and Housing Corporation guaranteed housing loans; the Canadian dollar, pegged throughout at ninety-two and a half cents in terms of the U.S. dollar, came under pressure from time to time but survived.

As I have said, I was fortunate to be minister of finance in the mid-sixties. At the time, of course, I was unaware of my good fortune. I thought that I had plenty of difficulties. So did everyone else. The opposition was scathing about my performance as minister of finance. Here are some of the things that were said:

We have the largest spending, the highest taxing, the highest cost of living and almost the greatest deficit in our history.

The finances of this country are out of hand.

How miserably he has failed to come to grips with inflation, unemployment and high interest rates.

The Minister's speech yesterday, in which he tried to defend his policies, reminded me of the surgeon who after an operation talks to his colleagues and says: 'Yes, the operation was a trememdous success, it was highly technical, everything was fine, but the unfortunate patient died.'

... he is guilty of pursuing a fiscal policy which is leading us to final disaster when he could prevent it.

My consolation is that the opposition has said much the same thing about every minister of finance, regardless of his record, regardless of his party. It's all part of the budget ritual.

What is striking about the years from the end of the war until 1970 is how closely the total of federal expenditures matched federal revenues. The maximum deficit, which occurred in 1958, was only 13.7 per cent of total expenditures in that year. It took twenty-four years for the net public debt to rise from $13 billion to $18 billion. (It is now over $450 billion.) Interest on the public debt absorbed less than 15 per cent of total revenues while I was minister of finance (it absorbed about a third in the 1980s). Those results are evidence of the prosperity enjoyed by Canadians during those years. They are also evidence that Canadian governments and Canadian finance ministers were, for the most part, cautious and careful in fiscal policy, as were the governments and finance ministers of most industrialized countries, regardless of their political orientation.

Why deficits later rose

My successors as minister of finance were not so fortunate from the early 1970s on. Expenditures tended to rise much more quickly than revenues. The political climate did not help. Our government was in a minority position from 1972 to 1974 and handicapped in its ability to resist popular and costly expenditures and to raise revenue. Not the only reason for the widening gap, but in my view a significant one, is that while payments under statutory programs such as family allowances, old-age security, medicare, and equalization payments to the provinces automatically increased as costs and prices rose, income tax revenues were restrained by legislation – introduced by John Turner in his 1973 budget and advocated by Robert Stanfield as leader of the opposition – that protected taxpayers from the effects of inflation on their rates of taxation.

However well-intentioned this protection may have been, it was not accompanied, as it should have been, by deliberately imposed tax increases of one kind or another to match rising expenditure. While it may have been unfair to individual taxpayers that inflation pushed their money (rather than their real) incomes up into higher tax brackets, revenues did rise and could be expected to rise in inflationary periods at a rate to match more closely increases in expenditures, thus performing an anti-inflationary role. To expect future governments to substitute legislated tax increases for this automatic, hidden system of tax increases was naïve. There were so many reasons why my successors found it difficult to raise tax rates so as to curb the rising deficit. Some were very good reasons, such as rising unemployment; some were not so good, such as impending elections.

External events were not kind to my successors as minister of finance. Because of the oil shock and the subsequent economic downturn, there might well have been substantial budgetary deficits in the 1980s even if income-tax brackets had not been indexed for inflation. The costs of social programs like medicare were soaring. Without income-tax indexation, however, the deficit would certainly have been smaller and more manageable; the government would have been left with greater mano-euvrability to deal with current problems and would have relieved substantially the burden on monetary policy. What lessons are to be drawn? Perhaps Talleyrand's advice to some over-conscientious advisers: 'Pas trop de zèle.'

Fiscal policy can be used – I have used it – to offset inflationary or deflationary tendencies in the Canadian economy. Exemptions from corporate tax (in modern parlance 'tax expenditures') or tax changes can be used – I have used them – to stimulate or restrain particular economic activities. I learned, however, as every minister of finance learns from experience, that the fundamental purpose of taxation is to raise revenues to pay the cost of government.

The Carter Commission

One of the challenges I faced as minister of finance came from an unexpected source. The Royal Commission on Taxation, better known as the Carter Commission after its distinguished chairman, Kenneth LeM. Carter, had been appointed by the Diefenbaker government on 25 September 1962 and presented its report to our government on 22 December 1966. It was an imaginative document, acclaimed in academic circles and by much of the press for its rigorous, logical approach to tax reform. One of its authors was Harvey Perry, former senior taxation official in the Department of Finance, and an acknowledged authority as head of the Canadian Tax Foundation. When questioned as to the acceptability of its recommendations, I gave the customary answer, that it would be studied by the government. I invited representations. And for this normal and neutral attitude I was criticized most severely by some newspapers, particularly the *Toronto Star*, which could not under-stand why I did not rush to commit the government to accept the principles enunciated in the report.

'A buck is a buck, is a buck, is a buck.' No need to consider the origins of the revenue accruing to the individual taxpayer in a year, just the total, whether earned income, interest, dividends, real and deemed capital gains, or inheritances. A revolutionary concept, with appealing ethics! It had never seemed fair to me that a working man should pay income tax on his hard-earned pay, while a rich man, for example, should not pay income tax on an inheritance that came to him without any effort on his part.

Taxes on corporation profits should be considered as withholding taxes collected on behalf of shareholders; another major concept underlying the recommendations of the Carter Commission. I thought that the resulting elimination of double taxation of corporation profits would make a strong appeal to the business community, if not to the ordinary taxpayer who did not own shares in corporations. In the event, the support of the business community, which had more pressing concerns about the commission's recommendations, was lukewarm. The idea was eventually accepted in principle but only partially implemented.

I left the Finance ministry in 1968 to become secretary of state for external affairs before it became necessary for me to take any action on the recommendations of the Carter Commission. That responsibility fell to my successor, Edgar Benson, who initiated and carried through an extraordinary process of consultations on tax reform. In the end, the results, while useful, bore little resemblance to the fundamental reforms recommended by Carter and his associates. There was too much inertia in the existing system of taxation, and there were too many uncertainties in shifting from known to unfamiliar and untested systems for the politicians to take the risks inherent in radical reforms, however logical they might be. A cautionary tale, to be heeded by enthusiasts for tax reform in the future.

Preparing budgets

Each minister of finance has his own approach to cabinet participation in the preparation of a budget. My approach was to make three presentations to the cabinet, at weekly intervals. The first presentation, made two weeks in advance of the budget date, was an outline of the economic situation and its implications for fiscal policy. A week later I presented my views on the alternative courses of action that could be followed, particularly the taxation alternatives. Finally, the day before the presentation of the budget, I asked for approval of the particular tax changes I had decided to include in the budget speech.

The reason for withholding from cabinet until the eve of the budget the final decisions on tax changes was not so much to minimize possibilities of a leak as to protect the cabinet from allegations that there had been a leak, or that ministers had profited from advance knowledge of tax changes that came into effect on budget day.

Although I did my best to give members of the cabinet the opportunity of presenting their views before I made my decisions (and in this respect I think I was at least as open as my predecessor and my successors in the Pearson and Trudeau cabinets), the need for secrecy about tax changes did mean that my colleagues had very little opportunity to express their views about my final decisions. I did, however, let the Prime Minister know some days ahead about what I had decided to do, and I had the advantage of his reactions. It will not come as a surprise to those who knew Pearson that he did not ask searching questions about economic matters such as tax changes.

I am in agreement with those who believe that there are many aspects of fiscal policy that could be discussed more openly in advance of the budget presentation. There is no particular reason, for example, to maintain strict budgetary secrecy on proposed changes in the personal income tax. On the other hand, advance knowledge of proposed changes in the corporation income tax or in commodity taxes could be immensely valuable to speculators on the stock market or to sellers and buyers of goods and services.

In the nature of things, budget speeches are sober, matter-of-fact documents. There is nothing very appealing about them that leads to enthusiastic applause, except when significant tax reductions are announced, which is seldom. Although my budget speeches were well drafted, logical, and persuasive, they were meant to be read and studied rather than listened to. I found them long and complicated to deliver and it showed. On one occasion, I accelerated my pace of reading to the point where someone in the opposition called out 'Whoa!'

In a simpler age, I am told, the minister of finance of Canada spoke from some notes scribbled on the back of an envelope. This is no longer feasible. Yet somehow it should be possible for the minister to present orally a résumé of his budgetary proposals accompanied by the full text to be included in *Hansard*. Television could carry his presentation live, followed by the full text on the screen, thus providing simultaneous release country-wide.

Federal-provincial financial arrangements

As described in chapter 1, I was an official of the Department of Finance when the wartime tax-rental agreements came into effect in 1942, and in 1947 when they expired and had to be replaced by new agreements with the provinces. I was there when the government of Quebec made its decision to drop out of the rental agreements and to reimpose its own personal income, corporation income, and inheritance taxes and when the government of Ontario decided to impose and collect its own corporation income tax. (The government of Ontario later thought better of its decision, and re-entered tax rental in 1952.)

The vision that in 1937 had inspired the members of the Rowell-Sirois Commission and, in the immediate post-war period, the deputy minister of finance and his associates, faded: the vision of a national income-tax system, uniform across Canada, facilitating the formulation and operation of national economic policy. The 1947 agreements began the process whereby the tax-rental agreements were converted into tax-collection and tax-harmonization agreements with all the provinces except Quebec.

In 1957, the function of redistributing tax revenues to help the governments of the poorer provinces, a function that had been incorporated in the tax-rental payments, was assumed by equalization payments, a system developed by my friend Bob Beattie, then deputy governor of the Bank of Canada.

At each five-year renewal of the tax agreements until I became minister of finance at the end of 1965, the federal government abated its rates of personal and corporate income taxes in order to leave room for the imposition of provincial taxes required to finance rapidly rising provincial expenditures. The federal government collected these taxes for the provinces, with the exception of Quebec.

Concurrently, the federal government had been legislating social programs, such as family allowances (1944) and universal old-age pensions (1950), and enlarging the availability of unemployment insurance. It had also been using the spending power to make grants to the provinces to encourage and enable them to increase their spending on higher education and health and welfare – fields of provincial jurisdiction that were of national importance – and also, from time to time, on capital projects and public works as a means of stimulating economic activity.

Thus, by its own policies and legislative program, by enabling the poorer provinces the better to discharge their constitutional responsibilities, and by using the spending power to promote national goals through the encouragement of provincial activities, the federal government gave national leadership in the post-war period, leadership that, in the end, achieved remarkable economic and social development country-wide, notwithstanding our highly decentralized federal system.

It was an awkward, often ad hoc, controversial process, involving continuous confrontation between the federal and provincial governments, particularly between the federal government and the government of Quebec. From the outset, Quebec resisted federal initiatives in fields of provincial jurisdiction (the decision to drop out of the federal-provincial tax agreement at the end of the war was a portent of things to come).

The election of the Lesage government in Quebec in 1960 and of the

Pearson government in Canada in 1963 marked the beginning of a new phase in federal-provincial relations. Under the banner 'Maîtres chez nous,' the Quebec government took a strong nationalistic stand, demanding among other things the right to withdraw from joint shared-cost programs, with financial compensation. And they persuaded Pearson, then leader of the opposition, to accept the idea; witness the following from a pamphlet issued by the Liberal Party of Canada in the 1963 election campaign: 'If some provinces wish, they should be able to withdraw, without financial loss, from joint programs which involve regular expenditures by the federal government and which are well established. In such cases, Ottawa will compensate provinces for the federal share of the cost, by lowering its own direct taxes and increasing equalization payments. This will be done also if some provinces do not want to take part in new joint programs.'

I was not consulted about this policy position, although I had been a Liberal candidate in the 1962 election as well as in the 1963 election. If I had been consulted I would have expressed misgivings. It seemed to me then, and I continued to hold this view when I became a minister, that it is inconsistent with the underlying concept of Canadian federalism that a Canadian taxpayer living in any province should pay a different rate of tax to the Canadian government than a Canadian taxpayer living in another province.

It was to be expected that at some point the federal government would withdraw from joint shared-cost programs that had served their purposes, particularly following the introduction of equalization payments to supplement the revenues of the poorer provinces. It disturbed me, however, when the only province that declared that it wanted to opt out of joint programs was Quebec.

The opting out of federal-provincial shared-cost programs by the only province without a tax-collection agreement with Ottawa, accompanied by lower federal tax rates, gave me serious concern about the future of Canada as a national entity. Consequently, although I voted for it, I was not enthusiastic when, on 3 April 1965, legislation giving effect to interim contracting-out arrangements was approved by Parliament. This offered personal-income-tax abatements in lieu of conditional grants covering hospital insurance, old-age assistance, allowances for blind and disabled persons, unemployment assistance to unemployables, vocational training, and health grants. Cash payments were offered in lieu of conditional grants for another list of less expensive joint programs.

The provinces were to notify the federal government by October 1965 if they wished to opt out of programs. Only Quebec exercised the option and did so for all the offered tax abatements and cash.

When I assumed the responsibilities of minister of finance at the end of 1965, in the midst of a fundamental review of federal-provincial financial relations, I was already concerned about the trend of events. I recognize that the federal spending power can be abused. Consequently, there is a case for constitutional curbs on its use. But I believed then, and still believe, that there is justification for its retention in a usable form. Education, for example, is under provincial jurisdiction. Yet those who are educated in provincially controlled schools and universities move about the country and benefit the Canadian community wherever they live. It is valuable for Canadians from Ontario to have centres of research in Quebec City in which to study. First-rate universities, regardless of where they are located in Canada, attract students from across the country and from around the world. It is surely a proper function of the federal authority and not an intrusion on provincial jurisdiction to encourage high standards of education and to offer to pay a share of the cost of particular activities. Indeed, to expect the provinces, rich or poor, to perform a national role without national help, is unreasonable, inefficient, and counter-productive.

Similarly with respect to health. Medical research wherever it is performed is for the benefit of all Canadians, indeed for the benefit of mankind. The health of the Canadian population, the rate of infant mortality, the control of contagious and infectious diseases: these are matters of more than local or provincial concern. It should not be inconsistent with the Constitution for the federal authorities to take action in the interest of national standards in health care as they did when they sponsored medicare.

The adamant opposition of the Lesage government to shared-cost programs, as they then existed, did, however, have one constructive result. It led federal officials to examine carefully the way in which the spending power was used. The Quebec authorities were particularly opposed to joint shared-cost programs – usually a fifty-fifty split of expenditures between the federal and provincial governments – that involved the audit by the federal authorities of provincial expenditures.

It was out of this examination that the form of federal participation in medicare evolved. Federal grants are made available to any province that meets four basic criteria: (1) comprehensive coverage of all physicians' services; (2) administration by the province, on a non-profit basis, of a provincial agency or a private authority designated by the province; (3) availability to all residents on uniform terms; (4) portability of benefits between provinces for persons temporarily away from home or moving to another province. In 1966, Quebec joined the medicare plan, notwithstanding its opposition to joint shared-cost programs.

Almost from the beginning, Quebec had refused to allow Quebec universities to accept federal grants. The solution: pay the province a sum equal to one-half of their own expenditures on post-secondary education. It was in 1966, during a cabinet committee discussion of shared-cost programs relating to post-secondary education, that for the first time I heard Pierre Elliott Trudeau, then parliamentary secretary to Prime Minister Pearson and representing the Prime Minister at that meeting, express his opposition to federal policies that resulted in special status for Quebec. That was, he contended, the slippery slope to separation. I was impressed. That encounter was one of the reasons why eventually I supported him as leader of the Liberal Party.

The decision by the Lesage government to have its own pension plan alongside the proposed Canada Pension Plan involved delicate negotiations to ensure portability of benefits. Since both plans were self-financing, taxation questions were not involved. Nevertheless, I was troubled in principle, as were many of my colleagues, by the fact that members of Parliament from Quebec would be eligible to debate and vote on a bill to establish or amend the Canada Pension Plan, which would operate everywhere in Canada except in their constituencies. Similar fundamental problems arose with respect to the overlapping of our proposed youth allowances, student loans, and municipal loan programs with areas of provincial responsibility in the province of Quebec.

Looking back, it is little wonder that in those early years of the Pearson government federal-provincial confrontations were frequent and often painful. Out of the conflicts emerged the establishment in 1965 of the Tax Structure Committee, composed of thirteen ministerial members, one from each province and three from the federal government. My predecessor in office, Walter Gordon, said in the House of Commons that the purpose of the committee was 'to conduct a complete and fundamental re-examination of federal-provincial fiscal arrangements.' A.W. (Al) Johnson, an assistant deputy minister of finance (and many years later president of the CBC), became secretary of the committee, at the suggestion of Premier Lesage.

It seemed to me that the time had come for the federal government to propose some general principles to guide federal-provincial fiscal arrangements in the future and, particularly, to halt the federal retreat from its principal tax fields. These are the principles I put forward on 14 September, 1966:.

Which Reminds Me ...

1. The fiscal arrangements should give both the federal and provincial governments access to fiscal resources sufficient to discharge their responsibilities under the Constitution.
2. They should provide that each government should be accountable to its own electors for its taxing and spending decisions and should make these decisions with due regard for their effect on other governments.
3. The fiscal arrangements should, through a system of equalization grants, enable each province to provide an adequate level of public services without resort to rates of taxation higher than those of other provinces.
4. They should give to the Federal Government sufficient fiscal power to discharge its economic and monetary responsibilities, as well as to pay its bills. In particular they should retain for the Federal Government a sufficient part of the income tax field in all provinces – both personal and corporate – to enable it to use variations in the weight and form of that tax for economic purposes and to achieve a reasonable degree of equity in the incidence of taxation across Canada.
5. They should lead to uniform intergovernmental arrangements and the uniform application of federal laws in all provinces.
6. The fiscal arrangements should seek to provide machinery for harmonizing the policies and the priorities of the federal and provincial governments.

I described my objective to the Tax Structure Committee as follows:

We must somehow fashion machinery which will permit a strong federal government to accomplish the economic and social responsibilities which properly belong to it, but without impairing the fiscal freedom and responsibility of the provinces. We must on the other hand fashion machinery which will strengthen the ability of the provinces to provide the greatly expanded and improved public services which are expected of them, but without at the same time hobbling the federal government or forcing it to have different laws for different parts of Canada.

I then went on to make some specific proposals designed to implement these general principles.

Because of rapidly rising education costs and the national interest in an educated Canadian population, the federal government offered to make a reduction or an abatement in its individual income and corporation income taxes, so that the provinces could raise their tax rates without increasing the overall burden on taxpayers.

To enable the provinces ultimately to assume full responsibility for continuing and well-established joint shared-cost programs in the social field, the federal government stood ready to substitute tax transfers for shared-cost grants. The proposals being made would, if accepted by all the provinces, lead in the direction of uniform federal laws across Canada.

To preserve its strength in the field of economic policy, the federal government would continue to use shared-cost programs to stimulate economic growth and development.

Equalization grants were to be reformed by a formula that took into account all provincial revenues rather than only the principal income-tax revenues. We offered to stabilize the revenues of provinces that suffered a significant decline.

Some neutral observers considered this as one of the most important statements on federal-provincial relations since the war. The provincial governments were less enthusiastic. They wanted the federal government to continue to withdraw from income and corporate taxes so that they could impose higher provincial taxes without an overall increase to taxpayers. The Quebec government, then headed by Daniel Johnson, advocated not only full withdrawal of the federal government from income and corporate taxes but also a wide extension of Quebec juris-diction, foreshadowing the confrontation with Ottawa that has continued until now. The provincial governments other than the Quebec government decided not to accept the offer of tax transfers in lieu of shared-cost programs and the offer was later withdrawn, leaving the unequal application of federal taxes to continue.

There were to be many more twists and turns in federal-provincial financial relations in the years to come. What I think we accomplished during my time as minister of finance was to bring more order and coherence to the negotiations.

The coordination of financial arrangements coincided with the decisions of federal and provincial leaders to consider fundamental changes in the Constitution. Thereafter, the two sets of discussions moved in tandem. The exercise of the federal spending power, for example, became a centre of constitutional negotiations, and the prin-ciple of equalization payments to the provinces was recognized in the 1982 Constitution.

Several of the provincial premiers were also their own ministers of finance – including W.A.C. Bennett of British Columbia and Robert Stanfield of Nova Scotia. Consequently, my meetings with the finance ministers to coordinate financial policies took on some of the characteristics of top-level federal-provincial meetings. They were far from pedestrian affairs, and, since they were held in private, participants were very outspoken. To support the Quebec minister of finance were Jacques Parizeau and Claude Morin, then competent and powerful officials and ardent Quebec nationalists.

I recall one meeting when I was urging the provinces to cooperate with the federal government in restraining inflationary pressures. Most of the provincial representatives were sympathetic, but not Premier Bennett of British Columbia. He expressed the view that inflation should not be resisted but encouraged as good public policy. In my view, 'Wacky' was an appropriate nickname.

The 1966 revision of the Bank Act

Walter Gordon introduced the decennial amendments to the Bank Act. The bill had not been debated, however, before Parliament was dissolved in 1965. It became my responsibility to reintroduce it when I succeeded Gordon as minister of finance, and I took the opportunity to make some changes. The principal change I made in the Gordon version of the bill was to include a provision to raise and eventually remove the historic 6 per cent ceiling on the interest rates that could be charged by the chartered banks. It was only in 1965 that interest rates on commercial loans by the banks began to push against the 6 per cent ceiling. The chartered banks had not yet begun to compete seriously in the market for personal loans, where prevailing interest rates were, of course, much higher than the bank interest ceiling.

My advisers and I were satisfied that the interest-rate ceiling on the chartered banks would not hold down the cost of borrowing and could in the future complicate the financing of Canadian industry. If interest rates generally rose above the ceiling, the banks would not lend at the ceiling unless the borrower agreed in advance to hold on deposit with the bank, without interest or at a very low rate of interest, a sufficient portion of the loan to raise the effective return on the loan by the bank to market levels or made some other arrangement to the same effect. On the other hand, if the general level of interest rates fell or did not rise significantly, competition would keep bank lending rates below the 6 per cent level.

The logic of the provision did not convince all the Liberal MPs, however, and particularly did not convince Walter Gordon, who had retained the ceiling in his earlier version of the Bank Act amendments. Some caucus members apparently believed that the ceiling on the rate that chartered banks could charge would keep the cost of borrowing down. Some did not want the government to appear to contribute to increased bank profits. Some simply thought that the lifting of the ceiling was bad politics. I had a hot debate in the caucus with the Gordon group. When the amendments were eventually approved and the ceiling was removed, the issue disappeared. I sometimes reflect on the financial mess that would have developed if the chartered banks had still been subject to that 6 per cent ceiling when, in later years, interest rates in Canada and abroad, over which the Canadian banks had no control, rose to several times that level.

I did not change the provisions of Gordon's bill that limited individual share ownership of Canadian chartered banks to 10 per cent so as to avoid control by any person or group, and that limited the activities of foreign-owned institutions defined as banks with more than 25 per cent foreign ownership. I shared Gordon's view that these were desirable amendments. Our quarrel erupted later after the Bank Act amendments had been introduced into the House of Commons.

The Mercantile Bank case

There was then only one foreign-owned chartered bank in Canada – the Mercantile Bank. It had been established in 1953 by a Dutch banking group and was a relatively small operation. Citibank of New York, controlled by a branch of the Rockefeller family, decided to buy it and made their intentions known to Gordon when he was minister of finance. Gordon told them in effect that he didn't want them in Canada and warned them that if they did proceed with their purchase there would be legislation to curtail their activities. Citibank nevertheless carried through their intention by buying all the shares of the Mercantile.

As Gordon had promised, the amendment to the Bank Act, which he introduced and I retained in the legislation when I became minister, imposed severe limitations on the expansion of any bank more than 25 per cent owned by foreigners. After the amendments to the Bank Act had been introduced, representatives of Citibank called on me and said that they intended to comply with the law by selling newly issued shares of the Mercantile Bank to Canadians until Citibank's ownership fell to 25 per cent.

When I told my colleagues of this Citibank proposal, Gordon, who meanwhile had returned to cabinet, was adamantly opposed. The intention of the new Bank Act, he asserted, was to require Citibank to sell existing shares, not newly issued shares, until its holdings fell to 25 per cent. That might have been his intention, I contended, but I was not aware of it and nowhere was this intention expressed in the law that he had approved. The Bank Act said only that when U.S. ownership of Mercantile had been reduced to 25 per cent of outstanding shares, it would be free from the restrictions imposed on foreign-owned banks. The Citibank directors had a plan to sell new shares to Canadians that seemed to comply with the law, and I was not prepared to tell them it was unacceptable because there was a hidden provision known only to me or to Gordon.

What Gordon wanted, I had to conclude, was to keep Citibank out of Canada. He had warned them that they were not welcome. They had not heeded his warning. So they should be frustrated in their plans to expand the Mercantile Bank.

Within cabinet the debate was rough and tough. Gordon held firmly to his position and I to mine. The Prime Minister asked some of our colleagues to try to work out a compromise, without much success. In the Commons committee examining the Bank Act amendments, chaired by Herb Gray, the confrontation was in the open and received widespread coverage in the media. The U.S. government protested, alleging discrimination against U.S.-owned banks.

The press kept a sort of score card. One day I was ahead; another day Gordon made gains. My alleged motives and strategy were analysed *ad nauseam*. Often I found it difficult to recognize myself. An American professor wrote a book on the Mercantile Bank case. In the end, the Bank Act amendments affecting foreign-owned banks as presented originally by Gordon and, when I succeeded him as minister of finance, by me, were, with minor amendments, approved by Parliament.

Eventually, after Edgar Benson succeeded me as finance minister and Gordon was no longer in the cabinet, Citibank did carry through its plans and sold newly issued shares in the Mercantile to Canadians, reducing its ownership to less than 25 per cent, thus freeing Mercantile from the restrictions on operation of foreign-owned banks. Mercantile opened a few branches, introduced some innovations to Canadian banking practices, got into difficulties, and in 1985 was absorbed by the National Bank of Canada. Now that there are many foreign-owned banks operating in Canada, the Mercantile Bank case appears as a historical oddity. At the time, it was representative of the struggle that went on within the Liberal Party over the issue of foreign ownership. It was not a confrontation between those who favoured foreign investment and those who were opposed. It was essentially a debate about how best to obtain what everyone wanted, namely a prosperous economy as much under Canadian control as is attainable in this increasingly interdependent world.

The 1966 debate on economic nationalism

The battle over economic nationalism was joined publicly on 9 October 1966 at the Liberal Party policy conference in the Château Laurier Hotel in Ottawa. Before the issue reached the floor of the conference for debate, Donald Macdonald, MP for Rosedale in Toronto, approached me on behalf of Walter Gordon seeking my support for a series of resolutions with a strongly nationalistic flavour. I was told that Gordon would be prepared to consider any amendments I might wish to suggest. I told Macdonald I did not wish to be associated with the resolutions. Accordingly, when the session concerned with the subject began, Macdonald got to the microphone first and moved the adoption of the resolutions he had shown me in advance. The second speaker to be recognized was from British Columbia. He wanted to propose a resolution advocating free trade with the United States (to which I was opposed). The chairman pointed out that Macdonald's resolutions were now before the conference and that he could not consider any other until those had been disposed of. Since he did not agree with the Macdonald resolutions, how could he get rid of them? the B.C. delegate asked. By moving that they be tabled, said the chairman. Which he did. Thereupon the debate was on the motion to table Macdonald's resolutions.

I took my place in line, but those ahead of me gave way so that I could speak immediately. My short speech (the limit was three minutes) was a conciliatory one expressing what I thought was a true Liberal approach to the question of foreign investment, moderate and not ideological.

Let me suggest to this workshop that our approach should be Canadian and Liberal.

By Canadian I mean that our approach should be designed to strengthen Canadian independence.

By Liberal I mean that it should be positive and outward-looking.
That is what distinguishes Liberals from Socialists and Tories.

There is no contradiction between wanting to strengthen Canadian independence and advocating policies that are positive and outward-looking. In fact the best way to weaken Canadian independence is to follow narrowly nationalistic policies. I see nothing to be gained and a great deal to be lost by narrowly nationalistic policies in a world of growing interdependence.

We have reason to be concerned about our continued reliance upon massive imports of capital. We cannot assume that the capital will always be available to us when we need it. Therefore, our policies should be designed to reduce our dependence on foreign capital. But these policies should be positive policies, not negative policies. They should be designed to generate more capital in Canada. They should be designed to exploit the most rapidly growing markets at home and abroad.

We have reason to be concerned about the extent of foreign ownership and control of our industries. Our policies therefore should be designed to encourage Canadian investment in Canadian industries. That is one purpose of the Canada Development Corporation. But we should avoid penalizing enterprise just because it is foreign. We need enterprise of all kinds to develop this great country of ours and to make it an attractive place for Canadians to live and work – and to resist the attractions of our great neighbour to the South.

Some vital sectors of our life must remain under Canadian ownership and control – like banks and financial institutions and newspapers and communications. Otherwise independence in any meaningful sense would indeed be in peril.

It is essential, too, that foreign-controlled enterprise should work in the best interests of Canadians. This is a special problem for Canada, because we live alongside the most powerful industrial nation in the world. Hence the importance of guidelines for good corporate citizenship and the need for disclosure of the operations of closely held foreign subsidiaries in Canada.

Mr. Chairman, we Liberals must provide Canada with positive opportunities for a productive, rich and outward-looking independence. We have the possibility before us of creating here in the northern half of North America a society whose independence will be based on achievements – in particular the achievement of creating a diversified, modern and outward-looking Canada – rather than creating a narrow parochialism. To my mind the test which we have to apply to any particular proposal in this regard is this: does it strengthen Canadian independence by excluding and limiting others and denying fulfilment to ourselves? Or does it strengthen Canada by enriching the Canadian society positively – by taking a full and creative part in this changing and exciting world? We Liberals choose this second alternative.

The applause indicated that I had struck the right note and, when the vote was taken, the Macdonald resolutions were by a large majority tabled and thus disappeared. I later worked with the Gordon group to propose resolutions acceptable to the majority of the delegates, and these were approved.

Some time later, Gordon congratulated me on what he termed my great victory in the 1966 conference, attributing it to superior organization. I don't think that was the reason my views prevailed. In fact, there was at least as much organizing on the Gordon side of the issue as among the opposition. My views were found acceptable because they better reflected the attitude of Liberals throughout the country. Liberals are a patriotic lot. Not all of them, however, equate patriotism with economic nationalism of the kind espoused by Gordon and his followers.

Some policies Gordon and I were agreed upon: For a country like Canada, located alongside the greatest power on earth and subject to a constant barrage of political, economic, and cultural influences across the border, it is preferable that our daily newspapers and our television and radio stations, through which we receive our news, should be owned and controlled by Canadians rather than by foreigners and that there should be a government-owned Canadian Broadcasting Corporation. Under these conditions, there was also justification for providing special support to Canadian magazines. We also agreed that no single owner or group of owners, Canadian or foreign, should control the big national banks that finance Canadian business and consumers. Because of the far-flung geography of Canada, it is better if the railways and airlines that link our regions are owned and controlled by Canadians.

As a Canadian, I want to see my fellow citizens owning and controlling as high a proportion of the country's industry as possible. I am more sceptical about the wisdom of laws and subsidies for that purpose, and particularly laws of general application that would limit or prohibit foreign investment.

For example, my attitude was ambivalent to the Foreign Investment Review Act, which Gordon strongly advocated, and to the resulting regulatory agency. I saw value and little harm in modifying, even rejecting, foreign take-overs of existing Canadian-owned enterprises, particularly when the intention was to close them in order to reduce competition. I was more sceptical about attempts to control new foreign investment. I couldn't imagine Ottawa turning down a proposed new factory in Cornwall or Halifax or St John or Winnipeg or Vancouver, even if it was 100 per cent foreign-owned. It was no surprise to me that a very high proportion of all investment applications were approved during the years that FIRA was in existence. What Canada needs are more industries able to hold their own against foreign competition at home and strong enough to export and to establish their own branches in foreign countries. It does not matter too much who owns the shares of such industries (although I would of course prefer Canadian owners), provided the head offices are in Canada, where the important decisions are made, and that research and development are carried out here.

Relations with Walter Gordon

The Liberal Party owes much to Walter Gordon. He was a central figure in the resurrection of the party, particularly in Ontario, after the catastrophic defeat of 1958. His personal support, financially and otherwise, was immensely valuable to Pearson at that time.

My personal relations with Gordon were good, but I was never part of the Toronto group of which Keith Davey and Royce Frith were principal members and of which Gordon was the inspiration. Our views on Canadian nationalism were very different. Gordon looked upon the extent of foreign ownership as the crucial test of Canadian independence. I found this far too narrow a focus within which to judge policy.

Strangely enough, in view of our respective origins and family circumstances, Walter Gordon was regarded by some of the media as being on the left in cabinet, while I was regarded as being on the right. I have had personal experience of poverty and hardship in a working-class neighbourhood during the Depression. I didn't have to be convinced of the necessity of fundamental reforms. Gordon was brought up in a well-to-do family. Moreover, as a westerner, I believed that those who advocated protectionist policies were on the right side of the political spectrum. So I have always been puzzled by the popular view of our respective positions. I suggest that the essential difference between Gordon and myself had nothing whatever to do with being on the right or on the left. It had to do with the fact that, although I had started my career in the business world and had for a few years been an executive of a big corporation, my essential discipline was in government. For sixteen years I was a senior adviser to ministers. I learned care and caution in offering advice. I found it necessary to think through the consequences of public policies, to look at the long run as well as the short term.

Gordon's discipline, on the other hand, was essentially in business. It is necessary, of course, to exercise care and caution in making business decisions, but, if mistakes are made, they affect only the financial fortunes of a limited group of people, whereas mistakes by governments may affect adversely the interests of millions of citizens. Moreover, it is much easier for business to remedy mistakes than it is for government. In short, because of our different experience and background, I was more cautious than my colleague, a characteristic that has nothing to do with being on the right or the left.

The introduction of medicare

At that 1966 Liberal Party conference, I not only took a leading part in the debate on economic nationalism, I had also to defend my insistence on a delay in the introduction of medicare. As a result, I found myself attacked on two fronts by so-called left-wing Liberals who, strangely, are also economic nationalists. I say 'strangely' because there was a time when right-wing Conservatives were the leading exponents within Canada of economic protectionism, following in the footsteps of John A. Macdonald and his National Policy.

As far as I was concerned, it was only the timing of the introduction of medicare that concerned me as minister of finance. I believed in a federal-provincial system of medicare and I wanted to see it in effect throughout the country. In my youth, I had had personal experience of the indignities suffered by the poor who could not afford the medical care they needed and had to depend upon the charity of the medical profession. My advisers warned me, however, about the administrative problems that would arise if the negotiations with the more reluctant provinces were pressed too urgently, and the governor of the Bank of Canada pointed to the adverse effects upon international confidence in the financial position of the government and in the Canadian dollar if hundreds of millions of dollars were added to annual budgetary expenditures in the immediate future.

I could not ignore this advice, and I sought delay in introducing the medicare legislation. The debate was bitter and divisive. Some ministers threatened to resign, including a Quebec Minister for whom I had a high regard and affection, Jean Marchand. I had to be content with a year's delay. It wasn't much. Some critics have argued that it wasn't worth all the trouble it caused me and the government. On reflection, the one-year delay didn't do much harm to the government or the party – it wasn't a significant issue in the 1968 election – and it facilitated the introduction of the program in the more reluctant provinces and helped to maintain confidence in the Canadian dollar at a time when some doubts were being raised about the willingness and ability of the government, then in a minority position and dependent upon support from the NDP, to be financially prudent.

Gordon returns to cabinet

Near the end of 1966, Prime Minister Pearson phoned me to seek my opinion about asking Walter Gordon to rejoin the cabinet. I gave a positive reply immediately. Gordon, I said, had resigned for what I considered a dubious reason: namely, that he had advised Pearson to call an election in 1965 that failed to produce a majority. I advised the Prime Minister that if he did not ask Gordon to rejoin the cabinet, there would be an inference that there was some reason for his resignation other than his election advice. Our conversation apparently confirmed Pearson in his decision and he asked me to be present when he met with Gordon.

We met at 24 Sussex Drive, the P.M.'s official residence, just the three of us. Gordon had a price for returning to the cabinet. Before agreeing to accept another portfolio, he wanted the Prime Minister to accept his conditions relating to the pursuit of policies of economic nationalism. I protested that it was unfair to the Prime Minister and unnecessary to place conditions on acceptance of membership in the cabinet. No other minister had done this. All ministers were free to resign if they were not in accord with government policy and to give their reasons. Gordon persisted, but it was not clear to me whether any or all of his conditions were in fact accepted by the Prime Minister. All I know is that they were not accepted during that interview.

The acceptance of the idea of an agency to review foreign investments was stimulated by Walter Gordon's return to the cabinet in early 1967. His support for the establishment of the 1968 Wahn Committee and of the publication of the Gray Report in 1972 – Herb Gray, the MP from Windsor, was the minister responsible, though not the author – was crucial. Alastair Gillespie, who sponsored the legislation that came into effect during the Trudeau administration, cultivated well-prepared ground.

Gordon's return to cabinet was brief – just over a year. His main interest was in expediting completion of the Watkins Report, which eventually appeared in January 1968. In the election of June 1968 Gordon did not run; he returned to Toronto where he remained an important political influence.

While minister of finance, Walter Gordon had proposed the creation of a government corporation to invest in Canadian industry that would sell shares to Canadians, the purpose being to give all Canadians an opportunity to invest in the industrial development of the country. This idea was approved as part of the government's legislative program in our first Speech from the Throne.

It was an attractive idea with broad appeal, but when I succeeded Gordon as minister of finance, I did not proceed with the legislation because of lack of agreement in the cabinet on several critical issues.

What is the purpose of the corporation – to maximize profits for the shareholders or to be an instrument of government policy designed to promote Canadian ownership? Should the government underpin the value of the shares in order to promote their sale and protect the small Canadian investor? These questions were not answered until several years later, during the Trudeau administration. I give credit to Eric Kierans, then Postmaster General, who insisted in cabinet that his colleagues make up their collective mind on the purpose of the proposed corporation. We decided that we could not hope to sell the shares unless the corporation was directed in the legislation to maximize profits for the benefit of the shareholders.

Kierans was a valuable minister, clear-headed, outspoken – perhaps too outspoken to accept for long the discipline that goes with cabinet solidarity in our system of government.

The Bank of Canada Act

The minister of finance has by law a close relationship with the governor of the Bank of Canada. I knew all the governors – Graham Towers, governor from 1934 to 1954; James Coyne, governor from 1954 to 1961; and Lou Rasminsky, who was governor throughout my term as finance minister.

Rasminsky was operating in the aftermath of a spectacular public quarrel between his predecessor, Coyne, and my predecessor, Donald Fleming. Fleming had eventually prevailed, in that the governor had resigned, but at great political cost and at the price of a crisis in the bank's morale and *esprit de corps*. These Rasminsky had repaired, and he was determined, as was the government, that a 'Coyne affair' should never recur in any form.

To this end, my predecessor as minister of finance introduced amendments to the Bank of Canada Act, drafted by Rasminsky, one purpose of which was to clarify the relationship between the Government of Canada and the Bank of Canada with respect to the responsibility for monetary policy. The 1965 election was called before the bill could be proceeded with. So I reintroduced the bill in almost identical form.

Following the recommendation of the Royal Commission on Banking and Finance (the Porter Commission), the amendment provided that, in the event of a disagreement between the government and the bank that cannot be resolved, after consultation has taken place between the governor and the minister of finance, the government may issue a directive as to the monetary policy that the bank is to follow. The directive must be in writing, in specific terms, and for a specified period. It is to be published in the *Canada Gazette* and tabled in Parliament within fifteen days.

The doubt about responsibility for monetary policy that had played a part in the uproar of the Coyne affair was removed. The government had ultimate responsibility. Equally important: if the government chose to direct the governor, it was to do so openly, for all to see, and must be prepared to defend its actions in Parliament.

In presenting the legislation to the House of Commons I expressed the view that if a government did direct the governor of the bank to execute a monetary policy that he felt was contrary to the public interest, he would resign rather than accept such a responsibility, providing another public occasion for the government to defend its actions.

Before this revision of the Bank of Canada Act most Canadians must have been puzzled, as I was, by the words appearing on our paper currency: 'The Bank of Canada will pay on demand X dollars.' If they went to the bank and asked for payment they would receive a similar note carrying the same words, or some token coins of equivalent face value. The words on the bills were a carry-over from the time when Canada was on the gold standard and one could demand payment in gold. The amendment to the Bank of Canada Act substituted the words 'This note is legal tender' for its face value.

Rasminsky did not suggest any changes in the preamble of the Act, which reads as follows:

Whereas it is desirable to establish a central bank in Canada to regulate credit and currency in the best interests of the economic life of the nation, to control and protect the external value of the national monetary unit and to mitigate by its influence fluctuations in the general level of production, trade, prices and employment, so far as may be possible within the scope of monetary action, and generally to promote the economic and financial welfare of the Dominion.

It is generally assumed that this preamble was drafted by Clifford Clark as deputy minister of finance under Prime Minister R.B. Bennett, who was also his own minister of finance, and who moved the legislation creating the Bank of Canada Act through Parliament in 1934. Clark liked preambles to acts of Parliament, and this particular preamble expressed the prevailing views of the functions of monetary policy as Canada struggled to emerge from the Great Depression. Before the war, the main problem for the first governor of the Bank of Canada, Graham Towers, and the government was to stimulate economic activity. Governor Rasminsky and I were in charge during a period of economic expansion and were more concerned about the risk of serious inflation. We emphasized price stability. It has been argued in recent years by the Bank of Canada itself that the preamble to the act is too general to be of much guidance in the conduct of monetary policy and that clearer direction from Parliament would enhance the independence of the bank. My experience as minister of finance leads me to be sceptical. One basic requirement of a successful economic policy designed to promote economic growth without inflation is coordination of fiscal and monetary policy, something that cannot be assured by words in an act of Parliament.

Rasminsky and I worked together with the greatest harmony, and we would have done so, I am convinced, even if these amendments to the Bank of Canada Act had not been made. The governor kept me fully informed on day-to-day operations of the bank and on the direction of overall policy, and I had no reason to question his judgment. His public utterances and reports were in the great tradition of central banking. It helped that fiscal and monetary policies were not inconsistent, as they became later in the 1980s and 1990s when budgetary deficits soared and remained stubbornly high during periods of rapid economic expansion, producing a great expansion in the national debt and throwing an impossible burden on monetary policy for the stability of the currency.

On several occasions, Rasminsky went to Washington to make the Canadian case – and to make it effectively -for special treatment when measures to deal with U.S. balance-of-payments problems, to which Canada had not contributed, threatened to cause a major financial crisis in Canada.

After he left the Bank of Canada, Coyne moved to Toronto and teamed up with Sinclair Stevens to try to form a Bank of Western Canada. In those days, banks had to be chartered by Parliament, a process that involved the presentation of a private bill.

As minister, I welcomed the creation of another chartered bank, especially one with a head office outside Toronto and Montreal. The legislation was approved in 1966. Unfortunately, in a series of dramatic events, Coyne and Stevens had a falling out and the venture collapsed without ever opening a branch. In the final stages of the drama, I had to intervene in the House of Commons Committee on Finance to reprimand both Coyne and Stevens, a painful occasion for me as Coyne's friend and associate over so many years.

Deposit insurance

Maintaining confidence in banks is always a concern of the minister of finance. This concern surfaced unexpectedly in 1966 in connection with one of Sinclair Stevens' businesses – York Trust. The superintendent of insurance, John Humphries, reported to me one day that there was growing concern about the liquidity of York Trust and some other institutions. He warned that there could be a run by the public to withdraw their deposits, precipitating a financial crisis that might extend widely. Very quickly, legislation was drafted to insure deposits up to $20,000, introduced in Parliament, and approved on 17 February 1967. The public were reassured about the safety of their deposits and the prospective crisis was averted. The chartered banks were unhappy, since they held the bulk of the deposits on which premiums had to be paid and were in no way responsible for public concerns about liquidity. Nevertheless, all of them wanted the public to know that deposits with them were also insured. As far as the chartered banks were concerned, there was no need for increased public scrutiny of their operations beyond what was provided by the superintendent of banks under the Bank Act. Deposit insurance did give the federal authorities, for the first time, machinery to supervise the activities of other deposit-accepting institutions, including those operating under provincial jurisdiction – except in Quebec, which established its own agency to insure deposits in institutions under Quebec jurisdiction.

For the most part these memoirs are concerned with matters for which I had primary responsibility as a minister. There were, however, subjects of general interest on which I had strong views as a member of cabinet. One such was the flag, which I discuss on page 124. Another was the Order of Canada. Both were projects of Prime Minister Pearson.

The Order of Canada

It might be concluded that, because I am an ardent Canadian, I would have welcomed and supported the establishment of the Order of

Canada. In fact, two other members of the cabinet and myself were not in favour. I didn't like to see official distinctions reintroduced into Canadian society. The Government of Canada had given up recommending to the Crown the conferring of titles on Canadians many years before, because titles seemed inappropriate in our kind of democratic society. Although appointment to the Order of Canada does not carry a title, it does confer an official distinction. There was bound to be envy and feelings of unfairness on the part of those not appointed, regardless of how carefully and objectively the appointees were selected. And so there is.

When it was offered to me many years later, I considered refusing the honour of becoming an officer of the Order, but I decided to accept lest people should think that I looked upon refusal as a mark of distinction.

Ironically, in view of my attitude towards the establishment of the Order of Canada, I found myself, because of the absence of the Prime Minister and other ministers more senior in precedence, presiding at the dinner given by the government on 24 November 1967 for the first companions of the order as well as the recipients of the Medal of Service, which is awarded for exceptional bravery. It was a brilliant occasion. At the head table flanking me were Governor General Michener and Mrs Michener, former Governor General Vincent Massey, Pauline Vanier, widow of General Vanier, also a former governor general, and former Prime Minister John G. Diefenbaker. Before us was as distinguished a group of Canadians as had ever been assembled in one place. I had prepared a short address in English and French, but I had not thought about a very simple matter, namely, what does one say at the outset of such a formal occasion – 'Please sit down'? It didn't seem adequate. Fortunately, Father Georges-Henri Lévesque, the inspiration of the Quiet Revolution in Quebec, who had been appointed as a companion in the Order of Canada, was standing a few yards from me. I asked him to say grace. And then we sat down.

Party leadership

I did not set out in life to become a politician. I did not, on becoming a member of Parliament, aspire to the leadership of the Liberal Party or the prime ministership. It is in the nature of politics, however, that the question of leadership of one's party is always under discussion, and the search for potential leaders goes on even when there is no challenge to the incumbent leader.

Because of its long years in power, and unlike the Progressive Conservative and New Democratic parties, the Liberal Party has had the opportunity to test its potential leaders in office. Blake, Laurier, King, St Laurent, Pearson, Trudeau, Turner and Chrétien had been federal ministers before they became leaders. By contrast, Bracken, Diefenbaker, Stanfield, Clark, and Mulroney had never been in a federal government when they were selected to lead the Conservatives. It was in line with tradition, therefore, that when Prime Minister Pearson decided to retire, the candidates to succeed him should, with the exception of Eric Kierans and one minor candidate, be members of his cabinet.

I was one of them and as eager to win as any of my rivals, although saddened and disheartened by the deterioration of my wife's health. There gathered around me a first-rate organization, the leading members of which were, of course, my loyal friends in Eglinton. In charge of my campaign was Jack Berkinshaw, who later became president of the Mony Insurance Company in Canada. In cabinet, four ministers declared themselves as my supporters – C.M. (Bud) Drury, Jean-Luc Pepin, Jean Chrétien, and Senator John Connolly, then leader of the government in the Senate. My campaign was launched early and got off to a reasonably good start. The media treated my candidacy seriously.

Here are some of the things I said when announcing my candidature on 19 January 1968:

There are some things that Liberals stand for because they are Liberals. We want – and I believe we can achieve – a rising standard of living for all Canadians, higher levels of public services of all kinds, a more equitable distribution of the wealth we generate. Above all, we want to get on with the job of eliminating poverty in Canada.

A constitution that has served for a hundred years without major amendment must have merit, but I am sure that the great majority of us would now prefer to have one that could be amended in Canada by Canadians and that reflects more fully both our ideals as a nation state and the peculiar and unique nature of the Canadian federation.

How to make a new society in this country, a society in which French Canadians can play their full part, is today Canada's greatest problem. It is also most certainly our greatest opportunity. The new idealism of Quebec can well be the decisive factor in the future of Canada, for without the full and enthusiastic participation in our national life of French-speaking Canadians, independence will not only be more difficult to defend but a good deal less meaningful.

I am one of those who think that Canada without Quebec is not only unthinkable, but likely to be very dull as well.

We are one of the most fortunate countries in the world. We have a high standard of living. We enjoy probably the most peaceful and one of the most satisfying lives in the world because we have great opportunities for the future.

I think that assistance to the less-fortunate countries of the world should remain one of our top priorities.

Maintaining perspective in a close bilateral relationship between vastly unequal partners is not easy. Some of the actions taken by Canada, and even some of the speeches made by Canadians, are no more than is necessary to protect our sovereignty and independence against powerful, even if benevolent, forces from below the 49th parallel.

I believe that increasing efforts should be made to overcome the commercial barriers that separate the Communist world from the free world, not only because I believe this is good economics but also because I believe it is good world politics.'

It was clear from the outset that among the other English-speaking ministers the one who would give me the greatest trouble, should he decide to run, would be Robert Winters, because he, like myself, had been in both business and politics, was considered, when in St Laurent's government, to have been a protégé of C.D. Howe, and was undoubtedly a fine figure of a man, tall and handsome, with an impressive voice.

When I was a civil servant, Robert Winters entered the St Laurent cabinet. I became acquainted with him at that time, and Winters regarded our association to be friendly enough that when we were both in business in Toronto he asked me from time to time to help him in preparing speeches and invited me to become a director of Rio Algom Mines Limited, of which he was chairman of the board – an invitation I declined.

Later, when I had entered politics, and he had not yet decided to try again to win a seat in the Commons, he accepted an invitation to speak on my behalf at a public meeting in Eglinton. No doubt it helped to have such a senior Liberal as Winters appear with me in a photograph on the front page of the *Globe and Mail*. It was evident, however, from the length and content of his speech that his purpose was as much to advance his own political future as to assure mine. After 1963, I was one of those who urged Winters to be a candidate in the next general election, as did the Prime Minister and many others. So we were all happy when he took the plunge and won a seat in Toronto in the 1965 election.

I did not know what, if anything, Winters was promised by Pearson, or what he believed he was entitled to by way of a portfolio. It was widely believed that he expected to be appointed minister of finance. Instead, Pearson recommended me to the governor general to succeed Gordon when he resigned, and Winters to succeed me as minister of trade and commerce.

In the run-up to the leadership convention, before either Winters or I had declared as candidates, Winters made a speech criticizing the financial policies of the government. I was very angry. I looked upon the speech as an attack on the minister of finance and asked Winters for an explanation. He said that he had not intended to criticize me and would be happy to write to me to that effect. He did write a private letter, which he would not permit to be published, a fact that added to my anger. This is one of the reasons why I did not support Winters for the leadership. I also resolved that, if he became leader and prime minister, I would not remain in the government. Perhaps I wouldn't have been invited.

When I took the plunge, Winters was still hesitating and there was no French-speaking candidate. Early on, the name of the minister of justice, Pierre Elliott Trudeau, began to be mentioned, and I took the opportunity to ask him directly whether he intended to be a candidate. His answer at that time – and I believe he was sincere – was negative. In the course of the conversation, he said that he didn't know any of the Canadian business leaders and only one provincial premier, whereas when he looked across the cabinet table there were Winters, Martin, Hellyer, and myself, all of whom had a wide circle of friends and acquaintances in both business and politics.

I asked Trudeau about his intentions because of my respect for him and my feeling, even at that stage, that he had qualities that fitted him better than any of the rest of us to lead the Liberal Party and the government.

Although I told him that I didn't think the idea would be consistent with the constitution of the Liberal Party, Marchand suggested to me one day during the leadership campaign that Trudeau and I should run for the leadership jointly, Trudeau as the French-Canadian leader and I as English-speaking leader. If we won the leadership a decision would be taken, perhaps by the members of the caucus, as to who would be leader and who deputy leader, and, if the Liberals were in office, who would be prime minister and who deputy prime minister. Some years later, the position of deputy prime minister was created, but the incumbent has never had much more authority than the senior ranking minister enjoyed when he presided, as I did, as acting prime minister in the absence of the prime minister. A deputy leader elected by the party, whether French-speaking or English-speaking, would be a different matter. It would give reality to the duality of Canadian politics, more reality than the tradition of alternation between French-speaking and English-speaking leaders of the Liberal Party. Whatever its merit, and it has its difficulties, the idea was not pursued.

The defeat of the 1968 budget bill

I had no reason to be unduly concerned about the approval of the 1968 budget and the passage through the Commons of the budget bills. There were no signs at any time that the opposition intended to 'gang up' on our minority government in the midst of the leadership race. This impression was confirmed by the approval on second reading of Bill C-193, which contained the major tax changes. If the opposition parties had intended to make it an issue, they could have put on the whips and defeated us (since they had more elected members than we did), thus precipitating an election. Although there may be some doubt as to what constituted a vote of lack of confidence at that point in time, the defeat of the bill on second reading certainly would have been one such vote. Six years later, in 1974, when John Turner's budget motion was defeated, Prime Minister Trudeau advised the governor general to dissolve the House and call an election forthwith.

When the House went into Committee of the Whole after approval on second reading, I had the task of obtaining approval of each clause of the bill. In Committee of the Whole the division bells do not ring to call members for a vote. Votes are called whenever the government side is satisfied that there are more government members in their seats ready to stand and vote than opposition members. It is a nerve-racking procedure when government is in a minority position. In that particular bill there were six clauses and therefore six votes, each of which had to be won.

Finally, all clauses were approved, much to my relief. I had agreed with the leader of the government in the House, Allan MacEachen, that third reading would not proceed that day. Unfortunately, the speaker's chair was temporarily occupied by Herman Batten, an MP from Newfoundland who was not thoroughly conversant with the rules. The chairman of the Committee of the Whole reported to him that the committee had considered and approved the bill. Whereupon, the acting speaker, reading from the sheet of paper handed to him by the clerk of the House, said, 'When shall the Bill be read a third time, now?' As agreed, MacEachen raised objections that would have been sufficient to delay third reading to a later day, since unanimous consent is required for immediate consideration. But Batten's eyes were glued to his paper. He did not see MacEachen, and went on to say: 'Moved by Mr. Sharp, seconded by Mr. Benson that this Bill be now read a third time.' I protested that I had not moved third reading. Confusion reigned. On the government side, some ministers wanted to go ahead, and the Liberal whip handed me a note that we had sufficient members to carry the motion.

At that point I should have persisted in saying that I had not moved third reading and drawn the attention of the chair to MacEachen's original objection. Instead I succumbed to the pressure and agreed to go ahead with the vote. The bells rang for seventy-five minutes. The Tories saw an opportunity to embarrass the government and sent out calls to all their members who were within calling distance. The vote on third reading was 84 to 82. Several ministers, candidates for the leadership of the party, were absent. However, I do not blame them for the defeat. It was my fault. Despite the pressure from our side as well as from the opposition to go ahead, I should have insisted upon delaying third reading until a later day when we could have mobilized our members for the vote.

Prime Minister Pearson, who was vacationing in Jamaica, returned immediately to deal with the crisis. The cabinet met and concluded that the defeat of the bill on third reading by two votes did not constitute a vote of lack of confidence. (Approval of a bill on third reading is usually a formality.) Following accepted parliamentary practice, the Prime Minister moved 'that this House does not regard its vote on February 19 in connection with third reading of Bill C-193, which had carried in all previous stages, as a vote of non-confidence in the government.' The motion was carried 138 to 119. This time the Social Crediters, who did not want an immediate election, supported the government.

The rules of the House of Commons forbid the presentation of a new bill similar to a bill that has been defeated in the same session. In order to restore public confidence in government finances, the government had, nevertheless, in one way or other to raise the revenues that would have been raised by the taxes included in Bill C-193. My officials demonstrated their capacity and ingenuity by drafting another bill, which the speaker ruled was sufficiently different to satisfy the rule. I presented it to the Commons and in due course it was approved.

Should I withdraw?

The third-reading defeat of Bill C-193 and the necessity of obtaining ap-

My parents on arrival from Scotland

Where I was born, on the outskirts of Winnipeg in 1911

Age thirty-one. Very serious

Tokyo, 1956. Touring Japan with C.D. Howe and T.C. Davis, Canadian ambassador

Mike Pearson and I at the dinner preceding the Kingston Conference that reinvigorated the Liberal party in 1960

Paris, 1964. J.H. (Jake) Warren, my deputy minister of trade and commerce, and I at a meeting of the Council of Ministers of the OECD

In the office of the mayor of Montreal, 1967. *Left to right*: Pierre Dupuy, commissioner general, Mitchell Sharp, federal minister responsible for Exposition 1967, Jean-Luc Pepin, parliamentary secretary to the minister, Mayor Jean Drapeau, Robert F. Shaw, deputy commissioner general

Sightseeing in Ottawa, 1971. The Minister of External Affairs shows the Queen and Prince Philip the new Lester B. Pearson Building.

Israel, 1969. A wonderful time to be in Israel. For some reason, Mrs Golda Meir reminded me of my mother.

London, 1970. The British government invited me to discuss Britain's proposed entry into the European Common market. I told Prime Minister Edward Heath that we were on their side.

Tanzania, 1971. With Julius Nyerere, one of the most attractive leaders I met on my African tour. Unfortunately, Tanzania had a disappointing record under his leadership.

Vietnam, 1973. Congratulating Canadian members of the International Control
Commission, who were withdrawn a few months later

Pierre Trudeau campaigned for me in Eglinton in the 1974 election. I persuaded his wife, Margaret, to say a few words, the first time she had spoken in public.

Washington, 11 February 1974. Before-dinner conference: President Nixon talks with West Germany's foreign minister, Walter Scheel (*left*), prior to a White House dinner for representatives to the thirteen-nation energy conference. Also at the head table are Mitchell Sharp and Japan's minister of foreign affairs, Masayoshi Ohira (*far right*).

Moscow, 1974. *From my left*: R.A.D. Ford, Canadian ambassador to the U.S.S.R., John Halstead and E.P. Black of External Affairs, Alexander Yakovlev, U.S.S.R. ambassador to Canada, Andrei Gromyko, foreign minister of the U.S.S.R., Nikolai Podgorny, president of the Presidium of the U.S.S.R.'s Supreme Soviet

Ottawa, 1975. Chatting with U.S. secretary of state Henry Kissinger on a social occasion, memorable for some indiscreet remarks made by him on the assumption that the microphone was dead when it wasn't

With my favourite cabinet colleague, Bud Drury

Playing the Andante movement from Mozart's Piano Concerto no. 21 with the
Toronto Symphony Orchestra under Victor Feldbrill

proval of substitute legislation forced me to reconsider standing as a candidate for the leadership. I asked Pearson for his advice, which confirmed my own view that I should stop campaigning in order to deal with the problems created by the defeat of the tax bill, but I should not withdraw from the race. Jean Chrétien campaigned on my behalf throughout the country, which undoubtedly did me a lot of good and introduced Jean to parts of English-speaking Canada he had never seen and where, in due course, he became a popular figure. I returned to campaigning on 20 March.

It became clear by the beginning of April, from the surveys of delegate support being made by my organization, that my chances of winning were deteriorating and that I was almost bound to be eliminated from the voting well before the final ballot. I met with members of my organization to consider what should be done. Almost unanimously, they shared my preference for Trudeau as leader. How best could we give him support, assuming that I would be eliminated at some stage of the voting if I stayed in the race? Was it better to wait until that point in voting and go to sit with Trudeau, or withdraw now and declare my support for Trudeau, before the voting began? To stay in the race until I was voted out ran two risks: first, that my attitude to Trudeau would appear ambivalent, and second, that my eventual move to Trudeau, after I was eliminated, would be interpreted, if he were ahead in the balloting, not as an expression of confidence in his qualities of leadership but as jumping on the bandwagon.

Once again, I consulted with Prime Minister Pearson. If I withdrew, should I come out in support of Trudeau? In an earlier conversation after the defeat of the tax bill, when I had stopped campaigning, we had exchanged views on Trudeau. At that time, both of us were impressed but puzzled. Now, I expressed more confidence in Trudeau and found that the Prime Minister's thinking had also advanced in the same direction.

I decided to withdraw in favour of Trudeau, a decision supported by all except one of my close advisers. Before my withdrawal became public, I felt it only common courtesy to advise Trudeau, who had been unaware of my intentions. I telephoned him immediately. My organization also learned that the editor of *Le Devoir*, Claude Ryan, was intending to announce his support for me in an editorial the following day. In order to avoid embarrassment we let him know that I would not be a candidate.

My withdrawal in favour of Trudeau before the opening of the convention was said by some media commentators to have tipped the scale in favour of Trudeau over Winters. While I have reason to believe that a high proportion of the delegates who had intended to vote for me followed my lead to Trudeau, equally significant, I believe, was the fact that my support carried with it the imprimatur of the minister of finance. Trudeau was largely unknown to many of the delegates at that convention. He had been in the Liberal Party for only a few years and in the cabinet for only a year or so. At one time, he had supported the CCF. There was understandable concern about his reliability on economic matters. What is he really like? Is he really a socialist as some allege? (My son, Noel, ran as a Liberal candidate against Jack Horner in Crowfoot, Alberta, in the subsequent 1968 election. He told me that his greatest problem was allegations made in the pulpits of the local churches that Trudeau was a Communist.) Why are you supporting him and not one of the other candidates, like Winters? These were the kinds of question I was asked as I circulated among the delegates in the days leading up to the voting. I did my best to give reassuring answers.

As the voting proceeded at the convention, candidates were eliminated one by one until the choice was reduced to three candidates; Trudeau, Winters, and Turner. Finally, Trudeau gained more than half the total, defeating Winters by 249 votes. Trudeau remained as prime minister, with one short interruption, for more than fifteen years, longer than any other prime minister except Mackenzie King and John A. Macdonald. In 1968, I thought the Liberal Party made the right choice. I have never had reason to change my opinion.

CHAPTER SEVEN

Secretary of State for External Affairs, 1968–1974

I. The Domestic Side of Foreign Policy

Replacing Paul Martin

As he set about forming his first government, Trudeau called me in and gave me a choice of portfolios. Although I had enjoyed being minister of finance, I wanted a change. The only senior portfolio that seemed to offer both change and challenge was External Affairs, where Paul Martin was the minister. That was my preference. Trudeau said he would see what could be done. Knowing what I came to know about Martin's great love for foreign affairs, I realize that he must have been disappointed when I replaced him. But never at any time did I hear him express, or hear that he had expressed, any lack of confidence in me as his successor.

Following my appointment, I was asked by the media whether there would be important changes in Canadian foreign policy. I replied to the effect that I didn't yet know, but that they should be aware that, whereas Pearson and Martin were professionals in the field of foreign policy, Trudeau and I were amateurs and our approach was bound to be different.

Pearson had been a diplomat, under-secretary and then secretary of state for external affairs, and had been awarded the Nobel Peace Prize before he became prime minister. Martin had never been a professional diplomat, but from the outset of his public career he had made a point of being involved in one way or another with the conduct of Canadian external relations, even before he became foreign secretary.

Trudeau had travelled abroad extensively both as a student and in later life. His involvement in the conduct of Canadian external relations, however, had been limited to membership on United Nations committees while parliamentary secretary to Prime Minister Pearson. He was certainly not part of what one might term the Canadian foreign policy establishment, centred in the Canadian Institute for International Affairs and its French-Canadian equivalent. His acidulous criticism of Pearson's reversal on the question of the presence of nuclear weapons on Canadian soil was a clear indication of his independent cast of mind.

My primary interest had not been Canadian foreign policy. On the other hand, as both civil servant and minister in the departments of Finance and Trade and Commerce I had extensive experience as a negotiator on behalf of Canada, especially with the United States, and had represented Canada at many international gatherings.

For six years, a longer period than any of my predecessors except Pearson, I was to be secretary of state for external affairs, serving under a prime minister who took office with strong and sometimes unorthodox views about both the content and the conduct of Canadian foreign policy. Our respective approaches to policy and administration were not always the same.

From time to time, Trudeau openly challenged the conventional wisdom in foreign policy and the foreign-policy establishment both within and outside government. I welcomed the debate because I was satisfied that the fundamentals of Canadian foreign policy would survive the challenge, which they did. I shared Trudeau's view that the time had come to express Canada's foreign policy in terms that shifted emphasis from our role in the world to the promotion of our interests and objectives, one of which was, of course, the promotion of peace and security. Together, during the six years I was foreign secretary, we took several decisive steps in the development of Canadian foreign policy, steps that were to have widespread repercussions.

Foreign policy is rarely subject to serious debate in Canadian general elections, partly because it is seldom a topic of popular interest and partly because over the years there has been a more-or-less non-partisan approach to foreign policy in Canada, at least as between the Liberal and Progressive Conservative parties. It was a portent of things to come that the Liberal Party platform for the 1968 election, at Prime Minister Trudeau's insistence and with my concurrence, included the promise of a review of foreign policy, especially of Canadian participation in NATO, and the establishment of diplomatic relations with the People's Republic of China. I helped to draft those planks in the party platform along with Michel Vennat, who, before joining the Prime Minister's Office, had been a special assistant in my office when I was minister of finance.

The principle of collegiality

I entered the Pearson government in 1963 aware that I shared responsibility for the decisions made by the cabinet. I knew that my political future was therefore, to a large extent, in the hands of my colleagues. Conversely, the political future of my colleagues depended, in part, upon how well I discharged my ministerial functions. To put it another way, each of us hoped and prayed that Prime Minister Pearson had done as well in selecting the rest of his cabinet as he had done in selecting each of us!

Prime Minister Trudeau gave new substance to the principle of collegiality. He insisted that, before making decisions for which there was collective responsibility, cabinet had to be better informed. No longer were ministers permitted to bring recommendations before cabinet directly and in a form that suited them. Suggestions were to be submitted in prescribed form in the first instance to cabinet committees, which made decisions subject to cabinet ratification or, if unable to reach a decision, reported the disagreement to cabinet.

In the first few months after the 1968 elections, under Trudeau's leadership, the Cabinet Committee on Priorities and Planning was a seminar on political science, participated in by a group of ministers, several with high academic qualifications. In 1968 the members of P and P were: Pierre Trudeau, Edgar Benson, Léo Cadieux, Bud Drury, Paul Hellyer, Don Jamieson, Arthur Laing, Donald Macdonald, Allan MacEachen, Jean Marchand, Bud Olson, Jean-Luc Pepin, myself, and John Turner. Some had been university professors. I don't think the debate could have been equalled for intellectual stimulation in any Canadian university. Our initial aim was to lay down in principle the priorities that should be given to the planning and actions of the new administration. Unfortunately – I use the word because it was such an enjoyable exercise – it wasn't long before the necessity to take decisions on urgent practical issues determined the agenda of the P and P Committee, to which major policy issues were referred. During my time in cabinet, the P and P Committee was not, however, an inner cabinet, although it did include the more important ministers (for geographic reasons it also included some junior ministers) and its decisions were referred to cabinet for final approval, like the decisions of all other cabinet committees.

Matters affecting the financial framework, the target levels of revenues and expenditures, were referred to P and P, and on such occasions the deputy minister of finance or the secretary of the Treasury Board was asked to attend. At one such meeting Simon Reisman, deputy minister of finance, was in attendance and taking a leading role by lecturing the ministers on their responsibilities. To relieve the tension, I intervened: 'Mr. Prime Minister, isn't it wonderful to listen to a civil servant who knows his place.' Everyone laughed, including Reisman. After a short pause, he returned to the attack, undeterred.

The effects of Trudeau's approach to decision making were revolutionary. First of all, there was a sudden and enormous increase in documentation. When I was a civil servant, our instructions were to limit our memoranda to two pages; otherwise ministers would not read them. By contrast, while Trudeau was prime minister, it was not unusual for a submission to exceed fifteen pages and for the documentation relating to a cabinet meeting to be at least a foot thick. It became necessary to summarize submissions to cabinet for the benefit of ministers who did not have time to read the whole document. Conscientious ministers with lots of time and energy to spare could become extraordinarily well informed, not only about their own departments and responsibilities but about government as a whole – and could become exhausted if they were too conscientious.

A second effect of the new procedure was to alter significantly the relationship between a department and its minister and between the minister and cabinet. Hitherto, the minister had looked to the deputy minister, as the permanent head of the department, for advice and for the preparation of recommendations to cabinet. The minister signed the recommendations and they went before cabinet for disposition. After 1968, cabinet documents had to be prepared in a stipulated form and submitted in advance to the Privy Council Office for approval as to form. At cabinet committees, where the submissions were first considered (except Priorities and Planning), ministers were permitted to be accompanied by civil servants, who often debated with one another and occasionally with ministers.

One result of this more complicated structure was to diminish the influence of individual deputy ministers, except possibly the clerk of the Privy Council. When I was a deputy minister to C.D. Howe, I had much more influence over government policy than any deputy minister during the Trudeau regime, not only because Howe was a powerful minister, but because the decision-making process was so much simpler.

The emphasis on collegiality also tended to raise the profile of the Prime Minister in relation to other cabinet ministers. In any event, Trudeau would have dominated his cabinet, simply because of his intellectual capacity. His performance in the Liberal caucus was equally impressive. No matter what the subjects under discussion, Trudeau was able in his summing up at the conclusion of the caucus meeting to be authoritative and reassuring, basic ingredients of effective leadership. By insisting upon adequate information from ministers and adequate debate in cabinet committee, Trudeau also became better informed than any of his predecessors, the best evidence of this being the ease and accuracy with which he answered questions from the opposition in Parliament and from the press in almost every area of government activity.

I did not, however, share the widespread view that, by monitoring the preparation of documents and by staffing cabinet committees, the Privy Council Office exercised undue influence upon cabinet decisions. On many occasions and for fairly long periods, I was acting prime minister and was briefed by the clerk of the Privy Council, Michael Pitfield, and his staff in advance of cabinet meetings and cabinet committee meetings. These briefings were informative. They drew my attention to significant issues. At no time did I detect what might be termed a Privy Council point of view.

Trudeau in cabinet

Trudeau was a remarkably effective chairman of cabinet – firm yet fair. I never knew him to anticipate a decision by giving his own opinion before asking the opinions of his colleagues, except, of course, with respect to constitutional questions. He asked probing questions rather than expressing his own opposing views, an approach that could be devastating to the proponents of a point of view that did not stand up to rigorous examination. He genuinely sought for consensus. His reorganization of cabinet procedure illustrated his insistence upon orderly debate and his support for collegiality.

Like all prime ministers, however, there were certain subjects that were his own specialty and on which he did not need or seek advice, at least not in cabinet. Foreign policy, for example, was seldom discussed in Pearson's cabinet. Pearson and the secretary of state for external affairs, Paul Martin, made the decisions. Trudeau had entered federal politics determined to keep Quebec in Canada and as a means to that end, to show Quebeckers that French-speaking ministers could play a significant role in the Canadian government. His appointments reflected this determination, and he gave direction to policy on constitutional issues and related aspects of federal-provincial relations. He was content to let his ministers give direction to economic and social policies, and he gave direction to foreign policy only from time to time and not always, in my view, constructively.

One day, somebody asked me the difference between being in Pearson's cabinet and being in Trudeau's. I replied: 'In Pearson's cabinet we looked at Mike and said to ourselves he is here because we're here. In Trudeau's cabinet, we looked at Pierre and said we're here because he's here.' Without him, Robert Stanfield would probably have led the Conservatives to victory in 1968, as he almost did in 1972. In that 1968 election, with Trudeau as national leader, all my opponents in Eglinton lost their deposits. In 1972, facing the same Conservative candidate, I managed to survive but with a greatly reduced majority.

From the outset of the Trudeau administration I was the senior minister in the House of Commons; consequently, I was acting prime minister in Mr Trudeau's absence, which happened frequently. It sounds more important than it was. An acting prime minister has no authority over his colleagues. At cabinet meetings he cannot express the consensus unless there is in fact agreement. There is no way he can discipline recalcitrant ministers. In the House of Commons, the acting prime minister does the best he can to cope with opposition attacks on government policy and to avoid contradicting his boss.

At the opening of the House on 5 March 1970, I had to deal with an unprecedented situation. The previous day Prime Minister Trudeau had left Ottawa for what he said was a skiing holiday and without notice had married Margaret Sinclair in Vancouver. Officials in the PM's office advised me to say nothing. I didn't agree.

Here, according to *Hansard*, is what I did say and the witty comment by Tommy Douglas, the leader of the NDP:

> **Hon. Mitchell Sharp (Acting Prime Minister);** Mr. Speaker, I apologize to the House for not having given notice yesterday of the intention of our esteemed Prime Minister to get married.
> **Some hon. Members:** Hear, Hear!
> **Mr. Sharp:** The trouble is he did not consult the members of his Cabinet on this essentially private affair, but I am sure all members of the House will join me in wishing great happiness and long life to the happy pair.
> **Mr. T.C. Douglas (Nanaimo-Cowichan-The Islands):** Mr. Speaker, the Acting Prime Minister need not have apologized for not having notified the House yesterday that the Prime Minister intended to embark on the sea of matrimony. We in the opposition parties are now accustomed to the Prime Minister doing things without giving us any advance notice.

The fact that he did not inform the cabinet is understandable. They would probably have insisted on the matter being considered by a study session, followed by a task force, and brought to a conclusion by a white paper, after which nothing would have been done.
Some hon. Members: Hear, hear!
Mr. Douglas (Nanaimo-Cowichan-The Islands): I suggest that at the Prime Minister's age such delay is unthinkable.'

Trudeau as party leader

Trudeau confessed to me one day early in his career as prime minister and party leader that he had difficulty in dealing with people. That was also my impression and I could understand why this was so. Until he became minister of justice, Trudeau had never been in charge of anything substantial, had never been the boss or, for that matter, been bossed. Nor had he been actively engaged as a leader in organized activity, like his friend Jean Marchand, who had led the largest trade union in Quebec.

It is not surprising that Trudeau found the Liberal Party side of his leadership responsibilities irksome and that he often disappointed the Liberal activists throughout the country by his reluctance to do the things that party leaders are supposed to do, such as giving pep talks at fund-raising dinners. In truth, he seldom acted like a conventional politician because he wasn't one.

Prime ministers are expected to know how to get people to do things, how to massage their egos by thanking them, and how, occasionally, to employ the art of flattery to get their way. My observation is that none of this appealed to Trudeau, who is himself so self-contained.

That Trudeau nevertheless led the Liberal Party for sixteen years and through five general elections with only one loss is a tribute to the power of his personality, the clarity of his thought processes, the vigour of his speech, and the strength of his convictions. He joined the Liberal Party because he saw it as the most effective political vehicle to achieve his purpose, which was to keep Quebec in Canada. He became leader of the Liberal Party and prime minister unexpectedly. He had been an MP for only three years. He had not been a party activist. He had not set out to become leader. In a sense, leadership was thrust upon him by those within the party, like myself, who recognized his potential.

By the time Trudeau became prime minister, the battle for official bilingualism, led by Pearson, had been won, although the legislation itself was not approved until 1969. Constitutional reform Trudeau embarked upon gingerly at first; at the end it became one of the major accomplishments of his long years in office.

Reflecting on those years when Quebec separatism first seriously threatened the unity of Canada, I realize that those of us in cabinet who represented constituencies outside Quebec were for the most part observers of political events in that province, whereas ministers from Quebec participated actively in political activities and debate in the rest of Canada. It wasn't that we were excluded from Liberal Party politics in Quebec. Rather, we realized that Quebeckers had to decide among themselves whether to stay or to leave and that our main contribution as English-speaking ministers was to give reality to Trudeau's contention that French-speaking Canadians from Quebec could play their full and appropriate part in the Government of Canada.

Organization of the department

When I took over the External Affairs portfolio in April 1968, the top departmental official, the under-secretary of state for external affairs, was Marcel Cadieux, an intellectual, French-speaking civil servant, a lawyer by training, and an acknowledged authority in the field of international law. In 1970, Cadieux and A. Edgar Ritchie exchanged places, Cadieux replacing Ritchie as ambassador in Washington and Ritchie replacing Cadieux as under-secretary. Ritchie was an economist by training with extensive experience in both political and economic affairs at home and abroad. Both were outstanding public servants, tough-minded and effective.

In those days, the top officials of the more important policy-making, departments, such as Privy Council, Finance, External Affairs, Trade and Commerce, and Health and Welfare, held their posts for fairly long periods and were replaced by experienced senior colleagues, thus providing continuity between ministers as well as between governments. In those days, too, those top officials spent most of their time on policy, as I did when I was deputy minister. Administrative matters were left in the hands of assistants, although, before he became ill and had to relinquish his position as under-secretary, Ritchie had the major task of endeavouring to coordinate the activities of several departments and agencies engaged in external activities.

Cadieux and, in turn, Ritchie were my principal sources of advice on foreign policy, for which I had reason to be grateful and was grateful. They were supported by an extraordinarily competent group of officials serving in Ottawa and abroad who, like themselves, had originally been selected on merit in competitions with extremely high standards. The under-secretary assigned to my office senior officials known as departmental assistants to help in the preparation of my ministerial statements and speeches. To me as a minister this was an imaginative innovation and it worked very well, mainly because of the intellectual quality of departmental assistants like Alan McGill, J.H. (Si) Taylor, and Reeves Haggan.

Although the attitude of superiority of External Affairs officials rankled with officials of other departments, they were probably justified in considering themselves to be an élite. With Pearson, who was a personal friend of most of the top officials, as prime minister, and with Martin, who himself maintained and enjoyed personal contacts with officials, as secretary of state for external affairs, they were in a privileged position within the Ottawa hierarchy.

The attack by Trudeau on diplomats

Consequently, Prime Minister Trudeau's double-edged attack on External Affairs, his questioning of the conventional wisdom with respect to foreign policy and his questioning of the value of ambassadors in the modern world of telecommunications and air travel, came as a great shock. It is a tribute to the resilience and intelligence of the department under Ritchie's firm guidance that it emerged from these initial attacks as well as it did. It wasn't until several years later, when misguided (in my view) efforts were made to turn External Affairs from a policy-making department into a central agency, with three ministers and three deputy ministers, that real damage was done to the prestige of the department and the morale of its officials.

Those who served abroad as ambassadors, high commissioners, and in other senior positions were as aware as Prime Minister Trudeau of the changes that had taken place as a result of the communications revolution. By the time I became secretary of state for external affairs in 1968, the long, detailed despatches over which the ambassador and his or her aides once laboured mightily were no longer in vogue. Instead, ambassadors spent a great deal of time not on dispatches but in advising visiting Canadian ministers, helping visiting Canadian businessmen, and attending a proliferation of international gatherings, which were also the result of the communications revolution. I therefore regarded the Prime Minister's comments about learning as much from newspapers as from diplomatic dispatches as superficial and unfair, and I was pleased when, after he had been in office for some time, he did not repeat them. His early comments may have served, however, to remind senior officials in External Affairs that they were not exempt from the public scrutiny and criticism that was accepted as normal by officials of other departments.

Two other developments affected the organization of External Affairs in those early years of my incumbency. One was the appointment by the Prime Minister in 1969 and 1970 of several senior officials of External Affairs as deputy ministers to other departments. This in itself was a tribute to the competence of External officials and, although it deprived the department of talent, it also opened the way for promotion of younger officers. When it happened, I recalled an off-hand comment made to me many years before by Norman Robertson, that it was a pity the government had devoted so much talent to foreign affairs and so little, relatively speaking, to federal-provincial affairs. Some of those who left later returned after seasoning, including three deputy ministers, Basil Robinson, Allan Gotlieb, and Derek Burney.

It also became necessary for the department, because of budgetary restraints at the beginning of the Trudeau regime, to reduce the number of personnel. This was done by eliminating a few smaller posts abroad and by reducing the number of personnel at most embassies and high commissions. It was a painful process, particularly for the undersecretary, who was responsible for the implementation of the cutbacks. My impression was that the department emerged leaner and trimmer and without impairment of any essential programs except, regrettably, its promotion abroad of Canada's cultural image. Cultural activity, at home and abroad, is always the first victim of such economy drives.

Before becoming secretary of state for external affairs, my experience both as official and minister had been in economic affairs – trade, foreign investment, international finance, and so forth. This proved to be useful in my new job, since Canada is far more important in economic than in political terms. I also recognized that our posts abroad should be headed by ambassadors, high commissioners, and consuls general who understood the importance of promoting Canada's economic as well as its political interests. I did not, however, believe that the Trade Commissioner Service should be absorbed into the Department of External Affairs. It was my opinion then – and still is – that trade commissioners should come under the discipline of the head of post while serving abroad, but should continue to report to the department that can provide the necessary back-up and support at home and direct contact with exporters, namely a department concerned with industry, trade, and commerce.

While secretary of state for external affairs, I found myself involved continually in external political matters – NATO, the Foreign Policy Review, the establishment of diplomatic relations with the People's Republic of China and with the Vatican, the International Commission for Control and Supervision in Vietnam, general policy on external aid, Biafra and Nigeria, Canadian activities in the United Nations, disarmament, nuclear non-proliferation, and official visits to many countries, to name a few. Whatever the Prime Minister or others thought about the redundancy of ambassadors or other officials with experience in the conduct of Canadian external affairs, I could not have got along without them. I needed a department that concentrated its efforts on defending and promoting Canadian external political and economic interests and that had competent officials at home and abroad to help me reach sensible decisions and to see that they were put into effect.

The Foreign Policy Review

Prime Minister Pearson and Paul Martin, his secretary of state for external affairs, had authorized a review of foreign policy before they left office and, when Trudeau and I succeeded them, the Department of External Affairs produced the resulting report, prepared by Norman Robertson, a former under-secretary of state for external affairs who was widely regarded as the foremost mandarin of his day. Trudeau rejected it as inadequate. He wanted a fundamental review that examined even such far-out alternatives for Canada as neutrality and non-alignment.

The review proceeded along two lines: one, which took precedence, centring on the North Atlantic Treaty Organization (NATO); the other consisting of a series of papers, prepared by officials of External Affairs in consultation with officials in other interested departments. These papers were eventually approved by the government and published under the general title *Foreign Policy for Canadians*.

Although officials were involved, the debate within cabinet about NATO centred on the differing views of ministers, some of whom – especially Marchand, Pelletier, Macdonald, and Kierans – wanted Canada to withdraw from NATO or, if that was not acceptable, at least to bring back our troops from Europe. The Prime Minister presided over the debate, which took place at the outset in the Priorities and Planning Committee and, at the end, in the full cabinet. Trudeau cross-examined, raised questions, and challenged officials and officers of the Armed Forces to defend their opinions, but kept his counsel. I am uncertain to this day what policy Trudeau would personally have preferred at that point in time. All he made clear was his determination not to be satisfied with the conventional wisdom and to shake up the establishment.

The debate in cabinet committee went on for weeks. We examined and rejected all the alternatives to membership in NATO, such as neutrality, non-alignment, and a defence arrangement with the United States alone. These alternatives being rejected, a continuation of membership in NATO seemed to be accepted and the debate shifted to the extent of our participation. Should we have troops in Europe and, if so, how many?

The NATO decision

The Prime Minister gave notice that the cabinet would meet over the weekend of 26 March and reach a decision. Defence minister Léo Cadieux and I, and our principal officials, met in my office to prepare for the discussion. We recognized that it would be virtually impossible to convince our colleagues to increase defence expenditures by the hundreds of millions of dollars necessary to equip for the tasks assigned to them the 10,000 men in our NATO contingent in Europe. We were reconciled to a substantial reduction. We also shared the views of many of our colleagues that the revival and prosperity of European members of the Alliance justified reconsidering of the size of the Canadian contingent.

In the midst of the discussion in my office, the agenda for the forthcoming meeting was delivered and included an item unfamiliar to either the minister of national defence or myself. We were puzzled and curious. Our curiosity was satisfied within a few minutes by the delivery of a document accompanied by a covering note to the effect that it was being distributed at the Prime Minister's request. I glanced at it to discover that it was a paper on defence policy. I turned it over to my cabinet colleague, Cadieux, and asked him not to resign immediately, that I would try to get in touch with the Prime Minister. Fortunately, I was able to do so by telephone. Did the distribution by the Prime Minister of this paper on defence mean that he had lost confidence in the minister of national defence? Trudeau protested that that was not the intention. He thought the paper was interesting for his colleagues to read, and that was his only purpose in distributing it. In view of my concerns however, he would withdraw it, which he did. It was never referred to in cabinet committee or in cabinet, although of course it was probably read by most of our colleagues. The Prime Minister did not tell me who had prepared the paper and I did not enquire. Later we learned that it was proposed by Ivan Head, who was then a foreign-policy adviser to the Prime Minister, and a group of senior officials seconded to the Privy Council Office. Later still I learned that the draftsman of the paper was Hume Wright.

An external affairs minister cannot be expected to be happy about the presence of a foreign-policy adviser in the Prime Minister's Office. I wasn't happy, nor was my department. I had no reason to complain, however, about Ivan Head's conduct. When he undertook missions abroad on behalf of the Prime Minister he spoke to me in advance and reported on his return. Head's greatest contribution was the drafting of Trudeau's speeches on foreign affairs, notably the Mansion House speech on the needs of the Third World. Eloquent as those speeches were, they did more to enhance the reputation of the Prime Minister than to influence the content of Canadian foreign policy.

Announcement of the NATO decision

The decision reached at that weekend meeting was to stay in NATO with troops in Europe, but to reduce the numbers. (Eventually a 50 per cent reduction was approved.) The minister of national defence and I had no difficulty in accepting this outcome of the review, which was about what we had expected; however, we strongly opposed announcing the full decision immediately. We requested time to consult with our allies and explain why we were reducing the size of our European contingent. Otherwise, we pointed out, our action might be interpreted as supporting the position of U.S. Senator Mansfield, who favoured withdrawing American troops from Europe. We failed to convince the Prime Minister, who felt that after the long weeks of discussion we could not avoid indicating publicly some change in our participation in NATO.

As Léo Cadieux and I had predicted, the governments of our allies in the United States and Europe were very angry at the way in which we had handled the announcement. The size of our contingent in Europe was not particularly important. What mattered was the strength of our commitment to the Alliance. Why hadn't we consulted in advance about the reduction in the number of our troops in Europe so as to minimize any damage to the Alliance?

The mishandling of the NATO decision had unfortunate repercussions for years on relations between Canada and our allies in Europe and the United States.

The Prime Minister himself discovered this when he sought to establish a contractual link with the European Economic Community (EEC) for economic purposes and eventually became one of the staunchest defenders of our continuing participation in NATO. From what I heard from contacts in Europe and the United States, the mishandling of the NATO decision in the early 1970s was one of the things that affected adversely the reception in the western world of Trudeau's peace initiative in the early 1980s, ten years later.

My experience as secretary of state for external affairs confirmed my view that membership in NATO suited Canada. That is why the Canadian government supported the formation of the organization in 1949 and succeeded in including reference in the treaty to the importance of economic cooperation. Within NATO we could call upon our European allies to counterbalance the enormous power of our friendly neighbour, the United States, and could call upon the United States when we sought to influence the policies of our Western European allies. In other words, within NATO we were better able to defend both our territory and our economic and political interests than if we had been isolated in our defence relations with either the United States or Europe. I was happy, and so I think were most Canadians, that we stayed in NATO with troops in Europe as part of the containment of the Soviet threat until the cold war came to an end.

In my opinion it would have been extremely damaging to Canada's interests and international reputation if we had withdrawn all our troops from Europe or, worse still, had withdrawn from NATO. I was confident that this wouldn't occur, so I didn't at the time consider what action I would take if either withdrawal happened. I felt so strongly that I probably would have offered my resignation as foreign secretary.

Periodic meetings of the NATO foreign ministers were excellent occasions to exchange views, both formally and informally, about the state of the world. Nowhere else could we better monitor the progress of the two-track approach – deterrence and détente – of Belgian foreign minister Pierre Harmel, or assess the prospects for disarmament, or exchange the latest gossip about conditions in the Soviet Union and Eastern Europe.

The debate among the NATO foreign ministers was as well informed as any I participated in. On one such occasion I was the first speaker and had the responsibility of welcoming ministers who were appearing for the first time as representatives of their countries. I remarked on the rapid turnover of foreign ministers and concluded that I now found myself as the most senior at the table. When William Rogers, the U.S. secretary of state, spoke, he challenged, in a friendly fashion, my assertion of seniority. (I had checked the record and knew that I had been appointed a short time before Rogers.) When it came his turn, Sir Alec Douglas-Home said that he didn't want to intervene between Canada and the United States, but 'did resurrections count?' It was his second term as Britain's foreign minister. In between, he had been prime minister.

It was one of the personal rewards of Canada's membership in NATO that, after a meeting of the foreign ministers in Brussels, I was flown to London to attend a party given by Prime Minister Edward Heath, a dinner at 10 Downing Street to celebrate Sir Alec's birthday. It was a magnificent occasion, a gathering of Britain's political élite. It was typical of Mr Heath, a fine musician, that instead of having grace said by the Archbishop of Canterbury, who was present, he had a choir appear at the end of the room to sing grace both before and after the meal.

'Foreign Policy for Canadians'

Never before 1968 had any Canadian government tried to express Canadian foreign policy in a single set of public documents. Until then, the content of Canadian foreign policy was to be found in ministerial speeches, in occasional documents, in the annual reports of the Department of External Affairs, and in papers and books written by academics. Nor, until then, had any Canadian government tried to place foreign policy within a consistent framework of Canadian interests and objectives. Foreign offices in other countries were astonished at our rashness.

At the time, I had some doubts about the value of publishing *Foreign Policy for Canadians*. Of necessity, it was full of generalities and was bound to raise controversy. Mr Pearson looked upon these papers as an attack on his record. Yet, many years later, when the Mulroney government undertook the same initiative, I came to realize how thorough our review had been in the early 1970s and how relatively clear and precise had been the descriptions of our policy, both the overall policy and the policies in relation to Europe, Latin America, foreign aid, the United Nations, and the Pacific, the subjects of the subsidiary pamphlets. So quickly did the world change that it wasn't long, however, before these papers became outdated and largely irrelevant.

The main criticism of *Foreign Policy for Canadians* was that it did not include a separate pamphlet on relations with the United States – rather like *Hamlet* without the Prince of Denmark. This was not an oversight. We had concluded, perhaps wrongly, that so pervasive were Canadian relations with the United States that the main paper was to a very large extent a discussion of Canada's relations with our southern neighbour.

Which Reminds Me ...

So let me digress to describe the nature of our relationship with the United States and my personal experience in negotiating on behalf of Canada with that great and powerful neighbour.

The special relationship with the United States

For about a quarter of a century, from the end of the Second World War until 1971, there was a so-called special relationship in economic matters between the governments of Canada and the United States. It was not a preferential relationship in any discriminatory sense, and it was never defined in any official document that I am aware of.

I observed the relationship in action when I was a civil servant and I operated within its framework as a minister. On the U.S. side, it consisted of an intelligent and self-interested consideration of Canadian needs. In so doing, the Americans were not being kind; they were acting in their own interests, which usually but not always coincided with our economic interests.

On the institutional side, one aspect of the relationship was the establishment in 1953 of the Canada–United States Joint Cabinet Committee on Trade and Economic Affairs, consisting of leading ministers on the Canadian side and leading secretaries on the U.S. side. The idea behind the Joint Committee was to try to anticipate problems in Canada-U.S. economic relations and, by informal consultations among top-ranking cabinet members, prevent them from becoming serious. The Joint Committee was not intended to be a negotiating forum and made no decisions. For a time it worked quite well, but eventually, as with so many similar institutions, the informal exchange of views was replaced by prepared statements by the two sides of their respective positions. More time was spent in approving the communiqué to be issued at the conclusion of the meeting than in discussing the outstanding issues between our two countries. The committee was eventually replaced by other forms of consultation.

Until I resigned from the public service in 1958, I accompanied the minister of trade and commerce to meetings of the Joint Committee (see page 70). From 1963 on I attended as minister.

When the Pearson government took office in 1963, it was decided to revive the committee, which had fallen into disuse. We met in Ottawa on 29–30 April 1964, the U.S. secretaries led by Dean Rusk, the secretary of state, and the Canadian ministers by Paul Martin, the secretary of state for external affairs. Prime Minister Pearson gave a dinner in honour of the visiting U.S. secretaries and made a speech in which he said that he had received a report from his colleagues about what had gone on at the meeting. It reminded him, he said, of a report of a murder that had appeared in the *News of the World*, a London weekly paper specializing in sex and crime. The news item included the report of the police constable involved: 'I found the young woman's body on 'ampstead 'eath. It was decapitated, dismembered, but not interfered with.' Addressing the U.S. secretaries, the Prime Minister concluded: 'You can decapitate us, dismember us, but don't interfere with us.'

The term 'special relationship' recognized the extensive and close ties between the Canadian and U.S. economies, unmatched anywhere else in the world in relations between independent countries. Consequently, the effect of U.S. economic policies upon Canada was far greater than upon any other country. Moreover, it was extremely difficult for the United States to apply restrictions on trade and investment transactions across the border that did not have adverse effects upon U.S. exports to Canada and upon U.S.-owned corporations, directly or indirectly. In other words, the United States was not likely to be able to improve its general economic position at the expense of Canada.

That was the line of argument that I employed and that other Canadian officials employed, with good results on several occasions when the U.S. government experienced balance of payments problems and began taking defensive action.

In the middle of 1963, just after the Pearson government had taken office, the secretary of the Treasury, Douglas Dillon, announced the Interest Equalization Tax on U.S. loan capital placed abroad. Because of our heavy dependence upon imports of capital, Canadian financial circles reacted with shocked surprise, quickly followed by serious weakness in the market. Canadian official reserves of gold and foreign exchange experienced a rapid and substantial decline. A team of senior Canadian officials went immediately to Washington. As a result of their discussions, a joint announcement was made that new issues of long-term Canadian securities in the United States would be exempted from the tax. That crisis was ended.

The basis on which my associates and I successfully argued for the exemption was twofold: first, Canadian borrowings did not contribute to the U.S. balance-of-payments deficit, and second, there would be no net gain to the United States from reducing them. Our government agreed that Canada would not make use of the exemption to a greater extent than was necessary to meet the current-account deficit. In other words, we wouldn't use the exemption to build up our exchange reserves.

During that period of concern by the United States about its balance of payments, which lasted some years, other measures were taken that would have had serious effects upon Canada if they had been applied in full. I was minister of finance for part of this period and spent a good deal of time talking to my counterpart, Henry Fowler, the secretary of the Treasury. I think I persuaded him that to apply the guidelines and other restrictive measures to Canada would be at least discomforting to the United States and very detrimental to the continued expansion of the Canadian economy.

The formal ending in 1971 of the 'special relationship' between Canada and the United States by Secretary Connally's tax on imports from Canada for a time altered the vocabulary of discourse between our two countries. For example, when President Nixon addressed Parliament on 14 April 1972, he said:

> Our policy toward Canada reflects the new approach that we are taking in all of our foreign relations, an approach which has been called the Nixon Doctrine. That doctrine rests on the premise that mature partners must have autonomous independent policies; each nation must define the nature of its own interests; each nation must decide the requirements of its own security; each nation must determine the path of its own progress. What we seek is a policy which enables us to share international responsibilities in a spirit of international partnership. We believe that the spirit of partnership is strongest when partners are self-reliant. For among nations, as within nations, the soundest unity is that which respects diversity, and the strongest cohesion is that which rejects coercion ...
>
> Our economies have become highly interdependent. But the fact of our mutual interdependence and our mutual desire for independence need not be inconsistent traits. No self-respecting nation can or should accept the proposition that it should always be economically dependent upon any other nation. Let us recognize once and for all that the only basis for a sound and healthy relationship between our two proud peoples is to find a pattern of economic interaction which is beneficial to both our countries and which respects Canada's right to chart its own economic course ...

Substantially, the relationship did not change, although we described it differently. Our economic ties were extensive and extremely close. It did change, however, when the Free Trade Agreement between Canada and the United States came into effect at the beginning of 1989. Thereafter, economic relations between Canada and the United States were governed not by understandings but by enforceable rules that were different from the rules that governed relations between Canada and any other country. We became part of a North American trading bloc in a world of regional trading blocs. Our relationship, economic and political, became very special indeed, to my regret.

Negotiating with the United States

I used to claim that over the years I had negotiated more with the U.S. administration than any other living Canadian. Not more successfully, mind you. I don't know how to measure success. With the aid of colleagues and officials, I simply did the best I could.

From my first contacts – nearly a half a century ago, when as an official I met an assistant to President Eisenhower to work out a deal to avoid the imposition by the United States of restrictions on imports of feed grains from Canada – I became aware of the crucial differences between the constitutions of our two countries. When negotiating either as an official or as a minister, I was authorized to speak on behalf of the Canadian government. Under our system, the Canadian government could, in most circumstances, assume parliamentary approval of the government's undertakings if that became necessary. My U.S. counterpart could speak with much less authority and, in particular, could not assure Canada that changes in the law, if these were necessary, would be approved by the Congress. All he could promise were his best efforts.

When I became secretary of state for external affairs in 1968, and with my approval, the Canadian Government dealt directly with the U.S. government; that is, the Canadian ambassador in Washington was instructed to make his representations to the secretary of state, leaving the U.S. administration to deal with the Congress.

After I had left that office in 1974, it became evident – the failure of the U.S. Congress to approve the East Coast Fisheries Agreement signed in 1978 with Canada was the best evidence – that where Canadian interests are at stake, the Canadian government is well advised to lobby the Congress as well as the administration. So far as I am aware, however, we have never lobbied the Congress against the wishes of the administration.

As an official and later as a minister, I led several delegations to Washington to protest U.S. giveaway programs for surplus grain under Public Law 480 that threatened commercial markets for Canadian grains. I recall one when the secretary of agriculture, Ezra Benson, honoured and surprised the delegation of eight Canadian officials by sweeping into the room where we were meeting our U.S. counterparts and delivering a prepared address from a podium on United States-Canada relations, concluding with the assertion: 'Let us never forget that we have a common ancestor, dear old England.' As a Canadian of Scottish origin I bit my tongue.

I learned from that experience that when domestic politics are concerned, such as the cultivation of the farm vote, the U.S. administration listens politely to our complaints but places them well down the list of their primary concerns. They are only likely to respond positively if they are seeking our cooperation and support in some other area, and we do well on such occasions to use such linkages to the limit to protect our interests. And it doesn't always work.

As minister, I engaged in that most remarkable – bizarre may be a more appropriate word – series of negotiations relating to the movement of Canadian petroleum across the border. In the United States, restrictions on imports of petroleum were imposed in 1959, in order to protect the domestic industry. The restrictions were quantitative and global, but for several years the Canada-U.S. border remained open – the so-called overland exemption – not only out of respect for the special relationship that existed between our two countries, but also because U.S. oil refineries located close to the border in the northwest depended on imports from Canada.

The resulting array of forces was this: the U.S. government wanted us, in return for maintaining an open border, to continue to import petroleum into eastern Canada from Venezuela (thus compensating that country for being subject to import controls into the United States) and to hold our exports of petroleum from western Canada to minimum levels; the U.S. northern border refineries wanted continued, unlimited acccess to Canadian oil; Canada wanted to export as much oil as possible to the United States, but the government was aware of the danger of the application of formal import restrictions by the United States if we were too successful.

For a number of years, by continuous consultation and mutual understanding between the two governments, the border was kept open. Our oil exports, although restrained by informal arrangements with exporters, increased steadily. Finally, in 1970, under pressure from other foreign suppliers and believing that its northern border refineries were less dependent on Canadian supplies than previously, as a result of the completion of a new pipeline serving the Chicago area, the United States, lowered the boom and applied formal restrictions on imports from Canada. Within a short time there was a sudden reversal of policy on both sides of the border. Consequent upon the emergence of the energy crisis in the early 1970s, the United States wanted all the oil it could obtain from Canada. We, on the contrary, became alarmed about the adequacy of our reserves to meet domestic requirements and applied strict limits on exports. 'Bizarre' is the right word to describe the negotiations.

In oil, grain, and finance, American policy making was delicate, complicated, and, naturally, self-interested. All these nuances were of great and prolonged concerned to me as minister, and to our government in general.

In the United States it was different. Relations with Canada are seldom at the forefront of American concerns, either of the administration, the Congress, or the public. On the other hand, relations with the United States are invariably at the forefront of Canadian concerns, of the government, Parliament, and the Canadian public. This imbalance has many implications, not least in the choice of methods for pursuing Canadian objectives.

Should we employ quiet diplomacy or make our views known publicly and loudly? Noisy complaints and representations by ministers made headlines in Canada and gratified those who had a grievance or an interest. We were lucky if they were mentioned somewhere in the back pages of the *New York Times.*

The fundamental reason why, over time, Canadian governments preferred to pursue their objectives more quietly, with less fanfare, was that results were better. Since we are looked upon as a friendly neighbour, non-threatening and seldom a cause of trouble, our requests received sympathetic consideration. It wasn't heroic stuff, but it reflected pretty well the attitude of Canadians towards the United States. Canadians want to be as independent as possible, but we also recognize the value of living alongside the richest and most powerful nation in the world.

The signing of the Free Trade Agreement changed the nature of the relationship, which has become much more formal. From now on, when Canada has a grievance against U.S. trade actions, the protest will usually take the form of an appeal to the Americans to adhere to the terms of the agreement, an appeal that will be made publicly to satisfy those who claim to have been injured by the American action. How the Americans respond will depend only partly on the efficacy of the dispute-settlement mechanism – although this should be helpful. It will also, as has always been the case, be influenced by the political clout of the interests that are arrayed against us. My experience leads me to predict that in order to protect our interests under the FTA Canadians will have to learn to be as outspoken, aggressive, and litigious as those on the other side of the border; in other words to become Americanized.

The Third Option

Curiously, the biggest change in our approach to foreign policy came about not as a result of the Foreign Policy Review or *Foreign Policy for Canadians*. It occurred, instead, when the U.S. government decided to bring its continuing foreign-exchange crisis under control.

As I mentioned earlier, the decision in 1971 of John Connally, U.S. secretary of the Treasury, to apply a surcharge on imports from Canada effectively ended the special relationship between our two countries. I was directed by cabinet, as secretary of state for external affairs, to undertake a special study of Canada-U.S. relations. My department prepared an inventory of outstanding economic issues between our two countries that was kept up to date and circulated among the ministers. Concurrently, arising out of a suggestion I made, Klaus Goldschlag, a senior official in External Affairs, drafted a paper discussing three options for Canada's economic policy in relation to the United States.

– Canada can seek to maintain more or less its present relationship with the United States with a minimum of policy adjustments;
– Canada can move deliberately toward closer integration with the United States;
– Canada can pursue a comprehensive, long-term strategy to develop and strengthen the Canadian economy and other aspects of its national life and in the process to reduce the present Canadian vulnerability.

This paper in its final form became known as the Third Option. It was discussed at length and over several months, in both the Priorities and Planning Committee and in cabinet, between February and its publication in the fall of 1972. Although I favoured the Third Option, I made it clear to my colleagues that its adoption as government policy would involve difficult decisions, greater Canadian control over Canadian economic activity, and improved industrial efficiency and competitiveness.

The ministers concerned with economic matters, at Finance and at Industry, Trade and commerce – and, in particular, their deputy ministers, Simon Reisman and J.F. Grandy – didn't favour showing our hand to our opponent while negotiating with the Americans. In general, they favoured a reactive, pragmatic approach; in other words, a continuation of the first option. Prime Minister Trudeau participated actively in the debate and strongly favoured publication of the Third Option paper as evidence of the determination of the government to maintain Canadian independence.

No minister or official favoured the second option, closer integration with the United States or the negotiation of a free-trade agreement with our great neighbour. Some who participated in the 1971 discussions – notably Donald Macdonald and Simon Reisman – changed their view on that issue in the late 1980s. I didn't.

I continued to be opposed to free trade with the United States and, many years later – in the late 1980s, when the Mulroney government negotiated an agreement – I spoke out against it.

My opposition to the FTA was not based on economics. I am an advocate of freer trade. I strongly supported various rounds of multilateral tariff reductions in the GATT, which played a central role in the expansion of world trade and in lowering trade barriers between Canada and the United States, thereby contributing to rising living standards in Canada. I spent a large part of my political life fighting the economic nationalists and protectionists within and outside the Liberal Party.

What I considered a deplorable error in terms of national policy was to shift from a multilateral or international approach to a continental approach, to accord better treatment to trade with the United States than to trade with Europe and Japan. Until then, we had done what we could to resist the overwhelming influence of the United States in our economy, our culture, and our politics. By entering into an exclusive free-trade agreement designed to integrate the economies of our two countries, we were not only abandoning our resistance, we were deliberately inviting ourselves to be overwhelmed.

To the proponents of the FTA who put economics first and down played the threat to Canadian independence, identity, and freedom of action, I responded by pointing out that if the primary goal of national policy is, as they contend, to ensure more and better jobs for the people who live north of the forty-ninth parallel, there is a better and more effective way than free trade to go: why did they not advocate joining the United States!

I digress. Let me return to 1971. The cabinet, after long and detailed discussion, approved the Third Option strategy.

I favoured and was authorized, as secretary of state for external affairs, to publish the paper on Canada-U.S. relations over my own signature, but not as part of *Foreign Policy for Canadians*. I did so in the publication *International Perspectives* in the fall of 1972. Whatever the purpose of this subtle differentiation may have been, the Third Option came to be accepted as government policy. Moreover, the Third Option came to be invoked enthusiastically by the government and by others to support policies that were far more nationalistic than my paper had proposed, a consequence that I deplored.

I intended the Third Option not only as an alternative to pragmatism on the one hand and integration with the United States on the other, but also as a preferred alternative to the more extreme kinds of nationalistic measures that were being advocated in some quarters at the time.

Did the Third Option succeed? For years after the publication of the options paper in October 1972, I was asked this question by journalists and university students writing essays or theses. It did succeed, I think, in prompting the government to give stronger support to national institutions like the CBC and the Canada Council, and to bilingualism, all of which helped to define and support Canadian culture and identity. On the economic side, the government did devote a good deal of effort to the promotion of overseas trade during the 1970s and 1980s. Nevertheless, the proportion of our total trade – exports and imports – that we did with the United States continued to increase. The Third Option had contemplated the adoption of policies to alter the industrial structure of Canada so as to diversify and strengthen our industries and thereby reduce our dependence upon the United States as an export market and as a source of imports. This was never really seriously attempted and, in retrospect, was probably far too difficult an undertaking for any federal government of Canada, given the crucial role of the provinces with respect both to resources and industry.

The battle of the flags

The problem of Canada's future was not confined, of course, to the temptations of the American economy. Throughout my years in political office, I also had to contend with the nationalist temptations of Quebec.

When I took office as minister of finance, one of my immediate and pressing troubling concerns had been federal-provincial financial relations, particularly with Quebec. I took office as secretary of state for external affairs in 1968 in the midst of a row with Quebec over responsibility for international relations. Both confrontations with Quebec had a common origin: surging Quebec nationalism.

The memory was still fresh of President de Gaulle's visit to Quebec when he uttered the words 'Vive le Québec libre,' the rallying cry of the separatists, from the balcony of Montreal City Hall, on 24 July 1967. When the cabinet met to decide our response, no one attempted to defend de Gaulle. I was impressed by the vehemence of the reaction of the French-speaking ministers from Quebec; Marchand, particularly, was outraged. They wanted the Prime Minister to tell de Gaulle to go home. Those English-speaking ministers who participated in the debate didn't want to go that far; a public rebuke was sufficient. De Gaulle interpreted Mr Pearson's statement that his speech had been unacceptable as meaning that he would not be welcome in Ottawa and went home without gracing us with his presence in the capital. After his visit, de Gaulle continued to wage verbal war on Canada. Unfortunately, he did more than that. From 1967 on, the French government encouraged the government of Quebec to seek international standing. The government of Quebec did not need much encouragement.

The British North America Act, which continues to be part of the Canadian Constitution, is silent as to responsibility for foreign policy and international relations, and for good reason. In 1867, responsibility for our foreign policy was located in London. We were a colony within the British Empire. In Britain, responsibility for foreign policy and international relations resides in the Crown. It is generally accepted that, when Canada became independent, responsibility for foreign policy and international relations resided in the Crown in the right of Canada, that is, in the federal government. There was no challenge to this assertion at any of the many federal-provincial negotiations on the Constitution. Nor, until the middle of the 1960s, was there any serious conflict between the federal and provincial governments in this area. Until then no province, not even Quebec, asserted the right to negotiate with foreign countries with respect to matters under provincial jurisdiction or sought international recognition as a sovereign entity.

The relatively calm waters were ruffled when, on the invitation of the host government, Gabon, Quebec decided to attend a conference of ministers of education of French-speaking states, mostly in Africa, but including France. The conference was held initially in the Gabon capital, Libreville, in February 1968; a few months later, in April 1968, the session resumed in Paris. The Government of Canada sought but did not receive an invitation.

Prime Minister Pearson wrote three letters to Premier Daniel Johnson expressing his serious concerns about what was happening and making proposals for cooperation between the federal and Quebec governments so as to avoid confrontation. The only reply was a personal letter from Johnson to Pearson that arrived on the day before the minister of education of Quebec publicly announced his government's decision to attend the resumed conference in Paris on 22–26 April 1968.

Premier Johnson was received by General de Gaulle in Paris in 1967 as if he were the head of government of a sovereign country. The Government of France treated the Maison du Québec as if it were an embassy. The Canadian ambassador, Jules Léger, was snubbed. There was a steady parade of French officials to Quebec City.

All of this was happening in the midst of federal-provincial negotiations on the Constitution. The government took advantage of the coincidence to issue two booklets in early 1968, one under Prime Minister Pearson's name, *Federalism for the Future*, which included references to foreign policy and international relations, and the other under the name of foreign secretary Paul Martin, *Federalism and International Relations*, which dealt in specific detail with the subject.

Quebec's participation in the conference of ministers of education of French-speaking states in Libreville and Paris led me, shortly after I became foreign secretary, to issue a supplementary booklet, *Federalism and International Conferences on Education*. The booklets issued by me and my predecessor at External were drafted by or under the direction of our deputy minister at the time, Marcel Cadieux, an ardent French Canadian who loved Canada.

I excerpt the following from the conclusions of my pamphlet:

'First – Foreign policy and foreign relations are by their nature indivisible, since no state can divide its external sovereignty.

'Second – Within the framework of Canadian foreign policy, the Federal Government seeks to protect and actively promote the interests of the provinces of all Canadians of both major linguistic groups. The Canadian Government will vigorously pursue this policy.

'Third – The policy of the Federal Government in arranging for Canadian representation in international organizations and at international meetings on education is to work closely with provincial governments to achieve balanced delegations which take full account of both federal jurisdiction in external affairs and provincial jurisdiction in relation to education ...

'Fourth – The Federal Government will work actively for the expansion of our relations with French-speaking states and for arrangements which will facilitate the participation of Canada in organizations of French-speaking states ...

These principles were to be tested at two francophone conferences. The first was a gathering of ministers of education of francophone countries in Kinshasa, now the capital of Zaire, in July 1969. The second, in Niamey, the capital of Niger, was to establish a permanent francophone organization.

The quarrel between Ottawa and Quebec was not about the substance of foreign policy, but about constitutional responsibilities for international relations. The quarrel between Canada and France related to the support by the French government of the pretensions of the Quebec government to represent the French-speaking population of Canada at international conferences.

Consequently, although as foreign secretary I strongly defended the indivisibility of foreign policy and foreign relations, it was the Prime Minister and my French-Canadian colleagues, particularly Gérard Pelletier, who bore the brunt of the 'battle of the flags' in encounters with the Quebec government and with representatives of the French government at home and abroad. Looking back, the battle was part and parcel of the constitutional negotiations that were proceeding at the same time and that came to an abrupt end when Premier Bourassa refused to sign the Victoria Charter in 1971.

The Kinshasa conference proceeded without too much trouble for our government. President Mobutu invited Canada to the conference, not Quebec. Marc Lalonde and Claude Morin worked out an ingenious arrangement whereby the Quebec delegation appeared under a plaque 'Québec-Canada,' with similar plaques for the New Brunswick and Ontario delegations.

Niamey proved to be more difficult. President Diori of Niger admitted to us that he was under pressure from the French government to invite Quebec and ignore Canada. He hoped the governments of Canada and Quebec could reach agreement on a single delegation, which they did, along the lines followed at the Kinshasa conference. Marcel Masse, who headed the Quebec delegation, did not like the Canada-Quebec agreement negotiated by Prime Minister Trudeau and Premier Bertrand (who had succeeded Daniel Johnson) and made his differences known. For three days, events in Niamey dominated the news headlines in Canada.

With de Gaulle's resignation from the French presidency in early 1969 the atmosphere improved, but there was no immediate change in the French support for Quebec government aspirations. A second conference in Niamey, designed to approve the organization of the Agence de co-opération culturelle et technique (ACCT) almost broke down over the question of the right of Quebec to membership. Pelletier, after discussion with the Prime Minister, finally agreed to a request by Quebec to be a participating government, explaining that this did not mean that Quebec had acquired any kind of external sovereignty; ultimate authority still rested in Ottawa.

The next round in the negotiations about the ACCT was in Canada in Quebec City and Ottawa in October 1971. Premier Bourassa had come to power in Quebec. He was not disposed to confrontation. I met with François Cloutier, the Quebec minister of cultural affairs, and reached agreement on procedure. Canada became a member country, Quebec a participating government, subject to the limitations that our government had insisted upon. The 'battle of the flags,' which must have appeared to most Canadians and Frenchmen as comedy rather than serious diplomacy, was over.

From the point of view of Quebec nationalists like Claude Morin, a senior adviser to the Quebec government (later a separatist), the province of Quebec made progress towards international recognition during those years. From the point of view of the Canadian government, the threat to the indivisibility of foreign policy and foreign relations had been turned aside. Giving Quebec and other provinces like New Brunswick with a substantial francophone population the opportunity to participate with the Canadian government in international conferences on matters under provincial jurisdiction, such as education, was a constructive development, encouraged by our government from the outset.

These events also coincided with and helped to bring about a change in the destination of Canadian foreign aid that better reflected the bilingual nature of Canada. Our foreign-aid program originated at the end of the war in the Commonwealth. For many years, the principal recipients were the countries in the Indian subcontinent, India, Pakistan, and Ceylon. In Africa, the principal recipients were former British colonies. During the late 1960s the emphasis shifted to former French and Belgian colonies, so that during my time at External Affairs there was an approximately equal split in the amount of Canadian foreign aid to English-speaking and French-speaking African countries. Quebec suppliers and teachers found it easier to participate in the Canadian aid program when that program included French-speaking countries. It is ironic that Paul Gérin-Lajoie, who as a Quebec minister expounded the Quebec case for the right to enter into relations with foreign countries on matters under provincial jurisdiction, was appointed to head the Canadian International Development Agency, which distributed foreign aid.

By 1970, relations between Canada and France were on the mend from their state of disrepair during the de Gaulle era. As part of the effort to strengthen the Canadian presence in Paris, a Centre culturel for the display of Canadian works of art, the playing of Canadian music, and the performance of Canadian musicians was constructed as an annex to the embassy. I went to Paris in April 1970 to make a speech at the formal opening.

This was not an official trip to Paris and I was, therefore, pleased and grateful when the French foreign minister, Maurice Schuman, greeted me on my arrival at the airport and gave me a lunch at the Quai d'Orsay.

Following lunch, he invited me to his office to see an inkwell that had once been used by Talleyrand, generally regarded as the first great practitioner of diplomacy. While I was looking at this historic piece, he said that his real purpose was to tell me privately that President Pompidou was determined to have better relations with Canada. And relations did continue to improve.

My next official visit to France was to attend de Gaulle's memorial service in Notre-Dame on 12 November 1970. It was a solemn and spectacular affair. De Gaulle's passing was the occasion; the purpose, I thought at the time, was to celebrate the glory of France in the presence of world leaders: kings and queens, presidents, prime ministers, princes of the church. The French do these things superbly well!

Although the larger provinces had established offices abroad, this practice did not raise concerns for our government. With the exception of the Maison du Québec in Paris, none of these provincial offices pretended to have representational or diplomatic functions. Their purpose was to promote exports of local products and tourism and to encourage foreign investment. As a deputy minister of trade and commerce and later as minister I organized and chaired federal-provincial meetings to coordinate activities of both levels of government at home and abroad.

Although many of the provincial offices were located in the United States there was none in Washington. Early in 1971, Premier Lougheed had hinted at establishing an Alberta office in that city to gather information, particularly about U.S. energy policy. This caused me concern, which was reinforced when Premier Davis announced in October 1971 that Ontario intended to do the same thing. In his press conference, Davis said that the proposed office would try to correct the U.S. government's ignorance of Ontario's economic problems and would seek and promote provincial interests in these matters.

I met with Davis and drew attention to the possibility of confusion and misunderstanding within the U.S. government if there were two spokesmen for Canada. They might play off the one against the other, from which both would suffer. I offered to attach an Ontario official to the Canadian embassy. Davis was attracted to the idea. In subsequent discussions at the official level, the Ontario government representative, Ian Macdonald, expressed misgivings about both the idea of an Ontario office in Washington and an Ontario official in the embassy. Instead, we strengthened our embassy staff by assigning an official with specific responsibility for determining and meeting Ontario needs for information. The same offer was made to any province that wanted it. During the 1971 provincial electoral campaign, and in the midst of the energy crisis, Premier Lougheed threatened to establish an independent source of information in Washington. But as the energy crisis disappeared, so did his pressure for a Washington office.

The FLQ crisis

During the morning of 5 October 1970, the chief of police of Montreal called to inform me of the kidnapping of James Cross, the British trade commissioner in Montreal. At first, I didn't believe the report; things like that didn't happen in Canada. But, shortly thereafter, the Front de Libération du Québec (FLQ) claimed credit and published their communiqué demanding, among other things, a ransom of $500,000 in gold, the freeing of more than twenty so-called political prisoners, and safe transport to Cuba or Algeria in return for freeing the British diplomat.

The British prime minister wrote to Trudeau saying that his government had 'the fullest confidence that the Canadian authorities in the exercise of their authority for the safety of Mr. Cross, will take every possible step to secure his release unharmed.'

As secretary of state for external affairs I had primary responsibility to the British government for the safety of Cross. I requested the Prime Minister to raise the matter at a meeting of the Priorities and Planning Committee to be held the next day. That meeting was inconclusive. There were suggestions that nothing need be done; that in effect the abductors were bluffing and only seeking publicity for the FLQ and would in due course release Cross. Some were not averse to paying a ransom. So I asked the Prime Minister to call a meeting of the full cabinet. Naturally, he asked me what would happen in cabinet that was different from what had happened in committee. I replied that this time I would put before cabinet the terms of a public announcement I would like to make. Did I have any objection, the PM enquired, if he asked the secretary to the cabinet, Gordon Robertson, to try his hand at an announcement? I had no objection.

Gordon Robertson is an elegant draftsman. After consideration, however, cabinet, which met in the afternoon, set aside elegance in favour of my shorter and simpler version, which my officials had helped me to draft during lunchtime. I delivered the announcement to television cameras in English and in French in reply to the demands of the kidnappers, including the following sentences: 'Clearly, these are wholly unreasonable demands and their authors could not have expected them to be accepted. I need hardly say that this set of demands will not be met. I continue, however, to hope that some basis can be found for Mr. Cross's safe return. Indeed, I hope the abductors will find a way to establish communication to achieve this end.'

I include these words from the announcement because they proved to be the key to the release of Cross. While the kidnappers' blackmail was rejected, the underlying message was that there might be terms that we could accept, including transport to Cuba. During the following week I made statements to the media along the same lines, which the kidnappers heard. Meanwhile, my department had cleared the way for the abductors to be accepted by Cuba if that became the outcome.

The kidnappers had included among their demands for Cross's release press and television publicity for a so-called political manifesto of the FLQ. The CBC came to me and offered their services if I decided that the contents of the manifesto should be read on television. This led me to read the manifesto. It was a lurid attack on existing institutions that made the FLQ kidnappers look like a bunch of wild and ignorant revolutionaries. I decided it would help the government if the people of Canada heard what the FLQ stood for and would not harm the negotiations for Cross' release. So I arranged with the CBC to have two of their experienced announcers read the manifesto in a flat monotone, in English and in French. The reaction from the public didn't help the FLQ. The Prime Minister, however, was angry when he heard what I had authorized the CBC to do. He thought I was succumbing to the FLQ blackmail. But he did not interfere.

On Saturday morning, 10 October, I telephoned from home to the minister of justice of Quebec, Jérôme Choquette, to tell him that I did not intend to make any further statements on the subject, that by now the FLQ kidnappers should know what we wanted them to do. Choquette, who had been the spokesman for the Bourassa government, said that he, too, had nothing more to say. A short time later the same morning, however, he telephoned me to say that, on advice from people who claimed to understand the FLQ, he had changed his mind and intended to give a press conference at 5:00 p.m. that day in which he would announce a new policy on behalf of the Quebec government. I asked him what he intended to say and he read me a long excerpt in French. I understood enough to be alarmed and asked him to put the proposed text on the teletype to my office. Meanwhile, I phoned my under-secretary, Ed Ritchie, to ask him and his team to meet me in the Operations Centre that had been established in the East Block of the Parliament Buildings.

When we read Choquette's proposed statement we were dismayed. He proposed saying that the government of Quebec was prepared in effect to release certain 'political prisoners,' FLQ sympathizers who had been found guilty of violent crimes, as had been demanded by the kidnappers in their communiqué.

Since Choquette had announced his press conference for 5:00 p.m. that day there was no point in asking him not to say anything, so we attempted a redraft of his proposed statement, eliminating the things with which we disagreed, and sent it on to the Quebec minister by teletype. Meanwhile, I had informed the Prime Minister of what was happening and obtained Trudeau's approval to tell Choquette that if he made his original statement I would dissociate the federal government from it. Choquette's first response to our redraft was to say that he did not accept the changes and intended to make his statement in the original form. I told him that if he did so I would dissociate the federal government from it.

I shall never forget those next few minutes, sitting in the Operations Centre with my officials contemplating the chaos if the Quebec and federal governments were to make conflicting statements. I decided to make one last telephone call to Choquette and to ask him this simple question: if he made the statement, did he have reason to know that Cross would be released? The answer was 'no,' and that he had decided to accept our suggested changes. We breathed a collective sigh of relief. That evening, after Choquette had held his press conference, Pierre Laporte, the Quebec labour minister, was kidnapped by another FLQ cell. The Cross affair was converted into a national crisis, and the Prime Minister became the spokesman for the federal government.

Laporte was murdered a week later. It took until 2 December for the police to find Cross and his kidnappers. I was in Brussels when the arrangements were finally worked out by my officials. The kidnappers would release Cross in return for freedom to go to Cuba and thus avoid immediate prosecution in Canada. (Eventually, they all returned, were prosecuted, served jail terms, and are now free.) I was attending a meeting of NATO foreign ministers on 3 December, when the message that Cross had been released was delivered to me, and I had the pleasure of passing it across the table to the British foreign secretary, Sir Alec Douglas-Home. As soon as the Brussels meeting had ended, I flew to London and greeted Cross on behalf of the Canadian government as he descended from his plane on 6 December.

Canada's handling of the Cross affair earned high marks not only in Britain but throughout the world. We did not give in to blackmail or panic. As the minister in charge, I give full credit for the safe delivery of the British diplomat to my officials, whose advice was invaluable. A particularly notable role was played by Claude Roquet, who later joined the Quebec public service, who planned and executed the dramatic exchange of Cross for temporary freedom for the kidnappers, and Orme Dier, who handled the matter insofar as the Cuban government was concerned. Both accompanied the kidnappers on the flight to Cuba.

The War Measures Act

The kidnapping of Cross by the FLQ was a profoundly disturbing event for Canadians. The kidnapping of Laporte by another cell of the FLQ produced trauma. The support that was given to the FLQ by labour leaders in Quebec at big public gatherings created the impression of a widespread movement favouring terrorist activities. Finally came the first bloodshed, the murder of Laporte.

Like my cabinet colleagues, I was conscious of growing public concern, bordering on panic, in certain places in Quebec and eastern Ontario. Something had to be done to restore public confidence. Ours was not a government of ministers that favoured resort to force to deal with public disorder. Indeed, there has probably never been a government that included more committed defenders of civil rights – Trudeau, Pelletier, Marchand, Macdonald, Turner, MacEachen, to name only a few. I had never had occasion to express publicly my views on civil rights, but when I lived in Winnipeg I associated myself in 1940 with the committee that defended local Italian-Canadians who were interned under the War Measures Act.

Confirmation of the extent of public concern arrived within a few days. First came the request of the Quebec justice minister, Jérôme Choquette, made under Part II of the National Defence Act, for Canadian armed forces to aid the civil power, to assist Quebec police in the protection of persons and property.

On 16 October, at 3:00 a.m. came an expected letter from Premier

Robert Bourassa of Quebec (there had been close consultation between Ottawa and Quebec City for several days): 'I request that emergency powers be provided as soon as possible so that more effective steps may be taken ... we are facing a concerted effort to intimidate and overthrow the government and the democratic institutions ... through a planned and systematic illegal action, including insurrection.'

At about the same time a letter from Jean Drapeau, mayor of Montreal, and Lucien Saulnier, chairman of the executive committee of the Montreal City Council, requested urgent aid: 'the assistance of higher levels of government has become essential for the protection of society against the seditious plot and the apprehended insurrection of which the recent kidnappings were the first steps.'

Several thousand Canadian troops were sent to Quebec as requested by the Quebec minister of justice.

The only legislation available to the federal government to deal with this kind of civil disorder was the War Measures Act, which could be brought into effect to authorize emergency action to cope with an apprehended insurrection. All of us in cabinet regretted that there was nothing more appropriate for peacetime emergencies. But there wasn't. So, reluctantly, after long discussion, we took the plunge.

At 4:00 a.m. on October 16, 1970, two Orders in Council were approved by the cabinet, one proclaiming the War Measures Act, the other establishing public-order regulations that authorized the Quebec police to arrest and detain persons suspected of subversive activity.

The following day Trudeau tabled the proclamation and the regulations and submitted a resolution requesting the support of the House of Commons for the government's actions. After two days of debate the resolution was approved by a vote of 190 to 16.

This was the sequence of events. Had we know what we now know about the limited extent of the FLQ operations, our government, the Quebec government, and the City of Montreal would undoubtedly have acted differently. But at that time we did not know, the RCMP did not know, and the Quebec police did not know. Ignorant as we were about the extent of the threat, we had to react to ominous appearances that included not only the kidnappings and the murder of Laporte, but also the series of previous terrorist acts by FLQ sympathizers that began in the early 1960s. One of the more extreme reactions in Ottawa to events was the attempt by an official in the PM's office to develop a scenario of the likely course of a revolutionary movement and how to deal with it, illustrated by coloured charts. I was bemused.

It was a rough time. All those involved wished that it hadn't happened. Those who were arrested and detained by the Quebec police had a grievance. Yet, in the end, when the kidnappers and the murderers had been brought to justice, there was no more terrorism.

In some respects, it was the Prime Minister's finest hour when he appeared on television on 16 October. 'This government is not acting out of fear. It is acting to prevent fear from spreading. It is acting to maintain the rule of law without which freedom is impossible.' On this point Trudeau spoke for us all.

The Canadian International Development Agency and the International Development Research Centre

My first contact with foreign aid came when Canada joined the Colombo Plan as a founding member in 1950 and the administrator of the Canadian Aid Program, Nik Cavell – with long experience in India – reported to me as associate deputy minister of trade and commerce. By the time I became secretary of state for external affairs and again had responsibility in this field, Canadian external aid, originally centred on Commonwealth countries in South and Southeast Asia within the Colombo Plan, had expanded from a $12.42-million to a nearly $300-million program of development assistance to Third World countries within and outside the Commonwealth. The program was under the administration of the Canadian International Development Agency (CIDA), which came into existence shortly after I took office as foreign secretary and reported to me.

Before entering politics in 1962, I had been the first chairman of the Canadian Freedom from Hunger campaign and in a series of speeches across the country had discussed foreign aid. We should be prepared to help less-developed countries to overcome poverty, I argued, not primarily because of the resulting trade benefits for Canada or because this would help reduce the spread of Communism, but simply because we are rich and they are poor. There might be incidental benefits to Canada in terms of economics and security. The underlying reason for providing foreign aid, I contended, is the same one that motivates Canadians to try to eradicate poverty and alleviate distress in Canada.

Those who have participated in campaigns to raise money for charitable purposes learn that needs far outstrip resources. Particularly is this true of campaigns to help the world's poor.

In the midst of the Freedom from Hunger campaign I was approached by Joe Hulse, then director of research for Maple Leaf Mills in Toronto. Would we be prepared to sponsor a project in Mysore,

India, for the training of food technologists? My immediate response was to say that I did not think the Freedom from Hunger campaign could raise the millions of dollars that would be required. Don't worry about that, Hulse replied. All we want is your sponsorship. We in the Canadian food industry will raise the money. And so they did. So successful was the project that the United Nations Food and Agriculture Organization borrowed the services of Joe Hulse to establish similar projects in other underdeveloped countries. In due course, he himself became a vice-president of the International Development Research Centre when this was established in 1970, as I describe below.

After my years in politics, I remain of the view that idealistic considerations such as social justice and charity (in the sense of love of one's fellow human beings) make a powerful appeal to Canadians and constitute the main justification for foreign aid. When I was young, Canadians supported more foreign missionaries proportional to population than any other country. As a Sunday school teacher in the 1920s I used to encourage the boys in my class to put their five cents in the collection plate rather than spend it on candy by telling them that their five cents would buy a whole meal for some poor child in China or India. Consequently, I was happy, on assuming office as the minister responsible for CIDA, that the government agreed to increase international development assistance, notwithstanding the policy of fiscal austerity that resulted in cutbacks in External Affairs personnel and foreign posts.

Canadian support for international development had to be mobilized so as to facilitate the approval by Parliament of the rising appropriations. This concern led to the appointment, successively, as the first and second presidents of CIDA, of two extraordinarily effective public advocates, Maurice Strong and Paul Gérin-Lajoie. Administration was neither their interest, their specialty, nor their skill. They conceived their principal responsibility as head of CIDA – and I think they were right – to be to popularize among Canadians the idea of external development assistance. They travelled and gave speeches and interviews at home and abroad as few non-elected public servants have ever done. I regret to have to add, however, that the pressure to spend – which came from the public and all political parties – had its inevitable price in terms of costs. If we had moved more slowly, we could have accomplished more by way of development assistance with the same number of dollars.

Since those years, we have learned much about international development. Some recipient countries have taken off; others are poorer than they were, notwithstanding substantial help from outside. There is less spending today and less emphasis on the quantity of assistance. More attention is given to the need for specific remedial action to deal with overwhelming problems such as drought, malnutrition, overpopulation, and environmental degradation, and there is a great deal more concern about the debt problems of the Third World.

Maurice Strong's appointment as president of CIDA was the first step in his remarkable career of public service both to Canada and to the international community. Born in a small town in Manitoba, he appeared on the Ottawa scene in the mid-1960s, sponsored by Paul Martin, with the reputation of having made a small fortune in business. He was full of ideas about how to help the people of the Third World. One of his principal contributions during my time in government was to persuade us in 1970 to create the International Development Research Centre, modelled on private organizations like the Ford and Rockefeller foundations. He became chairman of the board of directors of the centre. It was and is a unique institution. Apart from the chairman of the board and the president, who are Canadians, half of its directors are foreigners, some from the Third World. All its funds are provided by the Canadian government, and, apart from defraying administration costs, all are spent in less-developed countries to encourage local research. There are no arguments, such as arise from time to time with respect to CIDA, as to the pros and cons of tied-aid or the proportion of World Bank expenditures that are made in Canada.

The strongest supporters of foreign aid are often the strongest critics of tied-aid – aid that must be spent buying Canadian goods and services. I count myself among the strongest supporters of foreign aid, and I think there is a lot to be said, in practical terms, for the idea of providing Canadian goods and services rather than just money. Canadians who are motivated by idealistic considerations such as social justice and charity like to see a direct link with Canada with respect to at least a proportion of their aid contributions, as opposed to providing money to the World Bank to buy equipment manufactured in Germany, Japan or the United States to send to the recipient country. Nor should we discount the support for external aid that comes from those who produce the Canadian equipment or perform the services provided to the Third World.

The view from Ottawa

In all these affairs my main perspective was from behind the minister's desk in the Department of External Affairs, or from a seat around the cabinet table or a seat in the House of Commons. Or having lunch or dinner with visiting VIPs or local ambassadors, either as host or guest of honour – on the average about five meals of this kind a week. That is not, of course, how most people see a minister of external affairs. From television they get the impression of a distant figure who usually appears framed in flags and official bunting, inspecting ranks of soldiers, or shaking hands with a variety of impressive foreign figureheads.

But that was not how most of my time was spent. From NATO to the Third Option, to Quebec's foreign aspirations, to foreign aid, most of the work was done in overheated offices along familiar corridors – familiar, at least, until the Department of External Affairs moved from the East Block (as well as from offices in a number of other buildings) to new quarters in the Lester B. Pearson Building on Sussex Drive in 1973. I had the honour of escorting Her Majesty Queen Elizabeth when she officially opened the building.

Much time was also devoted to discussions with fellow Canadians who retain an active interest in the countries from which they or their parents had come: Canadians of Ukrainian origin who wanted me to support independence for Ukraine (which has been achieved); Canadian Jews who wanted me to support Israel in its quarrels with the Arab states; Canadians of Arab origin who wanted me to maintain neutrality in those quarrels; Canadians of Czechoslovak origin who wanted me to facilitate immigration from their homeland; Canadians of Baltic origin who wanted to have representation for their homeland in Ottawa, notwithstanding *de facto* incorporation in the Soviet Union (they too are now independent), and so on.

The truth is that the Canadian secretary of state for external affairs is at the very centre of 'internal affairs' – domestic politics.

CHAPTER EIGHT

Secretary of State for External Affairs, 1968–1974

II. Implementing Foreign Policy

Commonwealth summits

The most visible part of the job of foreign secretary that everyone sees is that of Canada's chief representative to the outside world. It has its pleasures – though not many – but it has its difficulties, too. Foreign policy and foreign travel appeal to other ministers besides the foreign secretary. And they often appeal to the prime minister himself.

Prime Minister Trudeau attended his first meeting of Commonwealth heads of government in London in January 1969. I went with him for the first and only time, except when the Commonwealth meeting was held in Ottawa. At the conclusion of the London meeting, I remarked to him that one of us was superfluous and I knew which one. I looked upon the Commonwealth as a useful organization but not one that plays a central role in Canadian foreign policy. I expected the Prime Minister, as a French Canadian, to be even less enthusiastic about this institution composed of former British colonies. But I was wrong. From the outset, Trudeau showed a keen interest in the discussions that took place among the heads of government and, eventually, worked hard and effectively to prevent the disintegration of the Commonwealth and to give the periodic meetings fresh impetus and direction. He found it particularly useful to have personal relations with the heads of government of Tanzania, Zambia, and Nigeria in Africa, and of Singapore, as representatives of Third World countries. I think he wanted to know how they were motivated, how they regarded the Western industrialized world, and how they intended to lead their peoples. There were periods when Trudeau was the only leader of a Western industrialized country with whom President Nyerere of Tanzania and President Kaunda of Zambia had any personal contacts. Sometimes Ivan Head travelled to see them on behalf of the Prime Minister and reported to me before going and on his return.

Diplomatic relations with the Vatican

After the close of the London Commonwealth meeting in 1969, the Prime Minister decided to go to Rome to visit the Pope and I travelled with him. On the way, he asked me if he should raise the question of the establishment of diplomatic relations between Canada and the Vatican. I supported the idea strongly and added that I thought that he should announce to the press, after his meeting with the Pope, that he had done so. In my opinion as a Protestant, I added, religious prejudice in Canada had diminished, and the time was ripe to take this long-delayed step to complete our structure of diplomatic contacts.

There were the expected questioning comments from some spokesmen for Protestant churches when news reached Canada of the Prime Minister's press conference in Rome but, as I had predicted, nothing very serious. I then advised the Prime Minister that neither of us should make any further comment publicly until we had found a suitable ambassador acceptable to the Vatican, one who, preferably, should be either a Baptist or a Methodist. The Protestant churches would expect the Canadian ambassador to the Vatican to be a Roman Catholic. They would be taken aback by the appointment of a Protestant, particularly a non-conformist, and would have to reconsider their traditional opposition.

I set about looking for a suitable candidate and luckily hit upon the name of a distinguished Canadian with whom I was acquainted when he was in charge of education statistics in the Bureau of Statistics in Ottawa – John Robbins, who was then the president of Brandon University, a Baptist college affiliated with the University of Manitoba. I telephoned him, he accepted the nomination, and his name was conveyed to the Vatican for agrément, as is customary with respect to all ambassadorial appointments.

Time passed and we had not received the name of the proposed Vatican ambassador to Canada. I sought an explanation from the Canadian cardinals and learned that the reason for the delay was that the apostolic delegate in Ottawa wanted the appointment and was busy enlisting support for his nomination. I called him in, explained to him the embarrassment caused by the delay, and said that when Parliament reassembled in two weeks I was bound to be asked a question that I could only answer by attributing the delay to the Vatican. My answer could well be interpreted as meaning that the Vatican had lost interest. He was shaken. Just before the reassembly of Parliament, he came to my office with a beaming countenance. He had been selected by the Pope as the first ambassador and sought our agrément. He was an excellent choice. When I told the Prime Minister, he was amused that a Protestant could successfully put pressure on the Vatican.

Recognition of the People's Republic of China

Included in the Liberal Party's 1968 election platform, which I helped to draft, was an undertaking to establish diplomatic relations with the People's Republic of China, 'recognizing the existence of another government on Taiwan.' We felt the time had come to recognize the effective government of the hundreds of millions of Chinese living on the mainland with whom we did so much trade, and, in particular, to whom we sold so much western wheat.

The reference to Taiwan was a hangover from the policies of the Pearson government, which had from time to time contemplated a two-government policy – recognition of the People's Republic government of mainland China and of another government having authority only on the island of Taiwan. There was, of course, at that time no such government on Taiwan. The government on Taiwan considered itself the government of the Republic of China, which had retreated from the mainland but still claimed jurisdiction over the whole of the country and included in its parliament non-resident representatives of mainland constituencies. That being so, separate recognition for Taiwan was a non-starter, equally unacceptable to the governments of the Republic of China and the People's Republic of China.

We studied the question within the department and sought approval of cabinet to open negotiations with the People's Republic, to approve the continuation of a one-China policy, and to abandon the effort to retain some sort of official recognition of a separate government on Taiwan. This departure in policy was approved, although not without difficulty and expressions of regret about the abandonment of Taiwan.

On 10 February 1969, we announced that Stockholm, where both Canada and the People's Republic of China had ambassadors, would be the site for the negotiations with Arthur Andrew, Canadian ambassador to Sweden, as the negotiator for our side. He was later succeeded by Margaret Meagher. From the outset, the Chinese laid down three conditions:

1. Canada must break relations with the 'Chiang Kai-shek gang';
2. Canada must recognize the right of the People's Republic of China to occupy the China seat in the United Nations;
3. Canada must recognize the sovereignty of the People's Republic of China over Taiwan.

On instructions, Andrew replied to the effect that Canada had a one-China policy now and intended to have a one-China policy in the future. It followed that if we established diplomatic relations with the People's Republic government we would break relations with the Republic of China government. It also followed that we would recognize the right of the People's Republic government to represent China in the United Nations. The third condition, Andrew told the Chinese ambassador, was irrelevant. We were not, in these negotiations, deciding the size of China.

For months and months, this was the substance of the negotiations, the Chinese reiterating their conditions, the Canadian ambassador reiterating our responses. At one point, Andrew suggested to his Chinese counterpart that it might be a good idea for the negotiations to adjourn until the two sides had something new to say to one another. The Chinese demurred. They wanted to go on and asked Andrew if he now understood the Chinese position, to which Andrew replied: 'I would be deaf if I didn't.'

Obviously, the negotiations revolved around the question of Taiwan. Meanwhile, in the House of Commons, there was a steady stream of questions to me from the opposition about the course of the negotiations, also centring on the question of Taiwan. To one of these I gave a spontaneous answer that provided the formula acceptable to the Chinese – namely, that while Canada did not accept the assertion by the Chinese government of its sovereignty over Taiwan, neither did we challenge it.

In the formal statement announcing the conclusion of the negotiations, we said only that Canada took note of the Chinese assertion that Taiwan is an inalienable part of the territory of the People's Republic of China. The accompanying explanation that I gave in the House of Commons had been shown in advance to the Chinese and forms part of the undertaking between the two governments. It contains these words: 'The Canadian Government does not consider it appropriate either to endorse or to challenge the Chinese Government's position on the status of Taiwan.'

The establishment of diplomatic relations between Canada and the People's Republic of China was a significant development for both countries. It is not often that Canada leads the world. Our recognition led a procession of some thirty other countries, which, very shortly thereafter, followed our example and exchanged ambassadors with the People's Republic of China, employing what came to be known as the Canadian formula about Taiwan.

I liked the ambassador from the Republic of China in Ottawa. In order to show my high regard for him personally, notwithstanding the transfer of our recognition to the People's Republic government, I invited him to have lunch with me on Monday, 12 October, the day before the official announcement on October 13. He came to my office accompanied by Ralph Collins, who was shortly to be appointed as our first ambassador to Beijing. The ambassador handed me an envelope, which, he said, contained a letter to me from his government. 'Do not read it before lunch, it will spoil your appetite.' I followed his advice and the three of us had a pleasant lunch at Madame Burger's, across the Ottawa River in Hull. There was very tight security at the site of our luncheon, not because of the presence of the Chinese ambassador but because of the FLQ Crisis, which had erupted a few days before.

Apart from an indictment of the government of the People's Republic of China and criticism of our intended recognition, the letter contained a significant statement to the effect that, from the moment Canada recognized the People's Republic of China, the Republic of China broke relations with Canada. In other words, we did not break relations with the government on Taiwan; it broke relations with us. Since the Chinese authorities had sold their residence about a year before and were leasing it from its new owners, there was no dispute about the ownership of premises hitherto occupied by the ambassador of the Republic of China; this was a great relief to all concerned in Ottawa.

I kept the U.S. secretary of state informed about the negotiations with the Chinese, and my officials did likewise with their counterparts in Washington. The U.S. administration was not pleased, which was no surprise. When I took office as secretary of state for external affairs in April 1968, Dean Rusk was just at the end of his term as secretary of state and I met him for a brief exchange of views. He told me then that, if and when the Communist government of China occupied the China seat, the United States would withdraw from the United Nations. I did not believe him, and William Rogers, who succeeded him as secretary of state, never repeated that threat to me.

Nevertheless, Rogers questioned me closely as soon as negotiations got under way as to how we would vote when the China question re-emerged in the General Assembly. I told him quite frankly that I thought we would probably want to change our vote to indicate greater sympathy for the People's Republic. Hitherto we had supported the position that the occupancy of the China seat was an 'important question' requiring a two-thirds majority to replace the Republic of China government by the People's Republic. We might want to revert to the ordinary majority rule. How could I justify the change? Rogers asked. Wasn't it still an important question? I tried an explanation that wasn't very convincing either to me or to Rogers, who expressed the hope that for the sake of our friendship he would not be around when I gave that explanation. Fortunately, it never became necessary for me to do so.

Although it took the United States another nine years to follow our example, within months after the conclusion of our negotiations, President Nixon met in Beijing with Chairman Mao. When the heads of state of two countries meet on a public occasion and exchange views, do they not recognize the authority of their respective governments?

In August 1972, I made my first visit to China, although I was not the first Canadian minister to do so after the exchange of diplomats in 1970. Jean-Luc Pepin has that distinction. While there, I officially opened the big Canadian trade exhibition in Beijing, organized by the Department of Industry, Trade and Commerce. For me, the highlight of the visit was the three hours I spent with Zhou En-lai. The Chinese prime minister opened the conversation in French, but quickly reverted to Chinese and the use of an interpreter. At the beginning, we exchanged views on a number of issues and then, seizing upon some remark I made, Zhou launched into a bitter hour-long monologue against the Soviet Union, listing China's grievances, item by item, year by year.

Much to my surprise and the surprise of my officials who, like me, had been reluctant to raise such a mundane matter with the prime minister of China, Zhou En-lai himself referred to the Ming Sung ships, originally built in Canada and delivered to the Nationalist government but still afloat. He offered to pay for them.

Thirteen years later, in 1985, I returned to China at the invitation of the Chinese government to celebrate the fifteenthth anniversary of the establishment of diplomatic relations. To my surprise and delight, I had the privilege of an interview, arranged by our ambassador, my old friend and former press officer Richard Gorham, with Li Peng, one of the rising political stars in modern China and an 'adopted son' of Zhou En-lai. (He became prime minister shortly thereafter.) I referred to my interview of thirteen years before and asked Li Peng, then deputy prime minister, about the state of relations between China and the Soviet Union today. Improved, he replied, but there will be no return to the situation that prevailed when the Soviet Union and China were allies.

What impressed me when I returned to China after an interval of thirteen years was the transformation in the appearance and conduct of the people. Mao jackets has been the universal dress in 1972. In 1985, there was colour and variety: officials who had at one time spouted the official line were prepared to discuss issues of the day freely and openly with foreigners like myself. The subsequent events in Tiananmen Square came to me as a tremendous shock and disappointment.

What a pity, it seemed to me, that economic and political freedom have not been permitted to develop concurrently. Even in 1985 it was evident that the Chinese economy was on the march, particularly in the countryside, where the farmers were taking advantage of the opportunity of selling their produce on the open market, and in the customs-free zones adjacent to Hong Kong.

Biafra

The most distressing issue I faced in my first year as secretary of state for external affairs was the attempt by Biafra to break away from the Nigerian federation and the resulting civil war. It started badly, when the Prime Minister was cornered by a group of reporters in a 'scrum'. What about Biafra? he was asked. From the moment the Prime Minister asked the rhetorical question 'Where's Biafra?,' the government appeared to be insensitive to the slaughter and to the needs of starving Biafran children. Day after day the newspapers and the television carried pitiful pictures of youngsters with bloated stomachs. There was a steady stream of questions in the House of Commons. Stanley Burke, the well-known TV personality, went on a lecture tour across Canada seeking support for Biafran relief. In conversation in my office, he supported the Biafran rebellion and he was far from alone. Canadian churches mounted dramatic relief operations. Dr Edward Johnson of the Presbyterian Church was particularly zealous.

Nowhere else in the world did the Nigerian civil war arouse such widespread public emotion as in Canada. Mark Press News Features Services, the Swiss advertising agency that handled public relations for the Biafrans, found a particularly receptive audience in this country.

The Canadian government was ready to provide humanitarian assistance throughout Nigeria, in Biafra as well as in those parts of the country under federal control. Unlike the private agencies, we had to try to do so in ways that were acceptable to the Nigerian government; otherwise Canada would appear to be supporting the Biafran rebellion. Our chosen instrument, acceptable to the Nigerian authorities, was the

International Red Cross, to which the government provided transport planes. The IRC itself encountered frustrations in its operations on both sides of the conflict. Our ambassadors and Ivan Head, who made a special trip on behalf of the Prime Minister, found there was very little support for the Biafran cause in other African countries. On one point they were agreed. They were strongly opposed to outside intervention. The Organization for African Unity put pressure on Biafra to cease its rebellion. Canadian efforts to organize a debate in the United Nations foundered because of the belief that the result would be a sterile debate on politics rather then on the need to alleviate human suffering.

All this had to be explained to Parliament and to the public, creating the impression that the government put politics ahead of human suffering. I appeared on a weekly TV program dealing on this occasion with Biafra. Unknown to me, because the questions were being asked in Ottawa and broadcast through Toronto, I was seen answering questions about complicated legal issues against a background of pictures of starving children. It was ugly, cheap journalism. Never again did I accept invitations to appear on that particular weekly program.

About a year after the rebellion was over, I visited Nigeria on a trip to several countries in Africa. By that time, international relief efforts in which Canada participated had become unnecessary. Reconciliation between the Ibos of Biafra and the other tribes had proceeded apace. One member of the Canadian media, who was with me on that trip and had supported Biafra, told me that he found it hard to believe the extent and rapidity of the reconciliation, which, he had been warned by the Biafran authorities during the war, would never take place. It became clear that most of the propaganda about starvation and threatened retribution against the Ibos, who were the dominant tribe in Biafra, had been exaggerated.

Before the war came to an end, I was invited by the Anglican clergy from the Eglinton area to meet with them to discuss Biafra. We were not able to fix a date until the war was over. I do not know what they might have said while the war was still going on. The message to me after hostilities had ceased was to ensure that I would be available to meet with them for consultation should a similar situation arise in the future. The emotional way the Biafra issue had been handled within their Toronto congregations had done damage to the Anglicans in Nigeria and they didn't want that to happen again.

Israel and Canadian Jews

In 1968, the boundaries of my Eglinton constituency shifted westward to embrace areas with a large Jewish population, including several leading members of the Canadian Jewish community, Rabbi Gunther Plaut among them. That was also the year I became secretary of state for external affairs. As I had done in other parts of Eglinton, I took the occasion in 1968 to visit clergy in the newly acquired parts of my constituency, many of whom were rabbis. When I met him for the first time, one young rabbi got right to the point: 'So you want to know about your Jewish constituents? There are three things about them you should know. They all remember the Holocaust. Whether or not they are Zionists, they all support Israel as the symbol of the survival of the Jews. They all believe in the virtues of family life; every Jewish mother worries when her son goes to school for the first time.' It was excellent advice.

There were and are two fundamental principles underlying Canadian policy towards Israel. First, as one of the countries that had played a leading role in the establishment of the State of Israel, we defend its right to exist. Second, we want a peaceful settlement of the conflict in the Middle East and, in the promotion of peace, try to follow an even-handed policy towards Israel and its neighbours.

Following the 1967 war, the Security Council of the United Nations formulated in Resolution 242, dated 22 November 1967, the principles for a peace settlement between Israel and its Arab neighbours that owed much to the drafting skills of George Ignatieff, then Canada's representative on the Security Council. Time after time, under pressure from both Israel and its Arab neighbours to side with them when conflicts arose, I called upon both sides, on behalf of the Government of Canada, to observe the terms of Resolution 242. Among other things, that resolution assumed the right of the State of Israel to exist and required Israel to withdraw from territories occupied in the 1967 war. In the English version, there is no definite article preceding the word 'territories.' The French version reads: 'des territoires.' Canada accepted the more flexible English version as expressing the intent of the resolution, since this was the language in which it was drafted and debated. This difference is of crucial importance. But it was my view and the view of my departmental officials that this difference will be resolved if and when Israel and its Arab neighbours (as Israel and Egypt were able to do eventually) get together to negotiate peace treaties. The borders of the State of Israel could not help but be a central feature of any negotiations of that kind.

Our attitude towards the State of Israel was basically friendly. As foreign secretary, I paid an official visit to that country in 1969, as well as to Iran and Egypt. My friend Sol Kanee from Winnipeg, who has served the Canadian Jewish community and international Jewry in many high positions, went to Israel to be there when I made my visit. He attended a gathering at which Abba Eban, the foreign minister of Israel, and I both spoke. In my view, Abba Eban was, and probably still is, the world's most eloquent English-speaking orator. I am not. Afterwards, I met my friend Kanee. We both agreed that Abba Eban had been in excellent form. What did he say? I asked my friend. I don't remember, he replied. Do you remember what I said? Oh, yes. The moral: there was less to remember and fewer sensual distractions in my simple speech. Nevertheless, I wish I were as eloquent in the English language as Abba Eban.

At the time of my visit, Israel was an exciting place. The war was over. There was no violence in the streets. Everywhere was evidence of the determination of the Israelis to make the desert bloom like a rose. The political leaders I met – Golda Meir was the prime minister – gave an impression of quiet confidence. This was the time, I thought later, for the process of healing and accommodation with the Arab world to have been set in motion. It was a missed opportunity.

Because of Canada's support for Security Council Resolution 242 and our policy of neutrality between Israel and the Arab states, I gave strict orders to Canadian politicians and officials to stay away from occupied territories when visiting Israel. But like all Christians, I wanted to visit the holy places when I was in Israel. Unfortunately, many of them were in East Jerusalem, which had been occupied by Israel in the 1967 war. So, what did I do? My colleague, Don Jamieson, made a speech at my nominating convention a few years later, at which a substantial number of Jewish constituents were present. He praised my integrity in exaggerated terms. Then he told how I had advised him to stay clear of the occupied territories when he visited Israel and, consequently, how he had arranged to cross into East Jerusalem incognito at night. At the Western Wall (the Wailing Wall) he told his Israeli guide how impressed he was. 'Exactly what Mr. Sharp said when he was here – incognito.' My Jewish constituents were delighted.

I attended Canadian Jewish public functions. I met from time to time with Abba Eban, who once said that he would have little to complain about if all countries were like Canada in their relations with Israel. I met with leading members of the Canadian Jewish community to discuss relations between Israel and Canada and the treatment of Jews in the Soviet Union and in other countries.

I did not always agree with the actions of the Government of Israel, however, nor did I always follow the advice of Canadian Jewish supporters of Israel. I knew that the Diaspora itself, including Jews living in

Canada, was sometimes divided in its attitude towards the policies of the Israeli government, even though they were strong supporters of Israel. What I tried to do was to be fair and never to mislead.

In the 1974 election, as in the 1968 and 1972 elections, my Conservative opponent was Murray Maynard. He was persuaded, apparently, that I had managed to survive the closely fought 1972 election because of the support I had received from Jewish constituents. In 1974, therefore, he attacked me publicly for not giving sufficient support to Israel. When I saw and heard this line of attack, I called in some of my principal Jewish supporters and told them that I did not intend to reply. It would not help Israel or Canadian Jews if it were alleged that Canada supported Israel because of pressure from Jewish constituents living in the foreign secretary's constituency. If my Jewish constituents did not agree with Maynard's accusations it was up to them to support me. As far as I could ascertain from the election returns, I did not lose support among Jews living in Eglinton in 1974.

I was urged on many occasions to protest the mistreatment of Jews in the Soviet Union and in other countries. There were occasions when this was appropriate, and from time to time I did protest publicly, so that Canada's point of view would be apparent to all. But more often I enquired of those who urged me to protest what their purpose was – to help the victims or to give satisfaction to Canadians that their government had expressed their abhorrence of the way the victims were being treated? I asked this question because sometimes a public protest by the Canadian government made it more difficult for the Canadian ambassador to be successful in his representations to the government of the country concerned on behalf of those who were being mistreated.

I had dramatic evidence of the efficacy of private diplomacy one Sunday afternoon in Toronto when I was invited to have tea by the president of a French-speaking Jewish group. Until that day, I hadn't known there were so many French-speaking Jews in Toronto. In the course of his remarks, the president reminded me that he and others had approached me some time before, urging the Canadian government to protest the treatment of Jews in a country of North Africa. I had put the question to him as to which was the better approach: to protest publicly or to make representations through the Canadian ambassador. We left the matter in your hands, he added, and as a result the ambassador persuaded the government of that country to let Jews who wanted to emigrate to Canada do so; that's why so many French-speaking Jews are here today.

Which Reminds Me ...

Vietnam and the
International Commission for Control and Supervision

On one occasion, early in my career as secretary of state for external affairs, I had described as a farce the continued existence of a commission (titled the International Commission for Supervision and Control [ICSC]) established in 1954 to supervise a cease-fire in Vietnam and of which Canada was still a member. I therefore did not react with enthusiasm, nor did my departmental officials, when on 25 October 1972 I learned from William Rogers, U.S. secretary of state, that another cease-fire agreement on Vietnam was imminent and that Canada was being considered for membership on another proposed supervisory commission, the International Commission for Control and Supervision (ICCS).

Most of my departmental officials, several of whom had served in the old ICSC, were opposed. They believed that the new commission would have the same fatal defects as the earlier commission and that, once in, we would find it impossible to withdraw. It would in effect be another farce.

I recognized the risks, but I also wanted to help the United States extricate itself from Vietnam and I didn't want Canada to be blamed for complicating the cease-fire negotiations. So I informed the Americans that, in order to meet the need for an international presence immediately a cease-fire went into effect, Canada was prepared to place at the disposal of the new commission, which we were informed would include three other countries – Hungary, Indonesia, and Poland – our delegation to the existing commission. We would then await further developments.

That peace was just around the corner proved to be a premature prediction. We had time to consider in depth the terms on which we would be prepared to participate in a new supervisory commission. We were not, of course, party to the negotiations between the Americans and the Democratic Republic of Vietnam (North Vietnam). The best I could do was to keep Secretary Rogers informed about our views, which I did by telephone on 28 November, supplemented by the usual contacts at a lower level.

On 3 December 1972 I went public in a statement in the House of Commons. If Canada could play a constructive role, we would. But the government required assurance that:
1. the new commission would be effective;
2. all four parties – the United States, South Vietnam, North Vietnam

and the Viet Cong – concerned in the peace negotiations would be bound by the agreement and would invite Canada to participate;

3. provision would be made for a continuing political authority to receive reports from the commission members;

4. the commission would have necessary freedom of movement in Vietnam; and

5. members could withdraw from it.

Once again, the cease-fire negotiations stalled, and the United States resumed its bombing of North Vietnam. Seizing the initiative from the NDP, who tried to make this their issue, I sponsored a resolution in the House of Commons on 5 January 1973, noting with grave concern the continuation of hostilities, deploring the recent bombing, welcoming its halt, and requesting the Americans to refrain from further bombing.

I was also able at that time to indicate to the House that Canada was acceptable as a member of the new control commission to all parties to the peace negotiations. I reiterated the conditions for our participation and stated that if all of them except for the one relating to the establishment of a continuing political authority were agreed to, Canada would be prepared to consider serving on the new commission for a minimum of sixty days. I also warned that the Canadian delegation would consider itself free to publicize proceedings as it saw fit – which in due course became known as the 'open-mouth' policy.

On 23 January 1973, the President of the United States announced the conclusion of an agreement on a cease-fire in Vietnam. The next day I informed the House of Commons that a preliminary study of the documents showed that we had had some influence on the terms of reference of the new supervisory commission and that in the circumstances, once the agreement had been signed, we would serve for an initial period of sixty days, notwithstanding our serious doubts. Our delegation would number 290. The head of the delegation would be Michel Gauvin, then Canadian ambassador to Greece, who my departmental officials told me had the right qualifications to exploit the 'open-mouth' technique. Major-General Duncan McAlpine would be the senior military adviser and commander of the Canadian military component, and V.G. Turner, of the Department of External Affairs, senior political adviser.

On 1 February I made it clear in the House of Commons that if the commission could be made to work, the government was prepared to make it work and that Canada was not representing any one party or side. Once again, I reviewed the serious inadequacies in the arrangements for international supervision. On 7 February, as a means of facilitating the work of the commission, I announced that Canada had recognized the government of the Democratic Republic of Vietnam (North Vietnam).

I went to Paris to head Canada's delegation to the International Conference on Vietnam, comprising the four parties to the cease-fire agreement, the four members of the ICCS, Indonesia, Hungary, Poland, and Canada, and the secretary general of the United Nations. We met on 26 February. My main purpose was to obtain some arrangement for a continuing political authority to which the ICCS could report. I thought the Security Council would be ideal. But enquiries indicated that there was little support for this idea, so instead, at the opening session, I tabled a draft resolution calling upon the secretary general of the United Nations to receive and circulate reports from the ICCS and any comments arising therefrom and providing for the International Conference to be reconvened by the secretary general under certain conditions. All the peace-keeping bodies then in existence, in all of which Canada was a member, were under the auspices of the United Nations.

That resolution was not approved. I thought the secretary general of the United Nations, Kurt Waldheim, was treated very shabbily. The best we were able to obtain was that those who received the reports from the ICCS, namely, the parties to the cease-fire agreement, would be responsible for forwarding such reports to other signatories to the Act of the International Conference on Vietnam and to the secretary general of the United Nations and that the conference would be reconvened upon a joint request of the United States and North Vietnam or upon a request from six or more signatories to the act.

When I returned to Ottawa, I reported these disappointing developments to the House of Commons and advised that I was considering going to Vietnam to see the situation for myself. Already, I reported to the Commons Standing Committee on External Affairs and National Defence, some of the difficulties we had foreseen were coming to pass.

Insofar as it was possible, I wanted the question of Canada's continuing participation in the ICCS to be dealt with on a non-partisan basis, so I invited the Progressive Conservative Party, the New Democratic Party, and the Social Credit Party each to nominate an MP to go with me to Indo-China. The NDP and the Social Credit accepted, naming Doug Rowland and Eudore Allard, respectively. The Conservatives didn't. Claude Wagner, the external affairs critic for the official opposition, regarded the trip as political propaganda. That was a serious error of judgment that deprived Wagner and his party of information that could only be obtained on the spot in Vietnam and that was obtained by Rowland and Allard.

We met the government leaders in Saigon in South Vietnam, Vientiane in Laos, and Hanoi in North Vietnam. To each of them I put the same questions about the way the ICCS was functioning and whether they wanted Canada to continue as a member. Each of them had a different view of events, but they were agreed that Canada should remain on the commission.

We also met with the Canadian members of the international control commission. We were impressed with their efficiency and deportment in a very difficult situation. Our visit, however, confirmed that, notwithstanding the best efforts of the Canadian delegation, the ICCS was not performing the tasks assigned to it under the cease-fire agreement. There were thousands of incidents; few led to requests for investigation; a very small number of commission reports emerged. When there were alleged violations by the United States or the South Vietnamese, the Poles and the Hungarians agreed to an investigation. When there were alleged violations by the North Vietnamese or the Viet Cong, they stalled. Clearly, these two Eastern European delegations regarded themselves not as impartial, as Canada did, but as representatives of the North Vietnamese and the Viet Cong.

In Vientiane, I met the prime minister of Laos, Prince Souvanna Phouma, an urbane and delightful politician. His main problem was that the North Vietnamese were sending reinforcements to the South along the Ho Chi Minh Trail, which crossed through Laos. As I left his office, he said he understood I was now going to Hanoi. 'When you meet the government there, please tell them to stop,' were his parting, plaintive words.

The end of the sixty-day trial period was approaching. Should we leave? On the positive side was the service performed by the ICCS in supervising the release of American and Vietnamese prisoners of war and the withdrawal of American forces from Vietnam. That alone justified the decision we had taken to join the ICCS. On the negative side: the cease-fire was not being observed and the ICCS was ineffective.

The Americans and other NATO allies and the Japanese urged us not to withdraw immediately at the end of the sixty-day period. Responding to these representations, we decided to stay for another sixty-day period.

The situation did not improve. It got worse. A helicopter carrying Canadian personnel of the ICCS was attacked, and Capt. C.E. Laviolette was killed. The government agreed with me that Canada should not continue to take part in the charade.

We let the Americans know that I was about to announce Canada's withdrawal from the ICCS. Henry Kissinger phoned me from the White House asking me to postpone my announcement because of negotiations he was then conducting with Le Duc Tho. I turned down his request but said that, although I would not postpone the announcement, I would postpone the date of our withdrawal by a month if that would be helpful. He said it would be.

So, on 29 May 1973, I announced Canada's withdrawal from the ICCS as of 31 July. A year later, Lee Kuan Yew, prime minister of Singapore, told me at a Commonwealth prime ministers' meeting in Ottawa that Canada was the only country that told the truth about what had been going on in Vietnam, a tribute to the open-mouth policy implemented so skilfully by Michel Gauvin, the head of the Canadian delegation.

The Iranians, for some reason, decided to replace Canada on the ICCS, which fell into oblivion and wasn't heard of again, notwithstanding innumerable breaches of the cease-fire the commission was supposed to supervise, the final collapse of South Vietnam, and the fall of Saigon. I am glad we were not there when the members of the ICCS had to scramble to get out before the collapse.

The Conference on Security and Cooperation in Europe

Canada's membership in NATO has paid off in many ways, not least in the entrée it has given us to international East-West conferences, such as the Conference on Security and Cooperation in Europe. Although not European states, the United States and Canada were both invited because we were involved in the security of our European allies.

One of the main purposes of the NATO countries in supporting the idea of the conference was to put the Soviet Union under pressure to accept a code of human rights for its citizens. For Canada, with its large immigrant population from the Eastern European bloc, there was a particular interest in promoting trade and cultural contacts and, to facilitate the unification of families, in the free movement of people across the Iron Curtain. As I said in my opening statement on 4 July 1973, 'If we can achieve gradual but meaningful progress in removing barriers to the movement of persons and information we will be well on our way to achieving our goals – creating the mutual understanding and confidence necessary for any enduring security and co-operation.' The main purpose of the Soviet government was to obtain international approval of the existing borders of the Soviet Union and its allies.

There were misgivings among our allies, to some extent shared by the

Canadian government, that the Soviet Union would not live up to any undertakings of a humanitarian character it might be persuaded to accept. I took the view that it would, nevertheless, be valuable to have a means of putting pressure on the Soviet Union with respect to cultural contacts, emigration, family reunion, and human rights. It was also my view that, on the other hand, while a declaration that existing European borders could not be changed by force might be useful to the Soviet Union, the NATO countries had no intention, in any case, of going to war for that purpose. Peaceful change was not ruled out.

I represented Canada at the first meeting of the conference in Helsinki in 1973, which led two years later, to the Final Act. I had forgotten the incident, but was reminded years later by an American who had been present, of a verbal encounter I had with Dom Mintoff, prime minister of Malta. Mintoff, who had a reputation for arrogance, did not like the Canadian position in relation to non-European countries bordering the Mediterranean. He warned me that if I persisted he would attack me publicly. I replied that I hoped he would do so. It would make me popular in my constituency and help me to get re-elected.

When I arrived in Helsinki, that remarkably modern city on the very edge of the Soviet Union, I was installed in a fine hotel, with a piano in my room, on which were some of the piano compositions of Sibelius, courtesy of the Finnish government. As a memento of that visit, I have a photograph of myself at that piano, clipped from the Paris edition of the New York *Herald-Tribune.*

How astounded those who attended that first meeting of the CSCE in July 1973 would have been if they could have foreseen the important role that this organization was to play fifteen years or so later in the reorganization of Europe following the collapse of the Berlin Wall and the Soviet Union and the end of the cold war. The CSCE seemed at the time – even to me – a rather forlorn hope. But operating on the principle that something is better than nothing, we forged ahead. For years Canadian delegates pounded away on human rights, and for years the Soviet bloc sat rigid and unmoving. They had signed *so many* meaningless commitments to human rights that one more, the Helsinki declaration, would surely make no difference. But it did.

Foreign travels

As every secretary of state for external affairs has done in the post-Second World War period, I travelled widely – hundreds of thousands of miles. Long gone are the days when foreign ministers depended upon ambassadors to be their messengers. One of my professors at the University of Manitoba, in a public lecture in the late 1930s, referred disparagingly to Anthony Eden as the peripatetic British foreign secretary because from time to time he crossed the Channel. According to the lecturer, he should have stayed home and attended to foreign policy.

When Prime Minister Mackenzie King (who was also the foreign secretary) left Ottawa for a foreign destination it was an occasion; his staff were expected to gather at the railway station to see him off. A trip to London or to the Continent involved an absence of several weeks. Today, in that same space of time, a prime minister can make several trips abroad by air and still spend a good deal of time in Ottawa.

Before the novelty of air travel to foreign lands had worn off, visits by foreign ministers attracted some attention. A couple of decades ago, it was (and it still is to some extent) an event when the U.S. secretary of state visited Canada. (It has never been much of an event when his Canadian counterpart visited the United States.) Provided, of course, that they were included in the visiting party, the Canadian media paid some attention when a Canadian foreign secretary visited a foreign country for the first time, as I did on a number of occasions, travelling to Scandinavia, Africa, the Middle East, and Latin America. The novelty has now worn off. There has to be a better reason than goodwill to justify foreign travel. International conferences of one kind or another constitute the principal reason. This was true during my term in office. Now the Canadian foreign secretary is expected to attend even more conference: the U.N. General Assembly and U.N. conferences on political matters, NATO ministerial meetings, the Commonwealth, La Francophonie, the Conference on Security and Cooperation in Europe (CSCE), the summit of the seven major industrialized countries, the Organization of American States (OAS), the Association of South-East Asian Nations (ASEAN), and ad hoc gatherings to discuss international emergencies. Canada has a reputation as one of the world's foremost joiners. We spread ourselves very thinly.

The role of the Canadian foreign secretary in international affairs is complicated by the fact that the prime minister also speaks for Canada. Personally, I tried to avoid travelling abroad with Prime Minister Trudeau. There are occasions for joint excursions, of course, like the summit, to which Canada was invited after I had left External Affairs, where detailed negotiations are involved in which the foreign secretary and his department are better equipped than the prime minister to participate.

218

As they say, foreign travel is broadening. I enjoyed and benefited greatly from my foreign travels. (Fortunately, I sleep well on planes and arrive at my destination ready to work.) Presumably, I was able to deal with foreign affairs with greater understanding and better judgment as a result of visiting many countries and areas of the world and meeting their leaders. For the most part, however, the purpose of foreign travel by the foreign secretary is not so much to learn (visits are too short to learn much) but to show the flag, to give evidence of Canada's interest and concern in the subject of whatever conference it may be or in the countries being visited.

In the course of my official activities I met many of the leading political figures of the day. The one who impressed me most was Willy Brandt, partly because of his remarkable career during the war and as mayor of West Berlin, but mainly because of his courageous and far-sighted advocacy of Ostpolitik – opening to the East – which has now come to full fruition with the end of the cold war, combined with his charming simplicity and lack of pretension.

When Brandt became foreign minister of the Federal Republic, our government invited him to visit Canada, which he did on 9 January 1969. I was invited to make a return visit to Bonn, which I did immediately following my visit to Paris to open the Centre culturel. By this time, Brandt had become chancellor, and my host was Walter Scheel, then foreign minister, a member of the Free Democratic Party, which was allied to the Social Democrats in the government of the Federal Republic. Scheel eventually became federal president.

Reading again the notes for a brief speech I made at a luncheon in my honour, I was struck by the enormous change that has taken place in Germany's position in Europe in the last two decades. On 6 April 1970, I said, among other things: 'We applaud your desire to normalize your relations with all European States. Recognizing, as you do, that the realization of that desire will not come easily or quickly, we commend your determination to continue its pursuit.' There was no hint then of the coming rapid ascendancy of West Germany in the European Community or of the unification of the two Germanies.

In 1970, I met and talked at length with President Tito of Yugoslavia, then the great proponent and leader of the non-aligned world. Whatever his faults, Tito kept Yugoslavia united. I remember the Yugoslav ambassador to Canada telling me, prophetically as it turned out, how concerned he was when Tito died and the presidency of the federation began to pass around the circle of republican leaders. On that same trip, I met President Ceausescu of Romania, who boasted of his independence within the Warsaw Pact, which was, of course, the reason why I included Romania in my schedule of foreign travel.

I had lunch with the Shah of Iran.Under the Shah, Iran was a friend of the West, surrounded on all sides, my host contended, by hostile countries supported by the Soviet Union. The Shah did not share the confrontational attitude of Arab countries towards Israel. The hospitality I received was splendid: magnificent dinners, tours, entertainment. In my mind's eye I can still see those overflowing bowls of grey Iranian caviar.

I was meant to be impressed, and in some ways I was impressed. If I had been more fully aware of the activities of the Shah's government I might have been sceptical. At the time my attitude was simply that, from Canada's point of view, the Shah's generally friendly attitude towards the West and towards Israel was a positive element in the disturbed Middle East situation.

In Cairo, I had the privilege of a conversation with President Gamal Abdel Nasser and decided to make the occasion more than a formality by asking him why he made such inflammatory speeches about Israel, using words like 'fields of fire and seas of blood.' He said he had been misquoted. At the subsequent press conference I was asked whether I had spoken to President Nasser about his speeches. I said yes and that he claimed to have been misquoted. The dispatches from Cairo did not mention either the question or my answer. They were censored to avoid disturbing the Palestinians, whom Nasser was supporting.

Travel is one of the perquisites of being secretary of state for external affairs. All these encounters were interesting, at least to me, and they provided insights into motivations that can only be obtained through personal encounters. Usually, they involved an exchange of views. In the nature of things, however, most of them, were far from momentous occasions for either party.

I add this: the very fact that national political leaders meet more frequently does modify their approach and their behaviour – it modified mine – particularly when they appear together on TV screens observed by an increasing proportion of the world's population. Slowly but surely, I believe, the human race is learning, through modern communications, that it has common goals and common problems that for their attainment or solution require cooperation and often joint action by national governments.

I travelled to meetings of organizations of which Canada was a member: to New York to attend annual sessions of the U.N. General Assembly; to Brussels, Rome, Bonn, Washington, and Lisbon to attend NATO ministerial meetings; to London in 1969 to attend a meeting of Commonwealth heads of government followed by a visit to the Vatican; to Helsinki in 1973 to represent Canada at the CSCE, as I have already described; and to Japan as one of a group of ministers to meet our counterparts in the Japanese government.

Every year, except when the Prime Minister decided to take the spotlight, I was expected to address the U.N. General Assembly and I did so, although not with enthusiasm. Because it reflected my frustration with the divisions and rigidities of the cold war, the speech I remember best, drafted by Reeves Haggan, began 'The United Nations is drowning in a sea of words.'

I went to Washington from time to time to meet with the U.S. secretary of state and to London, less frequently of course, to exchange views with the British government.

Relations with Latin America

Five ministers, Jean-Luc Pepin, John James (Joe) Greene, Gérard Pelletier, Otto Lang, and myself, participated in a tour of most of the countries of Latin America in 1968. I joined the group in Peru and went on to Chile, Argentina, Brazil, and Mexico. The new Liberal government had promised in its electoral platform to promote closer relations with Latin America. We tried, but in my opinion didn't bring about any significant change. We joined the Inter-American Development Bank and obtained observer status in the Organization of American States.

When I was vice-president of Brazilian Traction in the late 1950s and early 1960s, I discussed the question of Canadian membership in the OAS with many leading Brazilians. At that time, they didn't have much confidence in the OAS and thought that Canada would be more useful on the outside at least for the time being, a view that corresponded with my own feeling on the matter.

As I recommended, the government decided not to apply to fill the vacant chair reserved for Canada in the OAS, notwithstanding the strong encouragement to apply we received from the U.S. administration and some governments of Latin American countries. When I met with the secretary general of the OAS, I mentioned among other considerations that Canadians were reluctant to become associated in the OAS with so many non-democratic governments then in power in Latin American countries. In reply, Mr Galo Plaza Lasso pointed out that those governments were, generally speaking, led by military leaders, not personal dictators, who had taken power because of the failure of civilian political leaders and parties to govern their countries effectively. I had to admit that was only too true.

As Canadian secretary of state for external affairs I found it awkward visiting countries where non-democratic regimes were in power. The attitude towards authority is so different. In Buenos Aires, accompanied by the Argentine foreign minister, I was being driven at high speed through the traffic. There was a five-motorcycle escort clearing the way. Not only were sirens blaring but the motorcycle policemen kicked automobiles that did not move aside quickly enough. I said to the Argentine minister that if he had to get elected he wouldn't permit the police to kick the automobiles of voters. The following day the same thing happened. The minister spoke to one of the motorcycle policemen in Spanish, a language I do not understand. 'What did you say?' I asked him. That the president did not approve, was the response.

External Affairs and the monarchy

I am not an anti-monarchist. If I were a British subject living in the British Isles I would be a staunch defender of the monarchy. I admire Queen Elizabeth, with whom I had the privilege of spending many enjoyable hours in the course of my ministerial activities. I also believe that we should continue to model our system of government on that of Britain. Nor, to make it quite clear where I stand, do I favour the election of a head of state, as the president is elected in the United States. It would be sufficient that the Canadian head of state be selected by the government of the day for a fixed term, with the appointment confirmed by Parliament; in other words, a governor general by another name who would be head of state not vice-head of state.

I have held these views for some time and was confirmed in them by my ministerial experience, particularly as secretary of state for external affairs.

An official visit was arranged for Governor General and Mrs Michener to the Benelux countries in April 1971. Prime Minister Trudeau asked me, as foreign secretary to accompany them. We were received most hospitably, and Their Excellencies conducted themselves with grace and dignity. The presence of a governor general of Canada did, however, pose a special problem for our hosts. How was he to be treated – as vice-royalty or as full head of state? Queen Juliana and the government of the Netherlands decided to accord full head-of-state honours, and the Belgians and Luxemburgers followed suit.

These were generous gestures on the part of our hosts, but they illustrate the ambiguity of our institutions from an outsider's point of view. To the people of the Netherlands and Belgium, governors general are colonial officials, such as were appointed in the Netherlands East Indies and in the Congo. Many Dutch and Belgian people probably believed, when they saw our governor general in their midst, that Canada had not yet achieved full independence from Britain. In a private conversation at an official affair in Amsterdam, my dinner partner, a devoted admirer of Canada, didn't think that a visit by the governor general was worthy of us. I agreed.

A similar perplexity occurred during the ministerial visit to Latin America in 1968. Our purpose was to promote the sale of Canadian goods and make political contacts with the governments of those countries. We learned, after the trip was arranged, that Her Majesty would also be visiting some countries of Latin America at the same time. Her visit was intended, among other things, to promote British interests, including the sale of British goods. We couldn't ask Her Majesty to perform the function for Canada that she was performing for Britain on that Latin American trip because the Queen is never recognized as Queen of Canada, except when she is in Canada. When in the United States, for example, she is the Queen of Great Britain and promotes good relations between Britain and the United States.

The resulting confusion became very clear one day during the 1976 Montreal Olympics when Her Majesty visited the games after having spent a few days in the United States. An American reporter who had been with her on the American leg of her trip and who was ignorant of the subtleties of our Constitution, said on Canadian television that the Queen of England was in the stands.

Gradually, step-by-step, the governor general has taken over functions that were previously exercised by the monarch, so that within Canada the governor general is virtually head of state. Nevertheless, constitutionally the governor general is only the representative of the monarch.

Hence my strongly held view that Canada should have its own head of state who is not shared by others. The Queen and her successors could then have a special place as head of the Commonwealth as well as queen or king of Great Britain. In that capacity, the monarch would be received with enthusiasm and acclaim by Canadians in all parts of the country, including places Queen Elizabeth is now reluctant to visit.

My views on the monarchy were well known to my colleagues in both the Pearson and Trudeau cabinets. They were also known to some others. So far, however, I have obviously failed to rally a significant following. One would think that my views would have appealed to a

French Canadian like Trudeau. Perhaps they did. But, he did not act on them. He was prime minister when the monarchy was confirmed in our patriated Constitution.

A few years after I had left the ministry, I was asked by Prime Minister Trudeau to accept appointment as governor general. One of the reasons I declined the honour was my well-known attitude towards the institution.

CHAPTER NINE

President of the Privy Council and Leader of the Government in the House of Commons, 1974–1976

After External Affairs, what?

Shortly after I left External Affairs to become president of the Privy Council, I visited Paul Martin in London, where he was high commissioner for Canada. He asked me whether it was true that I said to the Prime Minister that I didn't want to be secretary of state for external affairs any longer. When I told him that was correct, he expressed his disbelief.

In many respects, External Affairs is the most attractive portfolio in Canadian government. It has prestige, challenge, some glamour (at least when travelling abroad), and seldom involves the kinds of problems that are routinely faced by, for example, the ministers of finance and health and welfare, with responsibilities for making decisions affecting the pocketbooks of Canadians. Nevertheless, after six years as foreign minister, I felt that I was losing touch with Canadian realities, and when Trudeau was forming his government after the 1974 election I asked for a change. But I didn't really know where I wanted to go.

President of the Privy Council and leader of the government in the House of Commons were not my choice. I just couldn't think of strong enough objections when the Prime Minister suggested them to me. By virtue of the title, the president of the Queen's Privy Council for Canada (which is the full title) has no responsibilities that I can find. He or she doesn't preside at cabinet and doesn't run the Privy Council Office. In the past, the prime minister often held the position. Once, when a reporter asked me what were the responsibilities of the president of the Privy Council, I used my imagination and told him, tongue-in-cheek, that he called the Canadian privy councillors together when there was a dispute as to the succession to the throne!

During my time in Ottawa, the president of the Privy Council has been assigned varying responsibilities by the Prime Minister. For example, when he returned to cabinet in 1967 to promote his economic nationalist policies, Walter Gordon became president of the Privy Council. Similarly, the government leader in the House of Commons has occupied various portfolios. It was under Trudeau that the tradition was established that the government leader should be president of the Privy Council – successively Donald Macdonald, Allan MacEachen, myself, Yvon Pinard, and, in the Clark and Mulroney governments, government House leaders Walter Baker and Ray Hnatyshyn.

The primary responsibility of the government leader in the House of Commons is to arrange the business of the House, that is, to ensure that government bills come before the House in an orderly fashion, that written questions on the order paper are answered, that the timing of debates on motions proposed by the opposition parties is agreed, and so forth, all of this in consultation with the House leaders of the opposition parties. I was fortunate in having such distinguished MPs as Jed Baldwin and Walter Baker as House leaders of the Conservatives and Stanley Knowles as House leader of the NDP. I didn't pretend to be an expert on rules of the House of Commons like Knowles. Indeed, I never claimed much expertise in that field; to keep me out of trouble, I relied on my parliamentary secretary, John Reid, an MP of exceptional quality from Kenora, Ontario, who later entered the cabinet, and on advisers like Jerry Yanover, in the office of the Privy Council president, who has devoted his life to parliamentary procedures.

Once every week, and sometimes more often, the leaders of the recognized political parties in the House met to discuss priority House business. As government leader, I informed the others of the government's plans and priorities. They listened and, if I asked that a particular bill be pushed ahead, they either assented or challenged the government to impose some sort of limit on debate – like closure. Generally speaking, it is in the interest of a government for its legislation to proceed through the House in an orderly way. It is often in the political interest of the opposition parties to prolong debate in order to draw public attention to what they consider to be shortcomings in a bill. Rarely is it the expectation of the opposition, when the government has a majority in the House, that it will be able to force the government to agree to substantial amendments of the kind that they are proposing.

When the government caucus met on Wednesday morning, it was my responsibility to inform the MPs of the business that would be before the House of Commons during the following week. On Wednesday, 14 April 1976, through my parliamentary secretary, J.-J. Blais, I sent a note to the chairman of the caucus that read: 'To Hell with House business, I am getting married.' Jeannette Dugal and I were married in Toronto at an ecumenical ceremony conducted by Angus McQueen of the United Church of Canada and Father Tom Hayes, a Roman Catholic priest, witnessed by our friends Bill and Mary Learmonth and their daughter Cathy, who played the flute for the six of us. Jeannette has brought me great happiness and as a proud French Canadian and a Roman Catholic, has advanced my understanding of the nature of Canada.

Ours is an adversarial form of politics. It is the responsibility of the opposition to oppose, not so much because they disagree with the government's proposals, but in order to force the government to explain and justify its policies, particularly when important issues are at stake. This is obviously true of the budget. If the opposition were in power, they might have followed similar financial and taxation policies. Hypocritical as it may appear, they perform a useful function by criticizing these same financial policies when they are in opposition.

It is in the House of Commons that leadership is tested. Before the advent of television, confrontations between the government leaders and the leaders of the opposition parties were described by the newspapers, and during election campaigns the public turned out to see the contestants in person at political gatherings. Because of TV coverage, there is now even greater exposure of the adversarial encounters in the Commons. I doubt that Mackenzie King would have survived for as long as he did as prime minister if TV had covered his speeches in the House. For the opposite reason, I think that TV had much to do with Trudeau's rapid rise to national leadership and his continuation in power for some sixteen years, with one short interruption.

After the 1974 election, the government once again had the support of a majority of Liberal members, so I was spared the kind of problems, inherent in minority governments, that were handled so skilfully by Allan MacEachen when he was government House leader. Looking back, I do not recall anything noteworthy in my handling of House business, unless the comparative absence of serious problems is in itself noteworthy.

During my term as House leader, however, there were four developments of significance – the emergence of freedom of information as an important issue, under prodding from Jed Baldwin, the Conservative House leader; redistribution and a substantial increase in the number of seats in the House of Commons (although I introduced the legislation, the underlying work had been done under the guidance of my predecessor, Allan MacEachen); the revision of the rules of procedure that gave Question Period priority; and, of greatest significance, the televising of House proceedings.

Access to information

While I favoured legislation to give the public access to information about government operations, I did not expect that much new and significant information would become publicly available, even with the most liberal rules about access. I thought public expectations about sensational revelations were certain to be disappointed. Under the Canadian version of parliamentary government, with its uninhibited Question Period, the government is under continuous scrutiny and questioning. In one way or another, most of the facts that matter in the decision-making process become known.

As a result of my sixteen years as a civil servant and another thirteen as a cabinet minister, I was very conscious, however, of the necessity of preserving the confidentiality of cabinet discussions, exchanges with foreign governments and provincial governments, and dealings between ministers and their public-servant advisers. Those involved in such contacts had to know that what they said or wrote to one another would not be revealed, at least for many years; otherwise they would not be prepared to be frank and open. I did not see how this confidentiality could be preserved unless the government itself retained full authority to withhold information it considered confidential. To entrust full responsibility for decisions about confidentiality to outsiders, however trustworthy – even to the courts, as was sometimes advocated – seemed to me to involve serious risks.

Baldwin and I debated the issue in the House on a number of occasions. We were not far apart, and if he had had my experience as a minister I believe our differences would have been even smaller. In 1982, long after I had left Parliament, the Access to Information Act was finally approved. It was a monument to Baldwin's persistence, although, of course, it was not entirely to his liking. It hasn't brought about any revolution in access to government information. It hasn't satisfied the media (which would like to sit in on cabinet meetings if they could), but it has been useful to people who feel they have been subjected to unfair or discriminatory treatment, to the legal profession which wants access to documents bearing upon the interests of clients, and to opposition MPs who diligently ask for and scrutinize the expense accounts and the travel of ministers on government aircraft. Historians are doubtful, since the operation of access has been slow and sometimes perverse. It is significant that his former Conservative friends, when they took office in 1984, did not amend the Access to Information Act along the lines that Baldwin advocated when he and they were in opposition.

Parliamentary reform

Reform of Parliament is always on the agenda of political parties, prime ministers, government House leaders, and MPs generally. To underline my own commitment to the reform of the rules of the House of Commons, I took the chair of the House Committee on Procedure and Organization, an unusual step. Ministers very seldom chair House committees. During my term as House leader and chairman of the committee, we debated a full range of fundamental reforms, but we could not agree to recommend major changes at that stage. Among other things, however, we did recommend one change in procedure, the implementation of which was later to prove of crucial importance to the introduction of television.

Question Period in the Canadian House of Commons is unique. Nowhere else in the world – unless possibly in Australia – are ministers at the national level subjected to the kind of questioning, without notice and on every conceivable subject, that is thrown at them daily in the Question Period while the Canadian Parliament is in session. By Canadian standards, Question Period in the British House of Commons is a comparatively tame affair.

When I arrived in Ottawa in the early 1940s, there was no Question Period in the present-day sense. Occasionally, the leader of the opposition would rise at the opening of the day's session and address a question to the prime minister, prefaced by words such as: 'Mr. Speaker, before the Orders of the Day are called, may I address a question to the Prime Minister on a matter of urgency.' Other questions were put on the Order Paper and answered in writing by the government.

Gradually over the years the scope of oral questions by the opposition was extended. It wasn't until the Diefenbaker years, however, that the opposition, led by the formidable four, Pearson, Martin, Chevrier, and Pickersgill, took full advantage of the opportunities to put the government on the spot by persistent questioning. Since there was at that time no formal oral Question Period, the questioning of ministers threatened to extend indefinitely and to interfere with the legislative process.

By the time I assumed the House leadership, a time limit of one hour had been put on the oral Question Period, but it did not begin until after routine procedures – such as reports of committees, questions on the order paper for reply in writing, and motions – had been disposed of, a process that took an uncertain period of time. Meanwhile, another problem had arisen. In order to put their views on the record, members had begun to make motions the acceptance of which for debate required unanimous consent – consent that was rarely given or, for that matter, expected. This procedure was also being used as a kind of filibustering, since there was nothing in the rule book that gave the speaker of the House of Commons authority to stop members from making such motions.

Having been to Westminster to observe the British House of Commons in action, our Committee on Procedure recommended – and our recommendation was accepted – that each daily session should begin with a fifteen-minute period for motions under Standing Order 31 (now replaced by brief statements by MPs, which is more sensible), followed by forty-five minutes of oral questions. We did not make that change with the expectation of televising House procedures. There is no doubt, however, that it greatly facilitated the introduction of television and added to its popularity by concentrating the intense drama of the oral Question Period in the first hour of the daily session. Indeed, to many Canadians, since the advent of TV in the House, the oral Question Period is Parliament in action.

Before the televising of House proceedings, ministers, having been questioned on matters of current importance, were routinely expected to appear before the TV cameras in Room 130S, in the basement of the Centre Block of the Parliament Buildings, to answer the same or similar questions put by reporters. As a politician, I didn't object to the exposure. I am told that my craggy face is made for TV. (Doug Fisher once remarked that my face was like a bowl of oatmeal porridge.) I did object, however, to the impression created among the public by this supposed replay of what had happened in the House. From what they saw on TV in those days, viewers would have had reason to think that Parliament consisted of ministers answering important questions from reporters gathered about them, pushing microphones into their faces.

There is, in fact, a tremendous difference between questioning by the media and questioning by opposition MPs in the House of Commons. Although House proceedings can be rough at times, the layout of the House separates the members of the government from the opposition members by a space said to be the length of two swords. Members do not address one another directly. They address the speaker (or at least they should). All members are 'honourable,' and their word must be accepted by other members. There are limitations on abusive language.

Televising the House of Commons

The question of broadcasting the proceedings of the House of Commons had been under active consideration for several years before I became government House leader. In March 1970, it was referred to the Committee on Procedure and Organization. In 1972, the committee approved in principle television and radio broadcasting of the House and its committees. The Speech from the Throne of 4 January 1973 declared that the government would recommend to the House of Commons the broadcasting of proceedings. This intention was reaffirmed in the Speech from the Throne delivered in September 1974.

On paper, this was progress, but from the time I became government House leader I campaigned personally and vigorously for action rather than declarations; if I hadn't, I am convinced that nothing would have happened for a long time.

I wanted the public to see for themselves the interplay between the parties and their spokesmen, see and hear for themselves the questioning of ministers by the opposition and the ministers' responses and watch the members they had elected do their stuff. I didn't think that TV clips of ministers answering questions by reporters or of opposition MPs attacking the government, or even newspaper articles on proceedings in the House were any substitute for observing Parliament in action. It seemed to me to be a pity not to take advantage of the miracle of TV to bring Parliament, the centrepiece of our democratic institutions, into the homes of the people. I wanted all Canadians to see what local inhabitants and visitors to Ottawa could see from the visitors' gallery.

I met with opposition, mainly from Liberal back-benchers who argued that while TV exposure might help ministers and opposition members who had the privilege of questioning them, it was of no benefit to the back-benchers on the government side, who rarely got an opportunity to ask questions and who would appear on TV screens only as background to the main actors. There were widespread fears that the TV cameras would seize upon MPs asleep in their chairs, or picking their noses, or reading newspapers, or would give the viewers a picture of empty chairs without making clear that the absent MPs were attending committee meetings or working for their constituents elsewhere.

There was also a concern about what the televising of proceedings would do to the behaviour of members. Would they become show-offs, strutting their stuff for the cameras, thus destroying the intimate, informal atmosphere of the Commons?

It took time to overcome the opposition, and I was particularly indebted to the skill of Robert Anderson, an experienced film-maker, who, among other things, produced a film that illustrated to MPs what televised proceedings in the House might look like and that included support for the idea from leading journalists including Charles Lynch.

Tom van Dusen, then in my office and later in the offices of Progressive Conservative ministers, played an active and useful role, and the CBC under the direction of Bruce Wilkinson did the technical work that convinced all of us that broadcasting would not interfere with the operation of the House of Commons and would project clear images and clear sound to the viewing public.

The key to the favourable outcome was the decision taken very early in the game to put TV cameras under the control of the speaker of the House of Commons and to feed the output to the stations and networks, which could use what they liked. (The broadcast of full proceedings on cable was to come a bit later.) Closely allied was the decision that the televising of House proceedings was, as far as possible, to be an electronic *Hansard*. This meant that the cameras would focus on the MP as he or she spoke. It would not roam the House looking for sleeping or nose-picking MPs or empty chairs.

I had resigned from the cabinet before the motion to televise proceedings was made and approved, but I had the satisfaction of seeing my efforts rewarded while still an MP. Since I was not a minister, however, only once or twice did I speak in the House after the introduction of TV.

The televising of the House has been a resounding success. Hardly anyone now questions the decision to televise the Commons proceedings. The provinces followed our lead and so, after a long time, did the British Parliament and the U.S. House of Representatives. Back-benchers on the government side may not get much exposure in comparison with ministers or opposition members who ask questions, but they get more exposure than if TV had not been introduced. The behaviour of MPs has not been much affected, except that they tend to dress better and they applaud by clapping rather than pounding their desks. The public may from time to time be upset by the rowdy behaviour of some MPs. The only difference is that now their behaviour can be seen by the multitude on their TV screens. Hitherto, only visitors to the House gallery had the privilege of observing the spectacle, which was just as rowdy then as it is now.

What gives me the greatest satisfaction of all is that, as a result of televising the proceedings of the House, Parliament has once again become the focus of public debate. Seldom does one hear it said now, as was said twenty years ago, that Parliament has become irrelevant. It cannot be ignored. Scenes from the Commons are broadcast daily when the House is in session, in newsclips and on cable.

The time has now come to build upon the success by removing some of the impediments to coverage that were necessary at the outset to quiet the fears of some MPs, so that viewers can see the House as visitors to the gallery see it, sometimes full, sometimes with many empty chairs (Speaker John Fraser put some of these improvements into effect), and to extend coverage to committees, where much of the work of the Commons is carried on and where back-bench MPs perform more conspicuously.

Redistribution of seats in the House of Commons

When an attempt was made in the 1972 Parliament to redistribute seats in the Commons on the basis of the 1971 census, calculated according to Section 51 of the British North America Act, the results were satisfactory to no one. So the matter was referred to the Standing Committee on Privileges and Elections. The committee was still at work when the House was dissolved and the 1974 election held, but it was close to agreement.

It became my job as House leader to place before the House a bill incorporating the principles in respect to which, I was informed, there was broad agreement of all the parties represented in the standing committee.

From the beginning of our history, representation by population has been an integral aspect of the distribution of seats in the House of Commons. There were also some special rules that, under the Constitution, had to be respected, and these produced results that in some cases varied widely from the strict application of 'rep by pop.' It was also thought desirable that no constituency should be so large geographically or in terms of population that it could not be adequately represented by an MP.

By the legislation I introduced, representation of the two largest provinces – Ontario and Quebec – continued to be determined strictly on the basis of 'rep by pop'. Quebec representation was raised from 72 to 75 seats. Dividing the population of Ontario by the average population of a Quebec constituency raised the representation of Ontario from 91 to 95 seats and raised it again after the 1981 census to 99. (It was projected that after the 1981 census Quebec would have 79 seats and Ontario 110 seats but this did not happen. Quebec remained at 75 seats and Ontario at 99.)

For the intermediate-size provinces the general rule was 'rep by pop' with special cushioning of the effect of declining population. Specifically, no province should suffer a reduction in its number of seats. At the lower end, there were special rules for the small provinces, principally the rule that no province should have fewer MPs than senators. This gave Prince Edward Island four MPs representing a population about the same as that of a large Toronto constituency.

One of the results of the redistribution was a substantial immediate increase in the number of seats in the House of Commons from 264 to 282 and, after the 1981 census, to 295 seats, and the likelihood, as Canada's population grew, of additional seats at each successive census. The seating capacity of the House of Commons had to be enlarged. It may have to be enlarged again as Canada continues to grow. Personally, I hope that the increase will be limited to what is absolutely necessary. The membership of the House of Commons is large enough; MPs, apart from ministers, are not overworked – even in populous provinces. They could represent and service a larger number of constituents. The main aim should be to adhere more closely to the principle of representation by population, achievement of which may depend, of course, on the future of the Senate.

Thanks to Jack Pickersgill, who introduced reforms in 1964, legislation relating to the determination of the borders of federal constituencies has been taken out of the hands of the party in power and given to neutral and impartial commissioners. So, too, the number of constituencies and their distribution among provinces no longer depends on partisan considerations. Gerrymandering at the federal level, at one time practised zealously by governments of all political stripes, has become a thing of the past.

Speeches from the Throne

There is one reform of parliamentary procedure that I advocated for many years on which I made no progress whatsoever.

From the time I entered Prime Minister Pearson's Cabinet in 1963, I took strong exception to the expansion of the Speech from the Throne from a simple announcement at the beginning of a new session of the legislation that would be placed before Parliament – which had hitherto more or less been the practice – to a long, detailed, quasi-political defence of the government's policies. I contended – unsuccessfully – that the proper person to defend the government's policies was the head of the government, not the local representative of the head of state, who should be kept well above the political fray.

At Westminster, the Queen reads a short, simple speech without argument, listing the subjects on the government's legislative program for the session. I am sure that Her Majesty would refuse to read the kind of speech that is given to the governor general to read and also to the lieutenant-governors of the provinces. In Quebec City, these constitutional proprieties are better observed than in Ottawa or in any other province. The Quebec lieutenant-governor reads a short formal speech opening the session and is followed by the premier, who announces and defends his government's policies. For reasons I discuss elsewhere in this book, I am not a Canadian monarchist, but so long as the British monarch is also the Canadian head of state, the monarch's representatives in Canada should not be asked to make speeches that could involve them in partisan politics.

The Speech from the Throne delivered to the Canadian Parliament on 13 May 1991 contained about 4,500 words. The Queen's speech at the opening of the British Parliament on 7 November 1990 contained about a thousand words. In the provinces the speeches of the lieutenant-governors are of varying length. The rule seems to be: the smaller the province the longer the Speech from the Throne. Several of them have been much longer than the speech delivered in the same year by the governor general.

I understand why this has happened. The opening of Parliament is a splendid, dignified occasion. The governor general is not going to be interrupted. His speech is going to be broadcast. Copies can be prepared in advance and distributed widely. What an opportunity to put the best possible face on the government's policies and accomplishments!

For constitutional reasons, the temptation should have been resisted! Not only so, but from a public-relations point of view, the Speech from the Throne is a dud, a one-day wonder, quickly forgotten and replaced by the cut and thrust of partisan contention when the session gets under way. It is not worth the enormous expenditure of time and effort on the part of the senior bureaucrats and ministers who work on the text and try to cram into it as much as possible.

Which Reminds Me ...

For years I tried my best to stem the tide, but finally I gave up and played very little part in the drafting of the Speech from the Throne, a process that I considered a waste of valuable time.

MPs' salaries

There was one occasion when I most regretted having accepted appointment as government House leader. That was when I had to take responsibility – in 1974 – for introducing legislation to raise the indemnities and expense allowances of members of Parliament, and the salaries of ministers and parliamentary secretaries. Both Prime Minister Trudeau and I had made it clear to the Liberal caucus that the government would not introduce such legislation unless we had assurance of support from the opposition parties. In other words, the government would be acting on behalf of all MPs, not only the government and its supporters. Mark MacGuigan was directed to make the soundings, and in due course he reported back that he had the support of Robert Stanfield, leader of the opposition, to an immediate increase of approximately 50 per cent in indemnities and allowances, and provision for annual adjustments equivalent to increases in average Canadian wage levels. Since indemnities and expense allowances had not been changed for years and had fallen far behind increases in the cost of living and standards of compensation in the community as a whole, these proposals were not unreasonable.

When I made the announcement in the House of Commons just before Christmas, however, there was a loud public outcry. Stanfield came to see me to say that he could not continue to support the proposals to which he had originally agreed and to suggest that we should seek a lower rate of increase. Which we did. Instead of a 50 per cent increase, we recommended about a one-third increase. It was still a substantial improvement in compensation to MPs and for the first time introduced an automatic annual adjustment similar to the increases that were taking place in salaries and wages of non-MPs.

Before the Second World War, Parliament met for only a few months in the spring of the year. MPs, other than ministers, earned their livelihood as businessmen, farmers, or professional men, or were independently wealthy. As MPs they received very small indemnities – really honoraria – free travel on the trains, but no expense allowances. Parliament now meets according to an annual schedule, with time off at Easter, in midsummer, and at Christmas and New Year. MPs have to be prepared to devote their full time to their official duties and therefore must receive adequate indemnities and expense allowances. Unlike British MPs, they are forbidden by law to accept compensation for acting as lobbyists.

While better pay, allowances, and staff are a response to longer sessions and increasing responsibilities, I regret to say that the process has also worked in reverse. MPs have had to justify their better treatment. They have had to prove to the public that they earn their pay.

When I review the transformation of the role of the MP over the forty-five years that I have observed it at first hand, I am inclined to think that one of the most important elements in the current struggle of MPs for greater recognition and influence is that they know they are relatively overpaid for being simply constituency ombudsmen and loyal party supporters in the House of Commons. They want to play a more important role in the decision-making process, whether on the government or the opposition side of the House.

On the government side, there is, of course, the traditional effort of MPs to become parliamentary secretaries and ministers. The big increase in the size of the cabinet under Trudeau and his policy of appointing parliamentary secretaries to all ministers and of rotating them every year or so gave more opportunities for advancement than ever before. It also altered the significance of appointments as parliamentary secretaries. Under Pearson and his predecessors as prime minister, appointment as a parliamentary secretary was recognition of merit and signalled possible advancement to cabinet office. It had no such significance under Trudeau, since nearly everyone got such an appointment if the government lasted long enough.

The struggle for recognition also manifests itself in other forms. Backbenchers on the government side, particularly since the advent of TV in the House, resent the fact that the speaker regards the Question Period essentially as a time for the opposition to cross-examine the ministry and allots only a couple of questions a day to MPs on the government side. The speaker might take a different view if Canadian political parties were less monolithic and there were on the government side MPs who wanted to cross-examine ministers on matters with respect to which they did not see eye to eye with the government.

Most important of all, the struggle of the ordinary Canadian MP for greater recognition and responsibility finds reflection in the increasing support for fundamental reforms in parliamentary procedure, particularly to give committees of the House greater independence and powers to initiate investigations and to amend legislation. I very much doubt, however, that the results will measure up to expectations.

Which Reminds Me ...

When a Canadian MP breaks party ranks, this is so exceptional that it rates special attention on TV and appears as front-page news in the newspapers. Why this should be so is puzzling, because in a country as widespread as Canada there are bound to be important regional differences within national parties and it is healthy that they should be expressed in Parliament. The British model is instructive. The Conservative Party is full of factions. So is the Labour Party. Yet the parties do not disintegrate, and debate in Parliament is vigorous.

If there were less party discipline, I believe Canadian parliamentary institutions would adapt themselves better, for example, to the realities of Canadian regionalism. There would be less talk of regional isolation. If party discipline remains as rigid as it is today, efforts at parliamentary reform are going to deal with appearance rather than substance.

An ordinary MP

In 1976, I was sixty-five years of age. I had been in cabinet for thirteen years. To hang on in the Government (even if I were asked) or in Parliament (if I were re-elected) for an indefinite period did not appeal to me. So I called on Trudeau and informed him that I did not intend to contest the next election and if he wished to replace me in the cabinet by someone who would be a candidate, I would be quite happy to resign.

Trudeau shuffled the cabinet and on 13 September 1976, I found myself for the first time an ordinary MP The following morning, I awoke to the realization that I no longer had to lead the House of Commons, attend cabinet and cabinet committee meetings, or participate in those agonizing sessions when controversial legislation or action was required of the government. It was a delicious feeling.

A dinner was held in my honour in Toronto on 16 February 1977, organized by Robert Stikeman, one of my loyal and active supporters in Eglinton. About 700 people attended, including the Prime Minister and several members of the cabinet. Pierre Genest chaired the dinner in his usual witty fashion.

It was a long night. Before I was called on to make my address, there were six speakers – Bob Bryce, Sol Kanee, Jed Baldwin, Jean Chrétien, Donald Macdonald, and the Prime Minister. Finally, at about 10:00 p.m. it became my turn. I was tempted simply to say thank you and let the guests go home. But I resisted the temptation, and said what I came prepared to say. My speech included some reflections on my career and on Canada. The part of the speech I enjoyed most, and so did the guests, were my opening remarks on the circumstances that might have surrounded my resignation from cabinet.

Let me begin by giving you the unpublished inside dope about my resignation from the Cabinet. Jed Baldwin has been campaigning actively for greater freedom of information. I stand before you as his first convert, ready to tell all, even to use my imagination, if necessary. I trust my example will not do too much damage to Jed Baldwin's campaign.

So here is the kind of story the media would like to hear. Early last summer I got a call on the telephone from Jim Coutts. 'Minister,' he said, 'how do you think things are going?' This is always Jim Coutts' opening gambit. It makes a Minister feel important when the Prime Minister's Principal Secretary asks for his opinion. After these irrelevant courtesies, he came to the real reason for his call. 'Keith was talking to me about you the other day.' 'Keith who?' I asked. 'Our Keith,' he replied. 'You know, the precipitator, the one responsible for our great Liberal victories in Western Canada. Senator Davey, the friend of K.C. Irving.' 'Oh,' I said. 'I thought it might have been Keith Spicer who was complaining about my French accent. I am told that he thinks I am trying to speak French the way Jean Chrétien speaks English. Anyway what was Keith Davey talking to you about?' 'Minister,' he replied, 'Keith's in trouble and he would like your help. He has been planting stories with the press for several months now that you will be leaving the Cabinet. Nothing is happening. It looks as if you are going to be there forever. His credibility with the media is crumbling. And when his credibility with the media crumbles, Keith is finished. The rain stops falling.' 'And what am I supposed to do to help?' 'Keith has a plan,' Jim told me. 'He wants you to offer to resign. He knows the Prime Minister will never accept your resignation. He has such a high regard for you but then at least he can justify all those planted rumours. Keith's credibility will be restored.'

As you know, I am first and foremost a loyal supporter of the Party and since Keith Davey has to retain his credibility with the media for the next general election campaign, I said I would co-operate.

So I went to see the Prime Minister and handed him my resignation in writing. Well, Keith may have restored his credibility with the media. Not with me. I expected the Prime Minister to protest. I expected him to be a teeny-weeny bit reluctant. I expected him at least to turn pale. But no sir. He took that resignation in his stride, like the strong resolute leader that he is. He even smiled.

After that experience, I have a fellow feeling for John Turner and

Bryce Mackasey. The gossip is that they didn't really expect the Prime Minister to take them at their word when they offered their resignations. And I hope the moral of this story will not be lost on my erstwhile Cabinet colleagues whom I see here this evening. Don't trust the bastard ...– I mean, of course, Keith Davey.

I am deeply grateful to the Cabinet members for being here and particularly, of course, to the Prime Minister who spoke so graciously and so generously. I know they all had to be here in Toronto for that Cabinet meeting tomorrow. On the other hand, they could have bought a cheaper dinner elsewhere, so it did involve a not-inconsiderable sacrifice apart from having to listen to me. If this were a speech in the House of Commons, they would by this time have quietly folded their signature books and silently slipped away, except those whom the Whip had bludgeoned into staying in order to maintain a quorum.'

A few days later, I met Keith Davey, who had been present at the dinner. He congratulated me on my speech. I replied by saying that I hoped people did not believe my story about his part in my resignation. 'I knew it wasn't true,' he said gruffly. It wasn't true, of course, but, as several of my friends remarked, it sounded like the sort of thing that could have happened.

Reflections on majority versus minority government, political parties, and business and politics

I conclude this final chapter about events in my political career by reflections on three subjects that have been of special interest to me: (1) whether majority or minority governments produce better results; (2) the nature of Canadian political parties; and (3) relations between business and government.

Since 1949 – that is, since the first election held after the end of the Second World War – there have been six minority governments at the federal level and seven majority governments. Adding together their respective durations, minority governments were in office about ten years and majority governments about thirty years.

With respect to minority governments, there was neither a coalition nor an explicit or public undertaking of support for the government from members of smaller parties in the House of Commons. The six minority governments were always at risk of being defeated in the House. Three of them were defeated on votes of non-confidence and dissolution followed. The remaining three chose the election date when they thought their prospects were favourable. No minority government lasted more than two years or so.

This simple summary confirms a fundamental characteristic of Canada's political culture during those years. Notwithstanding the relatively large numbers of minority governments, nearly as many as of majority governments in the post-war period, the norm was assumed to be majority government; minority governments were regarded as interludes of short duration, awkward interruptions to the exercise of power by the party with control in the House of Commons.

The corollary assumption was that power normally moved between the two major parties, the Liberals and the Progressive Conservatives. Or, to put it another way, Canada had two national parties vying for government office, plus fringe parties that were not serious rivals to either of the major parties and that, when they held the balance of power, did so for relatively short periods. This also helps to answer the question as to how much influence the parties that held the balance of power had upon the legislative program of the government.

I was a minister in three minority governments and two majority governments. Although I did not follow closely the meetings of the House leaders until I became government House leader myself following the 1974 election, my impression is that from 1963 to 1968, when we were a minority, we did not experience serious difficulty in obtaining parliamentary approval for our legislative program, nor do I recall that the government had to alter in any significant way the content of a program because of fear of being defeated. Looking back at those years of great legislative activity, I ask these questions: Could we have accomplished more or would we have put forward different legislation if we had had a clear majority of members in the House of Commons? I doubt it.

Without in any way depreciating the skills of such government House leaders as George McIlraith and Allan MacEachen, the main reason that we were able to proceed with so little resistance was that the NDP, which had the largest number of seats among the smaller parties, did not want to defeat us and precipitate an election, at least not before 1968, and neither did the Social Credit MPs.

The situation following the 1972 election was less stable and finally the pressure on David Lewis, the NDP leader, to show his independence led him to join the official opposition in defeating the 1974 budget. I remember expressing my disbelief when MacEachen told me that Lewis intended to do so; it looked to me like a serious error of political judgment. And so it proved to be for the NDP, which lost heavily in the ensuing election.

Neither the Liberals nor the Progressive Conservatives were faced with the necessity of forming alliances or coalitions with other parties in order to put together a government that could command the support of a majority of MPs. The party that elected the largest number of MPs took office and hoped for the best, sometimes with confidence, sometimes with fingers firmly crossed. Following the 1963, 1965, and 1972 elections, we Liberals proceeded, not as if we had a majority, but with care, in the belief that the parties holding the balance of power were not likely to join with the official opposition to precipitate an election.

The smaller parties, and particularly the NDP, which had an ideological approach, exerted their maximum influence during election campaigns. It was during those tests that the Liberals, in particular, had to decide how far to move to the left to win seats in constituencies where the main opposition came from NDP candidates. After the election was over, NDP influence on Liberal policy declined. It could only have been revived by a significant resurgence of support for the NDP during the period of minority rule; but no such resurgence occurred.

The Canadian political culture is changing rapidly and radically. The norm may no longer be alternation of power between the two main national parties, the Liberals and the Progressive Conservatives. There is the possibility that future Parliaments will be split among several parties, no one of which elects a sufficient number of MPs to be entrusted with government without the assurance of support from members of other parties, either by the formation of coalition governments or by alliances without ministerial participation.

In many ways the national parties have been the glue that kept Canada together as a functioning federation. Each of them had big followings among voters in all parts of the country. Their respective policies exhibited more similarities than differences because they both sought to reconcile the views of the different regions of the country and came to similar conclusions.

In my experience the main political parties at the national level in Canada were rather ramshackle affairs where policy making was involved. Their principal function was to elect the leader of the party, to select party candidates in the various constituencies when elections were called, and to raise the money and enlist the foot-soldiers during election campaigns.

Nothing issued by the Liberal Party of Canada, or by any of the other national parties, so far as I am aware, matched in scope and detail the publications of the research branches of the Conservative and Labour parties in Britain. During election campaigns, our parties printed a few pamphlets on policy. The British parties publish books with hundreds of pages for the guidance of candidates.

The paucity of documents on policy reflected accurately the way in which the Liberal and Conservative parties determined party policy. There wasn't too much to describe and there was danger in being too precise. Although party conventions discuss policy at great length, the purpose is more to encourage the party activists to express their views than it is to achieve consensus.

Out of power there is more scope for debate. But even in opposition the members of the caucus who are on the firing line in Parliament tend to be more influential in the determination of policy than are the members of the party gathered in convention or the party executive.

Very early in my political career – before I was an MP – I was campaigning on a university campus. A student held up a copy of a pamphlet stating Liberal Party policy. 'Do you agree with this?' he asked me. 'Not with all of it,' I replied. 'Then how can you be a Liberal?' 'Because,' I replied, 'I agree with more of the Liberals' policies than the policies of any other party.'

I might have added, if I had been pressed, that when I decided to become a Liberal candidate I did not pay much attention to the official policies of the Liberal Party. Diefenbaker repelled me. Pearson attracted me. I found that I had much in common on matters of public policy with Liberals among my acquaintances.

The reality was that people were more important than policies. Witness the competition between the Liberal and Progressive Conservative parties to persuade well-known and well-liked people to be candidates at forthcoming elections. It was assumed that the person being solicited would have no difficulty in accommodating to the generalities of either party's policies.

In Britain, on the other hand, younger aspiring politicians apply to a party to become candidates. The party of their choice decides in which constituency they will run, subject to acceptance by the local executive. If they win they are groomed for promotion. If they lose but show talent, they may be assigned a constituency with better prospects for success. Eventually they may become ministers and join the cabinet.

In Canada, the central offices of the national parties had little to do with the process. Pearson, as leader of the Liberal Party, urged me to be a candidate. I decided where I wanted to run and I made direct approaches to the executive in Eglinton constituency. If Pearson had shown any preference between my opponent, Russell Taylor, and me he would have been strongly criticized by the Eglinton Liberals. Even the usual categorization of the two main Canadian political parties, the PCs to the right and the Liberals to the left of centre, or reformist Liberals versus consolidating Conservatives, was no longer appropriate, even if it had been at one time. The New Democratic Party is now at the left of the political spectrum. The Reform Party is on the right. Once these parties assume national office – if they do – their political coloration will quickly fade when they have to deal with the real issues of governing this far-flung land of regional differences.

We have a few politicians who were elected when young and are still active, but we do not have a governing class of people who make politics their career as in the United States, Britain, and most European countries. Ours is a tradition not of professional politicians but of citizen-politicians who for one reason or another decide to stand for election to Parliament, and, even if elected, leave politics within a few years to return to private life. Even the central core of the national parties, the people who delight in politics and everything that goes with it, who raise the money and do all the things that have to be done, some with the hope of preferment, others just for the excitement, even this group changed most of its personnel from election to election. What has held the mainstream parties together was not, in my view, their structure, which was far from sturdy, but the traditional hard core support they could depend upon in all parts of the country. In other words, many people voted Liberal or Conservative because their families and friends did. The leadership of the parties changed; the loyalties of party supporters didn't. That loyalty depended upon adherence to a set of values, but these were general enough to permit policies to be adjusted by the leadership to changing circumstances.

All of this is changing and changing rapidly as I write these memoirs.

I have one final reflection on the political process in Canada during my time, namely, the relationship between business and politics.

Relations between the Government of Canada and the business community have never been better than they were during the decade or so following the end of the Second World War. There were several reasons for this. The government gave active encouragement, through tax concessions and other means, to industrial and commercial expansion in order to provide employment to returning servicemen. Foreign capital was welcomed. The minister who had organized defence production during the war, C.D. Howe, was in charge of post-war reconstruction and had the confidence of business leaders, most of whom he knew personally.

These business leaders not only knew C.D. Howe and his advisers. A high proportion of them had been personally involved in the operations of government as dollar-a-year men and as wartime officials in various government boards and agencies. They were familiar with the processes of decision making. They knew how the system worked. They knew the mandarins. They knew how to make representations and to whom.

In due course, that generation of business leaders who had worked in government retired or died. Thereafter, there has been limited infiltration of businessmen into government and of senior government officials into business, although a lot of senior officials retired and became consultants in the 1970s and 1980s.

In the United States, by contrast, businessmen accept appointment by the president as cabinet secretaries and as deputy and assistant secretaries at comparatively low salaries. After a few years they return to private life, having performed their public service and having acquired valuable experience, which, in most instances, enhances their private careers.

In Canada, cabinet ministers, equivalent to cabinet secretaries in the United States, have first to be elected to Parliament.

This is the principal reason why there are so few business-executive types in Parliament or in cabinet. Very few businessmen well established in corporations are prepared to interrupt their careers to try to become MPs, without any assurance whatever that they will become ministers. Not only that, the corporations themselves do little or nothing to encourage their senior executives to enter politics at the federal level. I know this from personal experience. The directors of Brazilian Traction did not grant me leave to contest the 1962 election. I do not complain. It did me no harm. I could have returned later as president. But it revealed an attitude only too common in the Canadian business community.

Contributions to political parties and to individual candidates at election time – campaigns by business groups for or against particular legislative proposals – these are the kinds of political behaviour favoured by Canadian corporations. To grant leave to a senior executive to stand as a candidate in a general election, accompanied by an understanding that his job is still there if he doesn't get elected and perhaps an understanding that he is welcome to return after a term as an MP – this is not normal practice in Canadian corporations. It is an interruption to the business of making money.

There is, in truth, a yawning gulf between business and politics in Canada. The Canadian business community should ask itself this question when criticizing government: Who among us are prepared to defend our views and slug it out with opposing candidates before the voters in a constituency at the next general election?

There wouldn't be many volunteers. It is so much easier to blame the mess, whatever it is, on the politicians, as if they were a class of people different from business people, or farmers, or professionals, or trade unionists.

It is one of the characteristics and I believe one of the virtues of Canadian society that, so far, we have no governing class, very few professional politicians, no body of people who spend a lifetime in active politics either as MPs or as MPs-inwaiting. Except of course for the senators. In the House of Commons, the average turnover from election to election has been high, though obviously highest when governments change. In any given decade half the population of the House of Commons will have been replaced. This is a healthy, democratic state of affairs, one that the people of Canada, including the business community, have good reason to preserve and in which they should be participants.

The Liberal and Progressive Conservative parties do not have ideological foundations. They are essentially pragmatic in their programs and in their actions. The NDP moves steadily from the left to the centre of the political spectrum when it assumes responsibility for governing and seeks office nationally or, for that matter, provincially.

It would be a profound error on the part of the business community to promote political polarization by deliberately supporting a party because of what is conceived to be its favourable orientation towards business interests – just as it was an error, in my view, for the leaders of the trade-union movement to have committed themselves to support the NDP. What the business community needs and should promote in its own interests is broadly supported national political parties with a businesslike approach and an enlightened social agenda.

As evidence, look at what happened from the end of the Second World War to the end of the 1970s. This was not only a period of steady economic expansion that was good for business. It was also the time when family allowances, old-age pensions, the Canada Pension Plan, medicare, and more comprehensive unemployment insurance were put in place. Those were golden years not only because Canadians grew richer at an unprecedented pace, but because governments actively intervened to distribute the wealth by giving a measure of social security to the mass of the population and, until the end of the 1970s, without incurring worrisome budgetary deficits.

CHAPTER TEN

Non-political Activities, 1978–1988

I had decided not to run for re-election, but I was not ready to retire. Although I was a couple of years beyond the normal age of retirement, my health was good. So I looked about for something interesting to do.

The Northern Pipeline Agency

In the early 1970s, the owners of the petroleum reserves discovered at Prudhoe Bay on the North Slope of Alaska in 1968 were developing plans for its transportation south. In retrospect, it is unfortunate that the Canadian government did not show more enthusiasm for an oil pipeline through Canada to the California market. That right-of-way could have been used for a pipeline to carry the natural gas that emerged from the wells with the petroleum at Prudhoe Bay as well as Canadian Arctic gas. With such a pipeline, the disastrous Exxon-Valdez oil spill in March 1989 could also have been avoided. In any event, it was decided to build the Alyeska pipeline to transport oil from the North Slope to the port of Valdez on the south coast for shipment by water to the lower forty-eight states.

How then was the natural gas to be transported south? The choice was between a pipeline to carry the gas to Valdez where it would be liquified and transported by ship to California, or a pipeline through Canada to serve California and the American Midwest.

On the Canadian side, there were also competing pipeline projects to carry the Alaskan gas, together with Canadian Arctic gas. Finally, the real choice narrowed down to two. One, the Canadian Arctic Gas Pipeline (CAGPL), supported by the leading gas and oil interests, would follow a route from Prudhoe Bay along the northern slope of the Yukon Territory to the mouth of the Mackenzie River, where the pipeline would tap Canadian Arctic supplies, and then south up the river valley, through the Northwest Territories and Alberta to the U.S. border. The other would run southward from Prudhoe Bay in Alaska to Fairbanks, where it would follow the route of the Alaska Highway through the Yukon Territory in Canada and south through British Columbia to Alberta. At Caroline, Alberta, 100 kilometres north of Calgary, it would divide into two legs. The western leg would take gas to California and other western states, through a line running to the border at Kingsgate in south British Columbia. The eastern leg would transport gas to the border at Monchy, Saskatchewan, where the U.S. part of the system would deliver it to the midwestern states. Canadian Arctic gas would be connected by a pipeline from the mouth of the Mackenzie Delta down the Dempster Highway to Whitehorse.

After long complicated hearings, the United States decided to accept the Canadian option and the Canadian authorities decided in favour of the Alaska Highway Pipeline, sponsored on our side of the border by Foothills Pipelines (Yukon) Ltd, headed by Robert Blair, a remarkable and unusual combination of business entrepreneur and Canadian nationalist. Within a surprisingly short period, so great was the urgency, the governments of Canada and the United States negotiated an agreement in the summer of 1977 to facilitate the building on both sides of the border of the longest pipeline ever contemplated anywhere in the world – some 5,000 miles, including the Dempster Link.

To supervise the building of the Canadian portion of the joint project, Parliament established the Northern Pipeline Agency (NPA). I was still an MP at the time the government put forward implementing legislation – the Northern Pipeline Act – and attended some meetings of the committee that reviewed the bill. The United States established a similar supervisory agency, the Office of the Federal Inspector, partly to prevent or minimize the kind of adverse socioeconomic and environmental impacts experienced when building the Alyeska oil pipeline.

For one reason or another, energy and pipelines have engaged my attention at critical stages of my career. It looked like an interesting challenge, so I indicated to the Prime Minister my interest in the job of commissioner of the NPA.

I was travelling when I received word from the Prime Minister's Office that immediately on arrival in Ottawa I was to go to the office of the clerk of the House of Commons and resign as an MP so that I could be appointed the next day as commissioner of the NPA. This I did, with the result that I never again occupied my seat in the House of Commons and never had the opportunity of making a farewell speech after fifteen years as a member.

The NPA was given extraordinary powers of supervision and regulation. It is a single window at the federal level for the conduct of virtually all dealings with the Foothills group of companies, jointly owned by Nova, an Alberta corporation, and Westcoast Transmission Co. and authorized to undertake the Canadian portion of the project. The NPA is also unique because all its costs, including the salary of the commissioner, are paid by the Foothills company on the principle that the costs of supervision and regulation are a cost of building the pipeline.

To my delight, I found myself working at the outset with Basil Robinson, a former under-secretary of state for external affairs, who had been in charge of the negotiations with the U.S. officials and had put together a staff seconded from External Affairs and other departments, some of whom, like Terry Cameron, who had been seconded to the agency from External Affairs and who became my principal assistant in Ottawa, stayed on as an employee of the agency for a considerable time. I was fortunate to inherit as my secretary Pauline Sabourin, who had been secretary to the under-secretary of state for external affairs. I was also fortunate that years later she typed the various drafts of these memoirs and made very useful suggestions.

In the late seventies and early eighties, so anxious were the Americans to obtain more natural gas that, instead of waiting until the Prudhoe Bay gas came on stream, they seized on an idea advocated in a report by the National Energy Board, under the chairmanship of Geoffrey Edge, in July 1977, and supported subsequently by President Carter in his report to Congress. The idea was to begin construction of the pipeline in the south rather than in the north, through which to move Alberta gas pending the arrival of Alaska gas a few years later. In other words, pre-build the southern portion of the pipeline.

Personally, I supported the idea of the pre-build and urged Allan MacEachen, who had signed the agreement with the United States and was the minister responsible for the NPA, to persuade his colleagues to approve the necessary changes in the terms and conditions governing the construction of the line.

Two basic kinds of assurance had to be received before pre-building could be approved by the Canadian government. First, there had to be as strong an understanding as possible that the line to Prudhoe Bay would be completed. The sponsors of the pipeline in the United States and Canada affirmed their intention to complete the line. In an exchange of letters with Prime Minister Trudeau, President Carter expressed full confidence that the project would proceed as planned. The U.S. Senate and the House of Representatives, responding to representations from the Canadian government, approved resolutions affirming the support of the Congress for completion of the joint project.

I had the unusual experience of drafting a letter from Prime Minister Trudeau to President Carter outlining Canadian concerns and of conferring with one of the president's staff in drafting the reply.

The second assurance required was that sufficient natural gas would be available in Canada to justify the pre-building. The National Energy Board conducted the necessary review and gave that assurance. When natural gas prices rose sharply during the energy crisis, the volume of gas surplus to Canadian requirements grew from an earlier estimate of 800 billion cubic feet to 4.5 trillion cubic feet, a substantial proportion of which was allocated for shipment through the proposed new western and eastern legs of the Alaska Highway Pipeline.

On 17 July 1980, the government, by Order in Council, concurred in an amendment to one of the important terms and conditions relating to financing contained in the Northern Pipeline Act. In effect, the amendment divided the Canadian section of the project into two stages to overcome problems retarding commencement of the northern segment of the undertaking. As a result, Foothills now had to establish to the satisfaction of the National Energy Board only that financing was available for the first stage, the pre-build, and could be obtained as required for the second stage – thus relieving it of its previous obligation to establish that financing was available for the entire project.

The Foothills group satisfied the requirements for the start of construction of the pre-build and, on 4 August 1980, the great project got under way in Canada, shortly after the start in the United States, on 30 July. The NPA had to be ready to supervise construction of the pre-build and at the same time to prepare for the construction of the remaining northern sections of the line, where unprecedented problems – technical, environmental, and social – were to be expected. The build-up of the staff proceeded under Harold Millican, who had been appointed administrator and was in charge of the operations office in Calgary and of regional offices in Whitehorse and Vancouver.

William Scotland, the designated officer, who was a deputy administrator of the NPA as well as an associate vice-chairman of the National Energy Board, worked out of Calgary. So did the third member of the top operating triumvirate, deputy administrator A. Barry Yates. A competent team.

It was a time of intense activity. Advisory committees were established, one in Yukon and one in British Columbia. We met regularly with representatives of the provinces and territories through which the pipeline would run. Millican and I toured the route of the pipeline in Yukon, holding public meetings, mostly with Native residents along the way. We went to Alaska to meet the governor and a group of business-men and politicians. I went to Prudhoe Bay to see for myself the extra-ordinary facilities where the gas that came out of the ground along with the oil was returned to the ground pending the building of a gas pipeline to transport it south. Foothills carried out tests to control pipe fracture of large-diameter pipe and to determine how best to lay pipe in permafrost and in soils subject to alternate freezing and thawing. There were parallel U.S. facilities in Fairbanks, Alaska.

My counterpart in the United States, the federal inspector Jack Rhett, and I met with our respective staffs from time to time to coordinate activities. The pipeline treaty required each government to ensure that the supply of goods and services to the pipeline in both countries would be on generally competitive terms. When Foothills called for bids on large items like pipe and valves these were sent to mills in the United States, in Europe, and in Japan. Canadian suppliers were very competi-tive and got a major share of the business.

Following extensive consultations with relevant federal, provincial, and territorial departmental agencies and a number of interest groups, socioeconomic and environmental terms and conditions aimed at maximizing the benefits and minimizing adverse impacts were drafted by the agency and approved by the government.

Standing committees were created in the House of Commons and Senate to supervise the supervisors, an exceptional innovation in our parliamentary system. I appeared on several occasions before those committees to report progress or lack of it, and so did Foothills.

Everything was go. The pre-build was soon delivering Alberta gas. Then the energy crisis vanished as a result of the recession of the early 1980s, the impact of conservation measures, and an increase in produc-tion and exploration, spurred on by higher prices. The contemplated shortage was replaced in the United States by what came to be known as a gas bubble – a surplus – that turned out to be more durable than most bubbles. The target dates for the beginning of construction of the northern sections of the pipeline in Canada and in Alaska were set back from time to time. Finally, in April 1982, the sponsors announced an indefinite delay. Meanwhile, more and more gas moved southward through the pre-build, until today, as I complete these memoirs, the pre-build carries some 27 per cent of total Canadian exports of natural gas to the United States.

The Calgary office of the NPA and its appendages were dismantled. When that was completed I asked the government to permit me to retire as a full-time employee and to revert to a part-time status on half pay. One of my friends in cabinet told me that they had never before been faced with a request from a public servant to reduce his salary. Apart from Pauline Sabourin, the agency personnel at head office in Ottawa were also part-time – Bruce Macdonald and Frank Gilhooly.

That period as commissioner of the NPA taught me much about gas pipelines, about Canada-United States relations, and particularly about Native people.

For the first time I met and conferred with Native people whose environment was going to be affected by the building of the pipeline. Their leaders, particularly in Yukon, were an impressive lot: articulate, responsible, and tenacious. As a representative of a Canadian government agency, I had two responsibilities under the terms of the Northern Pipeline Act – to ensure that their interests were not overlooked in determining the rules with respect to the construction of the pipeline, and to ensure that Native people would be offered the opportunity to work on the project. Sometimes I found that these two rules conflicted, because the Native people in Yukon at that time formally opposed the building of the pipeline until their land claims had been settled, although many of them wanted to accept jobs that were offered.

It helped me and my colleagues in our relationship with the Native people in Yukon to have appointed Ken McKinnon as head of the Whitehorse office. Apart from his background as a former member of the Yukon government, McKinnon is married to a gracious Native woman, who now shares with her husband the duties and responsibilities of commissioner of the Yukon Territory, the equivalent of lieutenant-governor in a province.

I have also, as a result of my experience, formed some views about the future of the Alaska Natural Gas Transportation System, the ANGTS as it is called south of the border. The agreement between Canada and the United States emphasizes that the pipelines in both countries are to be privately owned; the function of government is to facilitate and to regulate. One day, the United States will want and need to tap the Prudhoe Bay supply of natural gas. Having in mind the erratic history of the project, it would be natural for the sponsors to hesitate before committing themselves and for the bankers to be equally careful. The pre-building of the southern sections of the pipeline has opened big new markets for Canadian gas and has helped to reduce the risk in completing the line to Prudhoe Bay. Nevertheless, it is still an undertaking of massive proportions that runs the risk of being delayed too long, to the detriment of the U.S. economy, simply because the U.S. government adheres strictly to a hands-off policy. In my opinion, something more than facilitation will be in the American public interest, as the Canadian government found when it intervened to help to get the privately owned TransCanada Pipeline under way in the 1950s, to the benefit of the country and without cost to the taxpayer.

As my duties as commissioner of the NPA became less time-consuming, I was asked by the government in early 1983 to co-chair a Task Force on Conflict of Interest and in 1984 to help to negotiate an agreement between Canada and the United States on salmon fishing on the West Coast. I did not submit a bill for services rendered. It amuses me to think that, because Foothills Pipelines paid my salary as well as other costs of the NPA, this private company in effect reduced the cost to the taxpayer of the Task Force on Conflict of Interest and the negotiation of the Pacific Coast Salmon Fishing Treaty.

I was commissioner of the Northern Pipeline Agency for ten years, appointed by a Liberal government in 1978 and surviving three changes in government, in 1979, 1980, and 1984. The manner of my departure from office in 1988 was as follows.

From 1984 on, I had been prepared to step down as commissioner. This was not considered timely, so I proposed instead that I should no longer be on half pay, but should instead serve on a retainer basis. Before my proposal could be considered, Prime Minister Mulroney issued a statement listing the salaries of the heads of government agencies, including the commissioner of the Northern Pipeline Agency. I was credited erroneously with an annual salary of more than $200,000. I was very angry and told the press that my annual remuneration was less than $50,000. Mr Mulroney phoned to apologize, which was gracious of him. With that out of the way, I pursued my idea of reverting to a retainer basis. The clerk of the Privy Council, Gordon Osbaldeston, whom I had consulted, told me that the Prime Minister would not reduce my salary. So I retreated, but some months later revived my proposal to Donald Mazankowski, who put it forward to the Prime Minister for approval. Again I failed; I was informed by Paul Tellier, who had become clerk of the Privy Council, that Mr Mulroney wanted me to stay on but was still not prepared to reduce my salary. I was in a sense frustrated, but was grateful for this evidence of confidence.

Some weeks later, I had a telephone call from John Crosbie, who had become my minister. The call was to the effect that the government had decided to close the Northern Pipeline Agency. I knew this was impossible without parliamentary action. I suspected that Crosbie had been instructed to replace me because I had spoken publicly against the proposed Canada–United States Free Trade Agreement. By discreet enquiries I confirmed my suspicions.

Although I was working on only a part-time basis and my salary and other expenses of the agency were absorbed by Foothills Pipelines as an expense of the building of the pipeline, I would have resigned if Crosbie had asked me to do so on the grounds that it was inappropriate for me to express myself publicly in opposition to the Free Trade Agreement. Since he did not ask me to resign for that reason, I did not resign. I required the government in effect to fire me, an amusing way to end my long career in government. Fortunately, my replacement was a senior deputy minister in External Affairs, as I had recommended.

The Task Force on Conflict of Interest

There were no written rules about conflict of interest when I was a senior civil servant. We were expected to know what was right and what was wrong when public and private interests were in conflict. When I entered cabinet in 1963, there were still no written rules. There were unwritten rules that ministers would resign from boards of directors of business corporations and would find some way of disposing of personal investments that could be affected by the minister's public activities or by public policy. 'Frozen trusts' and 'blind trusts' were sophisticated devices for rich people to worry about, not for the likes of us.

During the years that I was a civil servant, there was even less concern about conflict of interest involving ministers. I can recall C.D. Howe reviewing his investment portfolio every week or so while he was a minister. He was a thoroughly honest man and would have strongly resented any suggestion that he might put his private interests ahead of his public responsibilities.

In those days, it appears that the public was more prepared to give the benefit of the doubt to a minister or a public official than it is today. And circumstances have changed fundamentally. There are many more public servants and ministers. Governments are more active in the economy, raising more possibilities of conflict of interest.

Gradually, during the Pearson years, the rules of conduct were codified and written down for the guidance of ministers and non-elected officials. In 1973, Prime Minister Trudeau developed a series of policies and practices affecting the conduct of present and former holders of public office that, he claimed, were as onerous as those in any parliamentary democracy. I was subject to them and I confirm his claim.

Ten years later, several troubling issues had arisen, particularly the 'Gillespie Affair.' The allegation was that Alastair Gillespie had contravened the existing conflict-of-interest guidelines when, after he left the cabinet, he sought financial aid from a Crown corporation for a project to convert coal into liquid fuel in Cape Breton. He was said to be in breach of the requirement that for two years after leaving office former cabinet ministers must not lobby any department or agency, including Crown corporations, for which they had been responsible.

This was the catalyst that led Prime Minister Trudeau to ask me and Mike Starr, who had been a minister in the Diefenbaker government, to co-chair a Task Force on Conflict of Interest. In his letter to us on 7 July 1983, he said:

> Judging from recent debate on this issue, it is clear that some would argue that any official dealing between present and former office holders gives the appearance of preferential treatment or wrongdoing. Such interpretations in my judgement not only go beyond the spirit and intent of the policies and practices developed by the Government of Canada but could also significantly and adversely affect the recruitment of highly-qualified individuals from diverse backgrounds to participate in public life.
>
> For these reasons and consistent with my prerogatives and responsibilities in this area, I believe that it is in the public interest that a study be undertaken of the policies and practices that should govern the conduct of Ministers, Parliamentary Secretaries, exempt staff, and full-time Governor-in-Council appointees during and after their period of public service. The results of such a study would be useful as well in reviewing policies in this area governing public servants ...

That was our mandate.

I shall always be grateful to Mike Starr for suggesting Patrick Boyer as executive director of our task force. At that time, Boyer was recognized as an authority in the field of election law. I had no doubt that he was also a good Tory (he was elected to Parliament as a PC candidate in 1984), but any reservations I may have had on that score were quickly dispelled by the quality of his analysis and writing.

I am not sure what Prime Minister Trudeau expected when he established the task force. Perhaps it was a few pages listing changes to be made in the existing guidelines. Instead, what he received was a treatise, entitled *Ethical Conduct in the Public Service,* probably the most thorough and detailed examination of the subject of conflict of interest ever put together anywhere. Starr and I made contributions from our practical experience in government. We held private hearings at which, among others, Paul Martin, Jr, appeared. He was then president of a shipping company and contemplating running for Parliament, the sort of person who should be encouraged to enter public life. He sought advice on conflict-of-interest rules that would govern the handling of his business interests if he decided to seek office. We received many suggestions in writing. Patrick Boyer reviewed practices in the United States, Britain, and the Canadian provinces and municipalities and wrote the classic report.

For the most part, the press ignored it. They regarded it as a gimmick to whitewash the 'Gillespie Affair.' At my press conferences, practically all the questions were on that affair, which it was not our responsibility to investigate.

Many of the task force recommendations were accepted in the revisions of conflict-of-interest rules by the Trudeau government and by subsequent Conservative governments. So far, however, no federal government has accepted one of our principal recommendations, the establishment of an Office of Public Sector Ethics, headed by an ethics counsellor with the status of a senior judge. Among other functions, the counsellor would advise the prime minister on procedures applicable to ministers to minimize conflicts of interest. When allegations were made that Ministers had broken the rules, the prime minister would ask the ethics counsellor to investigate and make a report. If the allegations were of a serious nature, the prime minister could – and probably would – make the report public, in this way ensuring impartiality and integrity at the highest political level.

It is very difficult to draft rules that fit all circumstances. We recommended that the ethics counsellor should have some discretion, so that if a minister or other public official, because of special circumstances, sought advice as to whether or not he or she had complied with the rules, the ethics counsellor could either issue a clean bill of health or give instructions to make changes to comply with the rules.

There have been several occasions when prime ministers must have regretted that they had not taken our advice. For example, the judicial enquiry that was appointed to investigate Sinclair Stevens' conduct was not, in my view, an appropriate procedure. Nor, in my view, did the enquiry make appropriate recommendations for the future.

The Canada–United States West Coast
Salmon Fishing Treaty

For some twenty years, officials of the Canadian and United States governments had tried without success to reach agreement on a treaty to define the respective rights of their fishermen to fish for salmon on the West Coast.

Early in 1984, a group of Canadian MPs visited Washington to discuss Canada-U.S. relations and learned that the U.S. administration, impatient with the lack of progress, had decided to add to their salmon-treaty delegation a trouble-shooter with a political background, a former congressman from Illinois, Edward Derwinski (later secretary of veterans affairs in the Bush administration). Returning to Canada, the parliamentarians recommended that our government do something similar by adding me to the Canadian delegation of civil servants.

In the midst of these activities, the Progressive Conservative government took office in September 1984. Almost immediately, John Fraser, the MP from the B.C. constituency of Vancouver South, who had become minister of fisheries, phoned me to say that he wanted me to continue as an adviser on the salmon fishing treaty and hoped to get the approval of his colleagues, which presumably he did.

I am not sure why, but it worked. Neither Derwinski nor I spoke at the negotiating sessions. We observed and we consulted with our respective teams. Occasionally, Derwinski and I met to assess the situation. What we provided was evidence that both governments wanted to reach agreement, and an assessment of the political risks. This helped the bureaucratic negotiators on both sides to make progress and at the end gave reassurance to our respective governments, which had to sign the treaty, and in the United States get it ratified by Congress.

The Canadian delegation was led by Garnett Jones, a director in the B.C. office of the Department of Fisheries. Jones and I kept closely in touch with Fraser, who had ultimately to take the responsibility for recommending and signing the treaty. I had known Fraser as a fellow MP and, when I was head of the Canadian group of the Trilateral Commission, appointed him as one of two MPs, the other, of course, being a Liberal MP, Herb Breau. The salmon negotiations gave me a new insight into Fraser's character – prudent, sensitive, unpretentious, the qualifications that have made him such an excellent speaker of the House of Commons. John Fraser and I spent literally hours on the telephone discussing the various aspects of the negotiations, particularly the effect of the proposed conservation measures on sport fishermen, which was a major political issue.

I appeared before the House Standing Committee on Fisheries and Forestry on 18 December 1984 to explain the proposed treaty, from which I quote the following excerpts from my statement:

> I was full of admiration for the way Mr. Jones carried the negotiations for Canada. He was very patient, very intelligent, persevering – far more patient than I would have been on many occasions during that very prolonged negotiation, which you may recall ended with a session that lasted from 9 a.m. in the morning until 8 a.m. the following morning. I think it was Garnett Jones, a little mad, who insisted we had to continue until we got all the matters cleaned up.

> ... Before the negotiations began I met several times with my counter-part, Ed Derwinski, and told him the United States delegation must get its act together. Canada is not negotiating with Alaska or with the States of Washington and Oregon; it is negotiating with the United States itself. I think those who recall the negotiations that went on in the past, particularly the more recent ones – it appeared sometimes as if it were Canada versus Alaska and Alaska versus Washington, and it is small won-der we did not reach a final settlement.

> ... It was obviously in the interests of both Canada and the United States to reach agreement, if only to eliminate the overfishing of species like the chinook salmon. Those who have ever had much to do with negotiations of this kind know, however, that it is not sufficient to say both sides have an interest in reaching an agreement which would have to impose temporary sacrifices on both sides and which would limit interceptions of United States fish by Canadian fisherman and of Cana-dian fish by Americans.

> Before ending these few remarks, Mr. Chairman, I would like to make one final point about an issue that was one of the most contentious we faced during these prolonged negotiations, and that was the issue relat-ing to trans-boundary rivers: rivers that rise in Canada and flow through the Panhandle of Alaska into the Pacific Ocean; rivers that for most of their length are in Canada but that emerge in American territory.

> As a Canadian, and not just as a member of this delegation, I express the hope that a significant presence of Canadian fishermen will be maintained on the Canadian section of those rivers. For too long the United States fishermen were permitted to assume, because of a lack of a Canadian presence on those rivers and the fact that they flowed into

the ocean in United States territory, that these were in fact Alaskan fisheries.

The Trilateral Commission

Not long after we were married in 1976, Jeannette and I were listening to a public-affairs broadcast on CBC radio. A commentator was waxing eloquent about a nefarious international conspiracy, said to be led by David Rockefeller and multinational corporations, called the Trilateral Commission. 'Darling,' I said, 'do you realize that, according to that speaker, you married an important man. David Rockfeller and I are trying to run the world.'

I had by that time stepped down from cabinet and had just become the head of the Canadian group and deputy chairman for North America of the Trilateral Commission. This private organization was formed in the early 1970s to promote understanding among the principal industrialized countries. The post-war Bretton Woods Agreement, which stabilized relationships among the major currencies, had collapsed. Relations between Japan and the United States, between the United States and Europe, and between Europe and Japan were at a low ebb.

The membership of the commission consisted and still consists of about 300 people, more or less equally divided among Japan, North America – the United States and Canada – and the democratic countries of Western Europe; hence the term 'trilateral.' The North American delegation consisted of some 85 from the United States and 15 from Canada. I succeeded Jean-Luc Pepin as the leader of the Canadian group when, in 1975, Pepin was put in charge of the Canadian government board to stabilize prices. Ministers and policy makers of national governments are excluded from membership.

What led to the charge of a deep, dark conspiracy was the election as U.S. president of Jimmy Carter, who had been a member of the Trilateral Commission when he was governor of Georgia, and his appointment of four members of the commission as cabinet secretaries and of a large number of other commission members as senior advisers. To add to the conspiratorial atmosphere: President Bush was a member before he became vice-president, Zbigniew Brzezinski was the first executive director, and Henry Kissinger has been a prominent member when not in office. In Japan and in Western Europe, the same interchange has occurred between government and the members of the commission. Here in Canada, John Fraser and Lowell Murray were Trilateral commission members before becoming ministers. In short, the politicians in the commission are either former members of government or aspirants to office.

None of this is surprising or ominous. The members are selected because they are considered to be influential people – in politics, in business, and in academic circles. They wouldn't be of much value if they were not influential. They meet from time to time both within their grouping and as a trilateral grouping to exchange views and to listen to the leaders of national governments.

The annual meetings rotate among Japan, North America, and Europe. Special delegations from the commission have visited the Soviet Union and China. As a member of the executive, I attended meetings in Tokyo, London, Paris, Rome (and the Vatican), Madrid, New York, Washington, and San Francisco.

The moving spirit was David Rockefeller. Without his enthusiasm and tireless travelling – and his personal charm – the Trilateral Commission might not have survived its first years.

Its greatest contribution to international cooperation, in my opinion, arose from the inclusion of Japan as a founding member of the triangle, equal in status to the United States and Europe. Until then, the membership of most such international organizations was drawn mainly from the Atlantic countries. At first, the Japanese members were slow to participate in this unfamiliar setting and in the English language. Within a decade or so they were taking up about a third of the discussion time at trilateral meetings, even differing among themselves. Discussions revolved around studies on important issues of the day selected by the executive and written by three authors, one from each region, ensuring that the Japanese point of view was never ignored. Over the years, there were a number of distinguished Canadian authors.

In the United States and in some European countries, leaders of trade unions accepted membership in the Trilateral Commission and took an active part in discussions. Leaders of the Canadian Labour Congress were offered membership but declined, to the regret of other Canadian members, like myself. We did, however, within the limitations of our group of fifteen, manage to recruit a representative group of businessmen, academics, politicians, and one former leader of a trade union and rotated the membership from time to time. The list appears in Appendix 2.

In 1986 I was succeeded as leader of the Canadian group and vice-chairman for the North American section by J.H. Warren, the distinguished diplomat and my former deputy minister when I was minister of trade and commerce.

What influence has the Trilateral Commission had? Sometimes we wished that we had been half as influential as our critics maintained we were. Such as it was, the influence was indirect. Our reports on international issues were among the best published anywhere, technically and in terms of comprehensiveness, because of the widespread consultations of the three regional authors with leading authorities throughout the world. No doubt, too, the contacts between businessmen and politicians at meetings of the Trilateral Commission helped to reduce tensions that had led initially to the formation of the commission and that still continue. The best evidence that the Trilateral Commission has influence is that monarchs, presidents, prime ministers, foreign ministers, and economic ministers found it worthwhile to accept invitations to attend meetings and to speak.

Canada's influence is modest, but useful. We cannot afford not to be there. Our presence helps to show that North America is not synonymous with the United States, that there is a distinctively Canadian point of view. There were times when I felt it necessary both in open meetings and in executive sessions to be less than enthusiastic about some aspects of U.S. foreign and trade policies.

In April 1984, the commission had a session called 'Living with the United States.' This is part of what I said as the head of the Canadian section of the North American group:

I do not regard this session on living with the United States as an occasion to express complaints about the conduct of our great friend and ally. I do regard it as an opportunity to make each other aware, and particularly the Americans present here today, of how the relationship looks from the point of view of other Trilateral members ...

The United States is the predominant force affecting Canada on the bilateral and worldwide levels, but tends to regard relations with Canada as essentially manageable and local while concentrating most of its energies on broader international concerns. But for Canada, these apparently mundane local issues like acid rain and U.S. interest rates are often of major importance, and because of our need to maintain our distinctness in the face of American bilateral and global policies. We are North American, but we are an independent country which has its own special interests to pursue in many areas.

We do not conceive our policies in terms of being pro-American or anti-American; what we need above all, I think, from the United States, is more understanding of the fact that we have our own character, our own history and a rich and complex society with its own requirements and dynamics. We submit, too, that since we are each other's principal trading partner, there are reciprocal benefits for both countries when the issues between us are handled with sensitivity.'

For me personally, it was a delight to meet again at Trilateral Commission conferences leading world figures in politics and business with whom I had worked as a Canadian minister.

For sheer drama, my most vivid recollection is of chairing a meeting of the Trilateral Commission in Washington, on 30 March, 1981, when I was handed a note saying that President Reagan had been shot. It took me a few minutes to convince the shocked audience that the report was more than an unconfirmed rumour.

East-West relations

The Trilateral Commission kept me in touch with leading players on the international scene. Early in March 1984, I was asked by the Aspen Institute for Humanistic Studies to be one of a group to prepare a study on 'East-West Relations: Past, Present and Future.'

Most of the group, like myself, were former members of government – 'eminent persons' I think was the term used to describe us. I had the privilege of chairing the meetings I attended, not because I outranked the others – far from it, in fact; several former prime ministers were included. Probably I was asked to chair the meetings because I am a Canadian, accustomed to negotiating consensus among contending points of view.

One of the members of the group was Britain's James Callaghan. He and I had parallel careers in our respective governments. For example, he was Britain's chancellor of the Exchequer when I was minister of finance. Our careers went in different directions, of course, when he decided to try for the leadership of the Labour Party, succeeded, and became prime minister. At dinner one day in London while he was in the opposition and before reaching the top, I asked him if he had abandoned his ambitions to lead the party. His answer was no. In return, he asked me the same question. I answered yes, that I was happy with Pierre Trudeau's leadership. After expressing some surprise, he went on to say that when he was walking down the staircase at Marlborough House, Trudeau had suddenly left his side and slid down the bannister. When he came to know Trudeau better he recognized his intellectual qualities as well as his athletic abilities.

When he was chancellor, I asked Callaghan to approve the transfer from London to Winnipeg of the headquarters of the Company of Gentlemen Adventurers into Hudson Bay, chartered by King Charles II on 2 May 1670 – now known as the Hudson's Bay Company. He was reluctant to lose this historic connection with the past, but he finally agreed and the transfer was effected in 1970.

It was during the Aspen Institute project that I met Shirley Williams, then a British MP and president of the Social Democratic Party. It turned out that she and I had similar views on many aspects of international affairs. Lord Carrington, about to become the secretary general of NATO, gave a dinner in London to which we were both invited and at which the newly arrived U.S. ambassador was present. The conversation turned to the Grenada affair, which had just happened, when the United States landed troops on that Caribbean island to restore order. Williams was very critical of the American action. In conclusion she added, without having consulted me, something like: 'and I know Mr Sharp, who is from a Commonwealth country, will agree.' Fortunately, I did.

Robert McNamara was a U.S. member of the Aspen Institute group on East-West relations. I knew about him, of course, when he was secretary of defence. I got to know him better when he was head of the World Bank, because he asked me to be a member of a committee to advise on the salaries of the executive directors of the bank, which I did for three years. Elliott Richardson, secretary of several departments in the U.S. government, was another member with whom I had worked on aspects of Canadian-American relations. Cyrus Vance, former secretary of state, and Theodore Hesburgh, president of Notre Dame University, completed the very distinguished U.S. representation on the Aspen group.

From Germany were Helmut Schmidt, former chancellor and a close friend of Trudeau's, Marion Doernhoff, publisher of *Die Zeit*, and Rüdiger von Wechmar, ambassador. From France, Edgar Faure, a former prime minister, Jean François-Poncet, a former foreign minister, and François de Rose, a former ambassador; from Italy Gianni De Michelis, Umberto Colombo, and Sergio Berlinguer; from Japan, Saburo Okita, a former foreign minister. From Canada, in addition to myself, was Ivan Head, then president of the International Development Research Centre. And there were others who made a contribution, including John McCloy, the distinguished American ambassador and public figure, who told us how President Truman made the decision to drop the bomb on Hiroshima.

The group met in Wye Plantation near Baltimore, in Venice, and in

West Berlin, where Dr Richard von Weizsäcker (now president of Germany) was mayor. I saw the Berlin Wall, the symbol of a divided Europe, before it was torn down in October 1989. Bruno Kreisky, former chancellor of Austria, attended the meeting in Venice.

It was a prestigious group. Under the direction of James Leonard, a former U.S. diplomat, Herbert Okum, ambassador-in-residence at the Aspen Institute in Colorado, and Martin McCusker, we produced a report entitled *Managing East-West Conflict. A Framework for Sustained Engagement.*

At the time, the recommendations of the report attracted widespread support, including that of Pierre Trudeau, Edward Heath, and George Kennan.

It was the fear of nuclear holocaust and the desire for an end to the cold war that led to the project and the preparation of the report. Both the nuclear confrontation and the cold war came to an end, not, I hasten to add, as a result of the implementation of our recommendations, but thanks to Mikhail Gorbachev, who had just come to power in the Soviet Union and who had a more radical agenda.

Cambodia

Like most people who follow the news, I was appalled by events in Cambodia – the killing fields of Pol Pot. Because my knowledge of the conflict was limited, however, I was surprised when I received a call from Donald Ranard of the Center for International Policy in Washington asking if I would chair an international conference on Cambodia in December 1985. When I expressed concern about my lack of expertise, he said that they had plenty of experts. I had been asked because James Leonard of the Aspen Institute said I was a good chairman.

One of the reasons I accepted was the site of the conference: the Rockefeller Foundation's Bellagio Study and Conference Center on Lake Como, Italy. Its serene beauty lived up to expectations, even in December.

For the first time since Vietnam invaded Cambodia in 1979, representatives from most of the countries involved in the conflict sat together to discuss the impasse. The twenty-eight participants included government officials from Vietnam, Thailand, Laos, and the Soviet Union; current or former diplomats from Australia, India, Japan, and the United States; retired military officers from Thailand and France; academics from government-related think tanks and universities in

Indonesia, Malaysia, the Soviet Union, and the United States; and several journalists with experience in Southeast Asia.

Representatives from Cambodia were not invited because the participation of officials from either Phnom Penh or the opposing coalition government would have prompted participants from many of the other countries to drop out. China and the United States declined to send official representatives.

I wrote to the Chinese ambassador in Canada urging that his government be represented at Bellagio, and I asked External Affairs to make the same pitch in Beijing. But to no avail.

The conference provided an opportunity for a candid discussion among participants representing opposing sides in the hostilities. The conferees did not agree on a solution, but they came away with a better grasp of the perspectives of the different protagonists in this conflict, which has brought enormous suffering to Cambodia and instability to Southeast Asia.

For me the conference was a learning experience. I was accustomed to dealing with the politics of East-West relations and had had to learn something about the problems of the Middle East because of our vital interests in that area. In Indo-China, Canada had been involved by membership in the international control commissions to supervise the so-called truce in Vietnam. We took on that responsibility fundamentally because we wanted to help the United States get out of Vietnam.

Cambodia was different. Here was a great human tragedy in an area in which Canada did not have important political or economic interests. We were concerned – I was concerned – simply because millions of innocent people had died needlessly in a conflict over political power and their country continued to be occupied, although not by those who had been guilty of the genocide.

The not-surprising conclusion I reached was that the well-being of the people of Cambodia was not the central concern of the contending forces in the Indo-Chinese area, although they all claimed that it was. Ideological struggles are involved. So were naked power politics involving at the time China, the Soviet Union, and, in a limited way, the United States. The recent end of the cold war has reduced the hostility that was still evident in 1985.

The corollary conclusion I reached is that the people of Cambodia are not going to be freed from their misery until the subject occupies a central rather than a peripheral place on the international agenda, and the underlying issues are confronted and resolved, which has not yet happened.

CHAPTER ELEVEN

Learning to Be a Canadian

Does any pattern emerge from this account of my lifetime of service in the government of Canada? For me it does: I was learning to be a Canadian. Although I was born in this country more than eighty years ago I am still learning to be a Canadian. The chances are I shall not complete my education before I die.

For my first thirty years, I lived in Winnipeg. Until I moved to Ottawa I had virtually no contact with French-speaking Canadians and knew little about them. I knew a good deal more about my fellow Canadians who had immigrated from the Ukraine, from Poland, and from Germany and more about my fellow Canadians from the Maritimes. I lived in the heart of one of our two solitudes.

It has taken me the rest of my life to realize that Canada is not what I thought it was in my younger days and to begin to understand the problem of national unity. If this were a unique personal experience I would not bother to describe it. I have found that far from being unique it is typical of my generation of English-speaking Canadians living outside the province of Quebec.

From this experience and observation I draw a simple and obvious conclusion: that there are two societies in Canada, one English-speaking society comprising various ethnic groups, to which I belong, and a French-speaking society.

The second simple and obvious conclusion is that the existence of these two societies is fully compatible with the development of our nation-state. Canadian history is there to prove it. Under its federal constitution and with its two societies, Canada has grown, prospered, and taken its place among the other nation-states and does not suffer by comparison with any. There is no better place in the world to live and raise a family.

I learned that French-speaking Canadians are determined to preserve their unique heritage and will undoubtedly do so. I can assure you from personal experience that this is by no means fully understood and accepted in all parts of Canada. To paraphrase the lyrics from a well-known musical comedy, there are many English-speaking Canadians who, like Professor Higgins, wonder plaintively, 'Why can't French-Canadians be like us?'

As I learned these simple facts, I abandoned any ideas that I might have absorbed from my youth about Canada being a great melting pot that in due course would produce unhyphenated Canadians, as much alike as possible. Instead, I began to catch a glimpse of the true destiny of Canada as a country in which diversity is something to be preserved and nurtured.

Then came the hard part, learning how to give substance to this vision in the governing of Canada.

I learned that not only is Canada a decentralized federation with extensive powers in the hands of the constituent provinces; it has few outward symbols of nationality. Unlike the Americans, we do not salute our flag; as a matter of fact, we got along for a century without one. There are few similarities between the English and French versions of 'O Canada,' our national anthem, apart from the tune. On our country's birthday, 1 July 1867, there was no great outpouring of national pride – just some speeches at political picnics. Subsequent July firsts have been quiet holidays, overshadowed by the boisterous fourth of July celebrations of successful revolution south of the border. We gained our independence not by revolution but gradually, without violence. Our head of state is still the British monarch, who visits Canada occasionally and is not a symbol of national unity.

Canada's 100th birthday party in 1967 was an instructive exception. That was a great national celebration lasting several months and one of the principal reasons was Expo 67, a first-class international exposition, held in Montreal, a bilingual city, jointly financed by the federal government, the Province of Quebec, and the City of Montreal.

Even when we were at war, when Canadian men and women were fighting and dying in Europe, in Asia, and on the high seas, domestic differences intruded on our patriotism. Vimy Ridge, where Canadians showed their courage and determination in battle, occurred in 1917, the year of the conscription crisis at home in which Canadians deeply disagreed about the conduct of the war and the nature of our commitment to our soldiers overseas.

Sometimes I have wished that it were otherwise, that there were some symbols of unity, some historical events around which Canadians, regardless of origin or language, could rally. After nearly half a century at the centre where the representatives of the people meet in Parliament I have concluded that it is futile to search for such national symbols. Ours is a country founded on compromise and political accommodation, not the stuff of popular celebration. A diplomat from a Commonwealth country, a historian by training, on arriving in Ottawa to take up his post told me that for such a young country Canada was very mature: 'You Canadians have no heroes.' That, I think, gets close to the truth about our beloved and fortunate country.

We do not have national heroes because the various communities that make up Canada have different origins and pursue goals and aspirations that are not always the same; French Canadians in Quebec are and want to continue to be a distinct society; French Canadians outside Quebec to survive; English-speaking people from Britain and Ireland and immigrants from Europe to build an affluent community from sea to sea; recent non-European immigrants to find a better life; aboriginal people to preserve their heritage.

What has enabled Canada to survive and to prosper, to be an example to the world of democracy and freedom in action, is our belief, borne out by our history, that the goals and aspirations of the various communities need not be in conflict – indeed have a better chance of being achieved within Canada than separately. This belief was the purpose and the inspiration of the Fathers of Confederation.

I have learned, over the years, that among the strongest unifying forces has been the desire of Canadians to be separate from the United States and to avoid being overwhelmed by the economic power and cultural influences of that great republic to the south. The desire to be independent reinforces the argument for unity. That is why I felt that the Canada–United States Free Trade Agreement, by promoting integration of our two economies, replacing internationalism by continentalism, reduced our ability to resist American economic and cultural domination.

I discovered from personal experience that the essential nature of Canada is always being redefined. We are never satisfied with the way things are. Quebec, the West, and the Atlantic provinces are always looking for a new deal. Fortunately, the constitutional framework devised by the Fathers of Confederation in 1867, plus a few amendments, has so far been sufficiently flexible to provide room for this continuous redefinition.

When I arrived in Ottawa in 1942 to take a job in the Department of Finance, the War Measures Act enabled the federal government to mobilize Canadian resources and manpower for the prosecution of the war. The federal government continued to give leadership during post-war reconstruction and the creation of the welfare state. Under the leadership of the federal government, a new industrialized, modern Canada emerged that bore little resemblance to the pre-war largely agricultural country of the dirty thirties.

I confess that when Quebec nationalism re-emerged I was disappointed. Canada, including Quebec, had been moving ahead so well and so vigorously that it seemed a pity to break the pattern of successful national action in which Quebec played a leading role and of which it was a principal beneficiary.

It was about this time – 1962 and 1963 – that I entered politics and became a minister in the first Pearson administration and Jean Lesage became Premier of Quebec under the banner 'Maîtres chez nous.'

So I and my contemporaries who shared my background had to learn to accommodate ourselves to the Quiet Revolution and the emergence of a revitalized Quebec society, determined to preserve and promote its distinctive character. Canada was once again being redefined and, significantly, without fundamental constitutional changes.

Some of the accommodations that had to be made were awkward, such as the agreement to compensate Quebec for dropping out of shared-cost programs and the decision by Quebec to have its own pension plan, insisted upon by the Lesage government. On the other hand, the introduction of medicare on a national basis, including Quebec, was encouraging from the point of view of national unity and national action. Conflicts with Quebec on foreign policy were resolved by ingenuity.

The rise of Quebec nationalism was one aspect of the redefinition of Canada during my years in politics. Another, which is sometimes overlooked, was the successful effort made by some of us 'mandarins' during the post-war years to encourage French Canadians to enter the public service of Canada and to attain senior levels; and by Pearson and Trudeau to appoint French-speaking ministers from Quebec to policy-making portfolios in the cabinet.

Today French Canadians occupy a substantial share of the top jobs in the public service of Canada, and French-speaking ministers from

Quebec have in recent years held every important portfolio in the federal government. What a contrast to the situation when I came to Ottawa in 1942! Then there were virtually no French Canadians in top jobs in the civil service, and French-Canadian ministers from Quebec usually got portfolios like Post Office, Public Works, Secretary of State, and Justice – never Finance.

In my continuing education as a Canadian I have learned an important fact of political life in this country, namely that the personal convictions and strengths and weaknesses of the party leaders have more influence on the course of events than the principles of the parties they lead, principles that in any event are not well defined.

It was fortunate that Pierre Elliott Trudeau arrived on the Ottawa scene when he did, a bilingual French Canadian from Quebec who believed in a strong federal government providing services in both official languages throughout the country and ensuring full participation of the French-speaking people of Quebec in the governing of Canada and in federal institutions.

My personal experience had led me to the same concept, but I do not believe I could have put it into effect successfully even if I had been elected leader of the Liberal Party and had become prime minister. Nor, in my judgment, could any of the other potential national leaders have done so, except Trudeau. Which of us English-speaking MPs from outside Quebec could have led the Liberal Party to win practically all the Quebec seats in Parliament at successive federal elections, notwithstanding the rise of Quebec nationalism and separatism, and without catering to Quebec nationalism in order to be popular? Trudeau won in Quebec by opposing separatism and special status, in contrast to the Mulroney government, which later cultivated the separatist and extreme nationalist voters. The Quebec extreme nationalists fought Trudeau tooth and nail.

After I resigned from Parliament in 1978, the Constitution moved to the centre of Canadian politics.

In 1982, the Trudeau government took the lead in patriating the Constitution from Westminster and amending it, notably by the inclusion of a Charter of Rights and Freedoms, with the consent of all the provincial governments with the exception of the government of Quebec.

In 1987, the Mulroney government, responding to five demands from the Quebec government, reached agreement with all the provinces at Meech Lake to amend the Constitution, including recognition of Quebec as a distinct society. Two provinces that had in the meantime elected new governments failed to ratify, and the Meech Lake agreement collapsed.

In the late 1980s the Mulroney government made another effort at constitutional reform and at Charlottetown reached agreement with the provinces on a series of amendments. This was put to the people of Canada in a referendum in October 1992 and rejected by a majority of them country-wide and by a majority of the residents of six provinces, including Quebec.

Although I took very little part in the debate on these constitutional events – I spoke out once or twice against the Meech Lake agreement because of its ambiguity – they did add significantly to my continuing education as a Canadian.

They confirmed the extreme difficulty and perhaps the impossibility of defining the nature of Canada, although such a definition was attempted in the Canada clause of the Charlottetown agreement. We are what we are; it doesn't matter much that we cannot find the right words, in poetry or in prose.

The failure of the Meech Lake and Charlottetown agreements leaves the issue of Quebec's place in Canada unresolved. On the other hand, if either of these amendments had been approved, there was no realistic expectation that the arguments would not continue. Even the advocates of the amendments affecting Quebec's powers regarded them as only the first step towards greater decentralization.

So for the time being, we are left with the status quo. Fortunately, the Fathers of Confederation bequeathed us a Constitution that, with a few amendments, has been remarkably flexible throughout the 125 years of Confederation and can be used in the future as in the past to deal with many of the practical issues of concern to all Canadians.

I look back at the years when I was actively involved at the policy level as a civil-service mandarin and as a minister. They give me confidence in the future. Somehow, without comprehensive constitutional change, Canada, under federal leadership, was transformed; Newfoundland joined the federation; Canada took its place at the economic summit among the richest industrialized countries; Canadians were provided with a social-security net that eliminated the kinds of hardships and deprivations that existed in my youth; we gained a deserved reputation as a diverse, tolerant, bilingual, multicultural society; and within this great federation existed Quebec's proud French-Canadian society, which flourished economically and culturally as never before, adding lustre to Canada's international image and a special quality to our identity.

Agenda, Kingston Conference, 6–10 September 1960

Speaker:	James Eayrs	'Defence'
Commentators:	Ronald Ritchie	
	C.M. Drury	
Speaker:	Michael Barkway	'How Independent Can We Be?'
Commentators:	Walter Gordon	
	William Hood	
	Harry Wolfson	
Speaker:	Harry G. Johnson	'External Economic Policy'
Commentators:	R.B. MacPherson	
	R.M. Fowler	
Speaker:	Maurice Lamontagne	'Growth, Stability and the Problem of Unemployment'
Commentators:	Russell Bell	
	Mrs Jean Edmonds	
Speakers:	Tom Kent	'Towards a Philosophy of Social Security'
	Claude Morin	
Speakers:	Monteath Douglas	'Programs of Social Security, Old Age
	Arthur Andras	Security, Unemployment Insurance,
	Dr Wendell Macleod	Medical and Hospital Care'
Speaker:	William Mahoney	'The Aims of Organized Labour'
Commentator:	Jean Marchand	

Speaker: David MacFarlane   'Agriculture'
Commentators: Lorne Hurd
                  Stewart Searle, Jr

Speaker: Alan Jarvis   'Policies and Plans for Urban Develop-
                                          ment and Land Use'
Commentators: William Kilbourn
                  Albert Rose

Speaker: André Laurendeau   'The Development of Canadian Values
                                          and Our Cultural Heritage'
Commentator: Kildare Dobbs
                  F.H. Underhill   Final Summing Up
                  Davidson Dunton
                  Hon. J.W. Pickersgill

Trilateral Commission Members, Canadian Group, 1976–1992

Ms Doris Anderson, President, Canadian Advisory Council on the Status of Women

The Honourable Robert Andras, PC, Senior Vice-president, Tech Corporation

Mr Michel Bélanger, Chairman and Chief Executive Officer, National Bank of Canada

Mr Russell Bell, Research Director, Canadian Labour Congress

Mr Conrad M. Black, Chairman of the Board and Chief Executive Officer, Argus Corporation Limited

Mr Robert Bonner, QC, Chairman, British Columbia Hydro and Power Authority

Mr Herb Breau, Member of Parliament, House of Commons

Mr Claude Castonguay, President and Chief Executive Officer, Laurentian Group Corporation

Dr Gail C.A. Cook, Executive Vice-president, Bennecon Ltd

Mr George E. Creber, QC, Vice-president and General Counsel, Canadian Arctic Gas Study Ltd

Mr David M. Culver, Chairman and Chief Executive Officer, Alcan Aluminum Ltd

Mr Louis A. Desrochers, McCuaig, Desrochers, Barristers and Solicitors

Mr Peter C. Dobell, Director, Parliamentary Centre for Foreign Affairs and Foreign Trade

Mr Claude A. Edwards, Former Member, Public Service Staff Relations Board

Mr Gordon Fairweather, Commissioner, Canadian Human Rights Commission

Mr Brian Fleming, Stuart, MacKeen and Covert, Barristers and Solicitors

Trilateral Commission Members

The Honourable John A. Fraser, PC, Member of Parliament, House of Commons

Mr Raymond Garneau, Member of Parliament, House of Commons

Mr Robert Gratton, Chairman and Chief Executive Officer, Montreal Trust

Mr Donald Harvie, Deputy Chairman, Petro-Canada

Mr Alan Hockin, Executive Vice-president, Toronto-Dominion Bank

Mr Edgar F. Kaiser, Jr, President and Chief Executive Officer, Kaiser Resources Ltd

The Honourable Michael J.L. Kirby, Senate

The Honourable Donald S. Macdonald, McCarthy and McCarthy, Barristers and Solicitors

Mr Claude Masson, Vice-dean of Research, Faculty of Social Science, Laval University

The Honourable James A. McGrath, PC, Member of Parliament, House of Commons

Mr W. Darcy McKeough, Company Director, McKeough Sons Company Limited

The Honourable Lowell Murray, Senate

Mr Arne R. Neilsen, President and General Manager, Mobil Oil Canada Ltd

The Honourable Duff Roblin, Senate

The Honourable Mitchell Sharp, PC, Commissioner, Northern Pipeline Agency Canada; Chairman, Canadian Group of the Trilateral Commission, 1976–86

Mr Maurice Strong, Chairman and President, Petro-Canada

Mr J.(Jake) H. Warren, Principal Trade Policy Advisor, Bureau du Québec à Ottawa; Chairman, Canadian Group of the Trilateral Commission, 1986–92

Mr G.A. Van Wielingen, President and Chief Executive Officer, NuGas Limited

Dr William C. Winegard, Member of Parliament, House of Commons

Index

Index

Index

Index

Index

Index